New Theology No. 4

New Theology No. 4

Edited by
Martin E. Marty
and Dean G. Peerman

The Macmillan Company, New York
Collier-Macmillan, Ltd., London

Permission to reprint the following is gratefully acknowledged:

"Crisis and Renewal in History of Religions," by Mircea Eliade, © 1965 by the University of Chicago

"On the Meaning of 'God': Transcendence Without Mythology," by Gordon D. Kaufman, Copyright © 1966 by the President and Fellows of Harvard College

"Language and Understanding," by Heinrich Ott and translated by Thomas Dean, © 1966 by Union Theological Seminary in the City of New York

"Theology and the Uses of History," by Justus George Lawler, Copyright © 1966 by Justus George Lawler

"The Dilemma of Identity for the Emancipated Jew," by Manfred H. Vogel, © 1966 by American Academy of Religion

"Toward a Theology for the New Social Gospel," by Max L. Stackhouse, © 1966 by Andover Newton Theological School

Library of Congress Catalog Card Number: 64–3132
SECOND PRINTING 1967

The Macmillan Company, New York
Collier-Macmillan Canada Ltd., Toronto, Ontario

Printed in the United States of America

Acknowledgments

OUR THANKS to the various writers, editors, and publishers who have made possible a fourth volume of *New Theology*. Again we call attention to the footnoted addresses of the publications whose material we have used; all are publications to be recommended to those who wish to become more knowledgeable about contemporary theology.

We are also indebted to Mrs. Joanne Younggren, our secretary-typist, for her able and sturdy assistance and to *The Christian Century* magazine for its benign attitude toward our editorial moonlighting.

Contents

Beyond the Secular: Chastened Religion   9

Crisis and Renewal in History of Religions
Mircea Eliade   19

Symbol, Myth, and the Biblical Revelation
Avery Dulles, S.J.   39

On the Meaning of "God": Transcendence Without
Mythology
Gordon D. Kaufman   69

Talk about Religious Talk
Jerry H. Gill   99

Language and Understanding
Heinrich Ott   124

Theology and the Uses of History
Justus George Lawler   147

The Dilemma of Identity for the Emancipated Jew
Manfred H. Vogel   162

The Issue of Transcendence in the New Theology,
the New Morality, and the New Forms
Gabriel Fackre   178

Veni, Creator Spiritus: The Doctrine of the Holy Spirit
Albert C. Outler   195

Problems of a Protestant Spirituality
John Kent   210

Toward a Theology for the New Social Gospel
Max L. Stackhouse   220

The Death of God and the Future of Theology
Harvey Cox   243

Beyond the Secular: Chastened Religion

As WE enter the last third of the twentieth century, it becomes clear that a new theological climate is upon us. When the 1960s began it was evident, throughout the areas where Western Christianity had found expression, that old modes of theological speech were being called into question. The neo-orthodox orthodoxy which had prevailed in Europe for a half century and in the United States for a third of a century was challenged and found wanting by many in the generation following Karl Barth, Rudolf Bultmann, Paul Tillich, and the Niebuhr brothers. The longer Christian past shared the fate of the recent past: iconoclasts questioned all the historic modes of theological speaking and —in the end—questioned the subject of theology itself.

During these years of change and experiment, *New Theology* was born to serve as an annual chronicle of such experiment. At the same time many were coming to speak of something called "*the* new theology." The editors of these volumes are not interested in exploiting the coincidence or in hitchhiking on the fame of anything called *the* new theology. Theological work today possesses too much variety to permit the use of a single covering term. If *New Theology*'s editors are keeping their eye on the serious theological journals of the day, it is not because they are trying to force homogeneity on a generation, to straitjacket its experience, to provide labels. We are interested in discovering the preoccupations and obsessions of the scholars, editors, and publishers, and in selecting varied materials that speak most clearly concerning the problems implied in these preoccupations and obsessions.

Some trends have begun to emerge in new theological writing, and we have taken pains to discern them. From the first we have made a point of the fact that theologians in the

9

1960s are more "world centered" and less church centered than in the years before. They have been obsessed with the attempt to pin down the meaning of "the secular." Indeed, almost no one writing in this field today can avoid placing this question at the head of his agenda. For historians, sociologists, phenomenologists, this means that they must analyze the secular as a possibility for theology. For theologians in the stricter sense of the term, it means that they must speak of "the problem of God."

From 1963, when we began to gather material for *New Theology No. 1,* until now, we have noted consistency in the way the problem of God was placed at the center, as it had not been during the ecclesiological and Christological conversations of the previous half century. In 1963, the event around which many essays were organized was the publication of Bishop John A. T. Robinson's popular *Honest to God.* During the year that *New Theology No. 2* was being compiled—1964—the question of language predominated, with Paul van Buren's *The Secular Meaning of the Gospel* serving explicitly or implicitly as a focus. Both 1963 and 1964 were years of apparent anarchy and confusion: iconoclasts, exorcists, prophets, and muckrakers were on the scene. In the spirit of the late, late Bonhoeffer, religion was being purged.

Our third volume, based on a content analysis of hundreds of journals, illustrated our belief that scholars and editors alike were trying to pick up the pieces. That year—1965— was a time of new constructive statements, of the first timid steps toward systematic work. Harvey Cox's anything but timid *The Secular City* symbolized the direction. In that volume, we were able to speak in our introduction about "the turn from mere anarchy." We put the book to bed at the publishers in late autumn. When it came out in early spring an event occurred which, in the popular view at least, suggested that mere anarchy had arrived: the press had discovered the "death-of-God" theology.

The American public, unused to recognizing atheists in the world, was now being trained to find atheists in the church and even in its seminaries. What sense did that make? What was constructive, ordered, and systematic about that half year's popular theology? Had we in *New Theology No. 3* prematurely killed the "death-of-God" talk? No. Whoever takes time to browse in the periodical rooms of libraries will find, as we found, that the journals had taken up the "problem of God" earlier and had begun to weary of "death-of-God" talk. Already, in our first volume, we had presented a specimen of the work of Thomas J. J. Altizer, one of the two better-known new radicals. But, in the winter of 1965–66, what the serious journals had begun to leave behind was picked up by *Time* and *Newsweek, The New York Times* and *Playboy,* and was discussed on a thousand campus platforms and in a hundred thousand Easter sermons. This public stir has prompted editors and writers to begin retracing their steps. A large number of recent articles in these serious journals return to the "death-of-God" theme. But it would not be accurate to say that this theme dominates the periodicals in the year under survey here. "Death-of-God" theology remained in the strictest sense of the term a two-man movement, whose leaders actually steered in opposite directions. We would be the last to say that the movement and the moment had no salutary effects or constructive purposes. They certainly enlarged the scope of theological debate; and—miracle of miracles—they succeeded in making theological themes in the precise and formal sense of the term a matter of public discussion.

Whether properly justified or not, however, most theologians were not attracted to the "death-of-God" talk. Their criticisms are too varied to be condensed here (though some of them appear in the essays which follow). Fundamental to these criticisms is a point that gives unity to our 1966–67 theme: Few theologians found the "death-of-God" analysis to be fully appropriate to the human situation, to say nothing of appropriateness to the Christian tradition and community. Typical of their concern is this paragraph from a speech given by David L. Edwards to the British Student Christian Movement in September 1965, and published in *The Student World* (No. 2, 1966):

The riddle of human existence remains, and many eminent humanists remain interested in this riddle. True humanism, I should say, believes that the most important business of man in his days on earth is to pierce the great riddle by the symbols of art and by storytelling, and in the light gained to live in peace and love. When that day of true humanism comes, the present impatient ignorance of philosophical and mystical theology, and the present bored refusal to study the subtle character of religious belief and religious language, will be seen as immature. It seems to me that those of us who remain religious believers, having accepted many rebukes, now have every right to call on our fellow humanists to be braver in their own dedication to the mature dignity of human wisdom. A book needs to be written called *Beyond the Secular*.

Beyond the Secular is being written, but it is being addressed as much to Christian humanists and Christian atheists as to humanists in general. And it is being written by the kind of men whose work is represented in *New Theology No. 4*.

The authors included in this volume are not intent on repudiating the main line of today's worldly, secular theology: indeed, they are a part of it; they have traversed the terrain which death-of-God theologians inhabit. We have not scoured among the defensive, crabbed, and cramped little magazines to find last holdouts against the theological agenda of our time. We know that here and there grand-scale metaphysicians are to be found; people to whom talk of "the supernatural" comes as easily as it did to medieval men may well be on the scene and may well be writing; arcane pietists are arguing their own particular case. More power to them. But we have corralled articles by people who want to be honest to God, who want to know the secular meaning of the Gospel, who have walked the streets and surveyed the towers of the Secular City and who want to be both humanists and theologians. They form no school; their language is not always consistent; they argue with each other. Often they, too, serve as iconoclasts and exorcists. They are not—most of them—shocked or disconcerted by "death-of-God" language. But neither are they satisfied with it. They want to go "beyond the secular" (though only by going *through* it). They are cautiously re-appraising the category of "religion," which was regarded with much suspicion both by the generation of Karl Barth and by the more radical era posthumously dominated by Dietrich Bonhoeffer. They see the world around them to be astoundingly secular and yet astonishingly fertile "religiously": in the new nationalism of the new nations, in the durable presence of world religions, in the quasi-spiritual strivings of men alone and in community, and in the superstitions as well as in the genuine gropings and hungers of "secular man" in a technological society.

A brief rundown of what is in store for readers of this volume will illustrate our point. In the concluding essay Harvey Cox, who is responsible for so much of the translation of "secular" theology to the American scene, points ahead (by way of attention to Pierre Teilhard de Chardin and Ernst Bloch) to a "theology of the future" which is a refutation of static metaphysical categories. Elsewhere we have heard Cox cautiously reintroduce the possibility of "religious" expression (shall we call it quasi-metaphysical concern reinforced with "liturgy" appropriate to it?). He has treated such religious possibilities as virtually eucharistic or play elements, in the spirit of "all those things which shall be added" unto him who has first sought the Kingdom and its righteousness.

If for Cox talk about religion comes with difficulty, it is the central concern of Mircea Eliade, one of the world's most notable students of man's religious impulse. If we wish to look to our roots, Eliade is a sure-footed guide as he discusses the significance of primitive religion and urges his fellow historians of religion to overcome their diffidence and to pursue with sophistication the larger dimension of their academic discipline, in particular in relation to the building of culture.

Another root for discussion of religious categories is the Bible as it has been responded to by Christians. Roman Catholic biblical scholar Avery Dulles, not unmindful of the problem of dealing with ancient and mythical or symbolic elements in a secular world, charts ways for dealing with them and points to the urgency and necessity of doing so. His is an essay concerned with "going beyond the secular" in biblical studies.

The most difficult piece in the book—newcomers to the subject may wish to postpone it until the last—is Gordon Kaufman's systematic parallel to Dulles' biblical article. While Kaufman considers myth to be in trouble in our secular world, he argues that it is possible to deal with transcendence (another "religious" category) apart from myth.

Since much of recent talk about the Gospel's secular meaning has centered in language analysis and in hermeneutics (the science of interpretation), it seemed advisable to include reportage from these specialties. Jerry H. Gill surveys the thought of several language analysts and proposes that empirical theologians "endeavor to map mystery." With an eye to Heidegger, Heinrich Ott, successor to Karl Barth at the University of Basel, carries this linguistic concern into hermeneutics and preaching. A moving and telling essay by Justus George Lawler, editor of the Roman Catholic magazine *Continuum,* continues along this line and implies a critique of unqualifiedly secular theologies from the viewpoint of philosophy of history.

When the discussions of the relation of religion to the secular came to prominence in Christian circles, some Jews were able to identify with the topic immediately. For they were experiencing a crisis of identity, trying to discern how their God-centered interpretation of history would fare in a world that saw only man at the center. Other Jews tended to shrug off the matter, arguing that to be an exilic people means that Jews have not borne the weight of a sacral culture for many centuries. But the debate that is going on in Christian circles finds an echo in Judaism, and Rabbi Manfred H. Vogel ponders the issues implied by both points of view and comes to an open-ended conclusion concerning Judaism's religious possibility in a secular age.

We have included four essays that involve applications of the secularity question to particular issues. Gabriel Fackre's criticism of new theology, new forms, and new morality might well provide newcomers with an opportunity to be brought up to date on the controversies implied throughout this book; his critical approach is typical of many who teach in the seminaries. Albert C. Outler, who has carried on a lively polemic against "radical theology" from the viewpoint of informed theological history, here relates contemporary issues to a group of ministers by reference to John Wesley. Britisher John Kent asks whether Protestants are ready to make up their minds about the enduring questions of human spirituality in a secular age. And Max Stackhouse argues that philosophical theology must not be lost in the shuffle while a new ethic is being propounded.

We are tempted to anticipate these essayists' arguments, to quote at length from their articles to substantiate our choice of motif for this volume. We resist the impulse, for the essayists express themselves in contexts that deserve sustained reading. They are united by their empathy for the secular and atheist thought of their time, their involvements in its problems, their discontent with its solutions. In many and varied ways they discuss human religion and spirituality, the question of philosophical theology, the religious *a priori* in man, and the phenomenology of religion in society. As Justus Lawler puts it—and surely we can be allowed *one* quotation—they do not want to let go, or better, they want to find that which "cannot be annihilated in the human heart because it is what makes the heart human."

M.E.M. and D.G.P.

New Theology No. 4

Crisis and Renewal in History of Religions

Mircea Eliade

Surveying the work done in comparative religion during the past fifty years, Mircea Eliade is not pleased with what he finds. In contrast to their nineteenth-century predecessors, contemporary historians of religion tend to specialize in non-committal monographs and to avoid synthesis and generalization; in effect, says Eliade, they have forsaken their calling, which is "to decipher and explicate every kind of encounter of man with the sacred, from prehistory to our day." Having chided his colleagues for their timidity, he then challenges them to pursue a "creative hermeneutics" which "would be able to stimulate, nourish, and renew philosophical thought." In passing, he seeks to quiet the qualms of both scientists and theologians, who—though for different reasons—are not likely to look with favor upon such a creative role for historians of religion. Dr. Eliade is Sewell L. Avery Distinguished Service Professor at the University of Chicago, and his article is from that university's periodical publication *History of Religions* (Summer 1965).* His wide-ranging researches have resulted in a host of books, among them *The Myth of the Eternal Return, Patterns in Comparative Religion, The Sacred and the Profane, Images and Symbols, The Forge and the Crucible,* and *Myth and Reality.*

LET US RECOGNIZE it frankly. History of Religions, or Comparative Religion,[1] plays a rather modest role in modern culture. When one recalls the passionate interest

* Swift Hall, University of Chicago, Chicago, Ill. 60637.

Translated from the French by Harry B. Partin, Duke University.

[1] These terms are distressingly vague, but as they belong to current language we are resigned to employing them. One generally understands "History of Religions" or "Comparative Religion" to mean the integral study of the religious realities, that is to say, the historical manifestations of a

with which the informed public in the second half of the nineteenth century followed the speculations of Max Müller on the origin of myths and the evolution of religions and followed his polemics with Andrew Lang; when one recalls the considerable success of *The Golden Bough*, the vogue of *mana* or of the *mentalité prélogique* and *participation mystique*; and when one recalls that *Les Origines du Christianisme*, the *Prolegomena to the Study of Greek Religion*, and *Les Formes élémentaires de la vie religieuse* were the bedside books of our fathers and grandfathers, one cannot contemplate the present situation without melancholy.

Certainly, one could respond that in our day there is no Max Müller, Andrew Lang, or Frazer, which is perhaps true, not because today's historians of religions are inferior to them, but simply because they are more modest, more withdrawn, indeed more timid. It is exactly this problem that intrigues me. Why have the historians of religions allowed themselves to become what they are today? A first response would be: because they have learned the lesson of their illustrious predecessors; in other words, they have taken account of the caducity of any premature hypothesis, of the precariousness of any too ambitious generalization. But I doubt that, in whatever other discipline, a creative mind has ever given up the attempt to accomplish its work because of the fragility of the results obtained by its predecessors. The inhibition from which historians of religions suffer at present surely has more complex causes.

Before discussing them I should like to recall an analogous example in the history of modern culture. The "discovery" of the Upanishads and Buddhism at the beginning of the nineteenth century had been acclaimed as a cultural event that presaged considerable consequences. Schopenhauer compared the discovery of Sanskrit and the Upanishads to the

---

particular type of "religion" (tribal, ethnic, supranational) as well as the specific structures of the religious life (divine forms, conceptions of the soul, myths, rituals, etc.; institutions, etc.; typology of religious experiences, etc.). These preliminary precisions are not at all intended to circumscribe the field or to define the methods of the History of Religions. We shall return to this problem in a special article.

rediscovery of the "true" Greco-Latin culture during the Italian Renaissance. One expected a radical renewal of Western thought as a consequence of the confrontation with Indian philosophy. As is known, however, not only did this miracle of the "second Renaissance" not take place, but, with the exception of the mythologizing vogue launched by Max Müller, the discovery of the Indian spirituality did not give rise to any significant cultural creation. Two reasons especially are invoked today to explain this failure: (1) the eclipse of metaphysics and the triumph of the materialist and positivist ideologies in the second half of the nineteenth century; (2) the fact that the early generations of Indianists concentrated on the editing of texts, vocabularies, and philological and historical studies. In order to be able to advance the understanding of Indian thought, it was necessary at any cost to establish a philology.

Nevertheless, grand and audacious syntheses were not wanting during the first century of Indianism. Eugène Burnouf published his *Introduction à l'histoire du bouddhisme indien* in 1844; Albert Weber, Max Müller, and Abel Bergaigne would not flinch before projects that today, after more than a century of rigorous philology, seem enormous to us; toward the end of the nineteenth century Paul Deussen wrote the history of Indian philosophy; Sylvain Lévi made his debut with some works that an Indianist of our day would attempt only at the summit of his career (*La Doctrine du sacrifice dans les Brāhmanas*, 1898; *Le Théâtre Indien*, 2 vols., 1890) and, while still young, he published his sumptuous three-volume monograph, *Le Népal* (1905–8); a Hermann Oldenberg did not hesitate to present his grandiose surveys of the religions of the Vedas (1894) as well as of the Buddha and early Buddhism (1881).

Thus the insolvency of the "second Renaissance," expected as a consequence of the discovery of Sanskrit and Indian philosophy, is not due to the orientalists' excessive concentration on philology. But the "Renaissance" did not come about for the simple reason that the study of Sanskrit and other oriental languages did not succeed in passing beyond the circle of philologists and historians, while, during the Italian Renaissance, Greek and classical Latin were studied not only by the grammarians and humanists but also by the poets, artists, philosophers, theologians, and men of science. To be sure, Paul Deussen wrote some books on the Upanishads and the Vedānta in which he attempted to make Indian thought "respectable" by interpreting it in the light of German Idealism—by showing, for example, that certain ideas of Kant or Hegel were found in germ in the Upanishads. Deussen believed that he served the cause of Indianism by insisting on the analogies between Indian thought and Western metaphysics; he hoped thereby to arouse interest in Indian philosophy. Paul Deussen was an eminent scholar, but he was not an original thinker. One has only to imagine his colleague, Friedrich Nietzsche, devoting himself to the study of Sanskrit and Indian philosophy, in order to realize what a true encounter between India and a creative Western mind would have been able to produce. As a concrete example, one considers the results of a creative confrontation between Western and Muslim philosophy and mysticism when he sees what a profoundly religious spirit like Louis Massignon learned from Al Hallaj, and how a philosopher who is also a theologian, such as Henry Corbin, interprets the thought of Sohrawardi, Ibn Arabi, and Avicenna.

Indianism, like Orientalism in general, has long since become a "respectable" and useful discipline, one among numerous other disciplines that constitute what is called the humanities—but the prestigious role that Schopenhauer had predicted for it has not been realized. If one dares to hope still for a stimulating encounter with the thought of India and Asia, it will be the result of history, of the fact that Asia is now present in the historical actuality; it will not be the work of Western Orientalism.[2]

And yet, Europe has shown several times that it is avid for dialogue and exchange with the extra-European spiritualities and cultures. Let us recall the effect the first exposition of Japanese painting had on the French impressionists, or

[2] The contemporary vogue of Zen is largely due to the uninterrupted and intelligent activity of D. T. Suzuki.

the influence of African sculpture on Picasso, or the consequences of the discovery of "primitive art" for the first generation of surrealists. But in all these examples, the "creative encounter" was with artists, not with scholars.

The History of Religions constituted itself an autonomous discipline shortly after the beginnings of Orientalism, in some respects relying on the researches of the Orientalists, and it has profited enormously from the progress of anthropology. In other words, the two principal documentary sources for the History of Religions have been, and still are, the cultures of Asia and the peoples whom one calls (for lack of a more adequate term) "primitive." In both cases it is a question of peoples and nations who, for a half-century, especially in the last ten or fifteen years, have divested themselves of European tutelage and have assumed their responsibilities in history. It is difficult to imagine another humanist discipline that occupies a better position to contribute both to the widening of the Western cultural horizon and to the rapprochement with representatives of the Oriental and archaic cultures. However exceptional may be their gifts, the greatest Indianist and the most eminent anthropologist find themselves forcibly contained within their domains, however immense. But if he is faithful to the aims of his discipline, a historian of religions ought to be able to know the essential aspects of the religions of Asia and of the vast "primitive" world, just as one expects that he is capable of understanding the fundamental ideas of the religions of the ancient Near East, the Mediterranean world, and of Judaism, Christianity, and Islam. Obviously, it is not a question of mastering all these domains as a philologist and a historian but of assimilating the researches of the specialists and of integrating them in the specific perspective of the History of Religions. Frazer, Carl Clemen, Pettazzoni, and Van der Leeuw endeavored to follow the progress in a multitude of fields, and their example has not lost its value, even if one no longer agrees with their interpretations.[3]

---

[3] We have cited these authors because they envisage the History of Religions as a "total science." But this does not at all imply that we share their methodological presuppositions or their personal valorizations of the History of Religions.

I have recalled these facts in order to deplore the small profit that the historians of religions have drawn from their privileged situation. Certainly, I do not forget the contributions made by the historians of religions during the past three-quarters of a century in all fields of research. It is thanks to these contributions that today one can speak of the History of Religions as an independent discipline. But one deplores the fact that the majority of the historians of religions have done only this, worked with devotion and tenacity in order to constitute the solid foundations of their discipline. The History of Religions is not merely a historical discipline, as, for example, are archeology or numismatics. It is equally a *total hermeneutics*, being called to decipher and explicate every kind of encounter of man with the sacred, from prehistory to our day. Now, by reason of modesty, or perhaps from an excessive timidity (provoked above all by the excesses of their eminent predecessors), historians of religions hesitate to valorize culturally the results of their researches. From Max Müller and Andrew Lang to Frazer and Marett, from Marett to Lévy-Bruhl, and from Lévy-Bruhl to historians of religions of our day one notices a progressive loss of creativity and an accompanying loss of interpretive cultural syntheses in favor of fragmented, analytical research.[4] If one still speaks of taboo and totemism, it is above all due to the popularity of Freud; if one is interested in the religions of the "primitives," it is thanks to Malinowski and some other anthropologists; if the so-called myth and ritual school still attracts the attention of the public, it is because of the theologians and some literary critics.

This defeatist attitude of the historians of religions (rewarded by the progressive disinterest of the public in their work) was crystallized precisely in an epoch in which knowledge concerning man increased considerably due to psychoanalysis, phenomenology, and revolutionary artistic experi-

---

[4] It is true that a Rudolf Otto or a Gerardus van der Leeuw succeeded in awakening the interest of the informed public in religious problems. But their case is more complex in that they have not exercised an influence as historians of religions but, rather, through their prestige as theologians and philosophers of religion.

ments and, above all, at the moment when the confrontation with Asia and the "primitive" world began. Personally we consider this fact both paradoxical and tragic, for this spiritual timidity became general exactly at a time when the History of Religions should have been able to constitute the exemplary discipline for deciphering and interpreting the "unknown universes" that Western man confronted.[5]

However, we do not believe that it is impossible to reestablish the History of Religions in the central position it merits. It requires, above all, that the historians of religions become aware of their unlimited possibilities. It is not necessary to let oneself become paralyzed by the immensity of the task; it is necessary above all to renounce the easy excuse that not all the documents have been conveniently collected and interpreted. All the other humanist disciplines, to say nothing of the natural sciences, find themselves in an analogous situation. But no man of science has waited until *all* the facts were assembled before trying to understand the facts already known. Besides, it is necessary to free oneself from the superstition that analysis represents the *true* scientific work and that one ought to propose a synthesis or a generalization only rather late in life. One does not know any example of a science or a humanist discipline whose representatives are devoted exclusively to analysis without attempting to advance a working hypothesis or to draft a generalization. The human mind works in this compartmented manner only at the price of its own creativity. There exist, perhaps, in the diverse scientific disciplines some scholars who have never gone beyond the stage of analysis—but they are victims of the modern organization of research. In any case, they ought not be considered models. Science does not owe any significant discovery to them.

For the History of Religions, as for many other humanist disciplines, "analysis" is equivalent to "philology." One does not consider a scholar responsible unless he has mastered a

[5] We have discussed this problem a number of times, most recently in the Preface to our book *Méphistophélès et l'Androgyne* (Paris, 1962; English translation, 1965).

philology (understanding by this term knowledge of the language, history, and culture of the societies whose religion he studies). Justifiably, Nietzsche spoke of philology (in his case, classical philology) as an "initiation": one cannot participate in the "Mysteries" (i.e., in the sources of Greek spirituality) without first being initiated, in other words, without mastering the classical philology. But none of the great classicists of the nineteenth century, from Frederich Welcky to Erwin Rohde and Williamowitz-Moelendorff, remained within the bounds of philology *stricto sensu*. Each, in his own way, produced magnificent works of synthesis, which have continued to nourish Western culture even when, from a strictly philological point of view, they have been surpassed. Certainly, a considerable number of scholars belonging to various humanist disciplines have not attempted to go beyond "philology." But their example ought not to preoccupy us, for the exclusive concentration on the *exterior* aspects of a spiritual universe is equivalent in the end to a process of self-alienation.

For the History of Religions, as for every other humanist discipline, the road toward synthesis passes through hermeneutics. But in the case of the History of Religions, hermeneutics shows itself to be a more complex operation, for it is not only a question of comprehending and interpreting the "religious facts." Because of their nature these religious facts constitute a material on which one can think—or even ought to think—and think in a creative manner, just as did Montesquieu, Voltaire, Herder, and Hegel when they applied themselves to the task of thinking about human institutions and their history.

Such a creative hermeneutics does not always seem to guide the work of the historians of religions because, perhaps, of the inhibition provoked by the triumph of "scientism" in certain humanist disciplines. In the measure that the social sciences and a certain anthropology have endeavored to become more "scientific," the historians of religions have become more prudent, indeed, more timid. But it involves a misunderstanding. Neither the History of Religions nor any other humanist discipline ought to conform—as they have already done too long—to models borrowed from the natural sciences, still more as these models are out of date (especially those borrowed from physics).

By reason of its own mode of being the History of Religions is constrained to produce *oeuvres*, not only erudite monographs. Contrary to the natural sciences and to a sociology that strives to follow their model, hermeneutics ranges itself among the living sources of a culture. For, in short, every culture is constituted by a series of interpretations and revalorizations of its "myths" or its specific ideologies. It is not only the creators *stricto sensu* who reassess the primordial visions and who reinterpret the fundamental ideas of a culture; it is also the "hermeneuts." In Greece, along with Homer, the tragic poets, and the philosophers from the pre-Socratics to Plotinus, there is a vast and complex category of mythographers, historians, and critics, from Herodotus to Lucian and Plutarch. The importance of Italian humanism in the history of thought is due more to its "hermeneuts" than to its writers. By his critical editions, philological erudition, commentaries, and correspondence, Erasmus renewed Western culture. From a certain point of view one could say that the Reformation and the Counter-Reformation constituted vast hermeneutics, intense and sustained efforts to revaluate the Judeo-Christian tradition by an audacious reinterpretation.

It is useless to multiply examples. Let us recall only the considerable repercussion of the *Kultur der Renaissance in Italien* (1860) of Jakob Burckhardt. The case of Burckhardt illustrates admirably what we understand by the expression "creative hermeneutics." Indeed, his work is more than a respectable work, one volume among others in the vast historiographic literature of the nineteenth century. This book helped to *form* the historiographic consciousness of the nineteenth century. It enriched Western culture with a new "value" by revealing a dimension of the Italian Renaissance that was not evident before Burckhardt.

The fact that a hermeneutics leads to the creation of new cultural values does not imply that it is not "objective." From a certain point of view, one can compare the hermeneutics to a scientific or technological "discovery." Before the discovery, the reality that one came to discover was there, only one did not see it, or did not understand it, or did not know how to use it. In the same way, a creative hermeneutics unveils significations that one did not grasp before, or puts them in relief with such vigor that after having assimilated this new interpretation the consciousness is no longer the same.

In the end, the creative hermeneutics *changes* man; it is more than instruction, it is also a spiritual technique susceptible of modifying the quality of existence itself. This is true above all for the historico-religious hermeneutics. A good History of Religions book ought to produce in the reader an action of *awakening*—like that produced, for example by *Das Heilige* or *Die Götter Griechlands*. But in principle every historico-religious hermeneutics ought to have similar results. For in presenting and analyzing the Australian, African, or Oceanian myths and rituals, in giving a commentary on the hymns of Zarathustra, Taoist texts, or the shamanistic mythologies and techniques, the historian of religions unveils some existential situations that are unknown or that are imaginable only with great difficulty by the modern reader; the encounter with these "foreign" worlds cannot continue without consequences.

Obviously, the historian of religions himself will feel the consequences of his own hermeneutical work. If these consequences are not always evident, it is because the majority of historians of religions defend themselves against the messages with which their documents are filled. This caution is understandable. One does not live with impunity in intimacy with "foreign" religious forms, which are sometimes extravagant, often terrible. But many historians of religions end by no longer taking seriously the spiritual worlds they study; they fall back on their personal religious faith, or they take refuge in a materialism or behaviorism impervious to every spiritual shock. Besides, excessive specialization allows a great number of historians of religions to station themselves for the rest of their days in the sectors they have learned to frequent since their youth. And every "specialization" ends by making the religious forms banal; in the last instance it effaces their meanings.

Despite all these failures, we do not doubt that the "creative hermeneutics" will finally be recognized as the royal road of the History of Religions. Only then will its role in culture begin to show itself to be important. This will be due not only to the new values discovered by the effort to understand a primitive or exotic religion or a mode of being foreign to Western traditions—values susceptible of enriching a culture as have *La Cité antique* or the *Kultur des Renaissance Italien* —it will be due above all to the fact that the History of Religions can open new perspectives to Western thought, to philosophy properly speaking as well as to artistic creation.

We have often repeated it: Western philosophy cannot contain itself indefinitely within its own tradition without the risk of becoming provincial. Now the History of Religions is able to investigate and elucidate a considerable number of "significant situations" and modalities of existing in the world that are otherwise inaccessible. It is not just a matter of presenting "raw materials," for the philosophers would not know what to do with documents that reflect behavior and ideas too different from those familiar to them.[6] The hermeneutical work ought to be done by the historian of religions himself, for only he is prepared to understand and appreciate the semantic complexity of his documents.

But it is exactly at this point that certain grave misunderstandings have occurred. The rare historians of religions who have wanted to integrate the results of their researches and meditations in a philosophical context have contented themselves with imitating certain fashionable philosophers. In other words, they have compelled themselves to think according to the model of the professional philosophers. And that was a mistake. Neither philosophers nor men of culture are interested in second-hand replicas of their colleagues and favorite authors. In deciding to "think like X" about archaic or orien-

---

[6] It suffices to examine what some rare contemporary philosophers interested in the problems of myth and religious symbolism have done with the "materials" they have borrowed from ethnologists or historians of religions in order to renounce this (illusory) division of labor.

tal thought the historian of religions mutilates and falsifies it. What one expects from him is that he will decipher and elucidate enigmatic behavior and situations, in brief, that he will advance the understanding of man by recovering or re-establishing meanings that have been forgotten, discredited, or abolished. The originality and importance of such contributions reside precisely in the fact that they explore and illuminate spiritual universes that are submerged or that are accessible only with great difficulty. It would be not only illegitimate but ineffectual to disguise archaic and exotic symbols, myths, and ideas in a form already familiar to contemporary philosophers.

The example of Nietzsche ought to encourage and, at the same time, guide the historians of religions. Nietzsche succeeded in renewing Western philosophy precisely because he attempted to formulate his thought with the means that seemed adequate to it. Certainly that is not to say that the historian of religions ought to imitate the style or mannerisms of Nietzsche. It is rather the example of his freedom of expression that should be underlined. When one wants to analyze the mythical worlds of "primitives," or the techniques of the Neo-Taoists, or shamanistic initiations, and so forth, he is not at all obliged to borrow either the methods of a contemporary philosopher or the perspective or language of psychology, cultural anthropology, or sociology.

This is the reason we have said that a historico-religious creative hermeneutics would be able to stimulate, nourish, and renew philosophical thought. From a certain point of view, one could say that a new *Phenomenology of the Mind* awaits elaboration by taking account of all that the History of Religions is capable of revealing to us. There would be important books to write on Modes of Existing in the World or on The Problems of Time, Death, and Dream, based on documents that the historian of religions has at his disposal.[7]

---

[7] There are, above all, urgent rectifications to bring to so many clichés still encumbering contemporary culture, for example, Feuerbach's and Marx's celebrated interpretations of religion as alienation. As one knows, Feuerbach and Marx proclaimed that religion estranges man from the earth, prevents him from becoming completely human, and so on. But, even if this were

These problems have passionate interest for the philosophers, poets, and art critics. Some of them have read the historians of religions and have utilized their documents and interpretations. It is not their fault if they have not profited from these readings as they expected.

We have alluded to the interest that the History of Religions holds for artists, writers, and literary critics. Unhappily, historians of religions, like most scholars and erudites, have interested themselves in modern artistic experiments only sporadically and in a kind of clandestine manner. There is a preconceived idea that the arts are not "serious," for they do not constitute instruments of knowledge. One reads the poets and novelists and visits museums and expositions to find distraction or relaxation. This prejudice, which is fortunately beginning to disappear, has created a kind of inhibition whose principal results are the uneasiness, ignorance, or suspicion of the erudites and scientists vis-à-vis modern artistic experiments. It is naïvely believed that six months of "field work" among a tribe whose language one can scarcely speak haltingly constitutes "serious" work that can advance knowledge of man—and one ignores all that surrealism or James Joyce, Henry Michaux, and Picasso have contributed to the knowledge of man.

The contemporary artistic experiments are capable of aiding the historians of religions in their own research, and, conversely, a truly historico-religious exegesis is called to stimulate the artists, writers, and critics, not because one finds "the same things" in both cases, but because one encounters situations which they can clarify reciprocally. It is not without interest to note, for example, that in their revolt against the traditional forms of art and their attacks on bourgeois society and morality the surrealists not only elaborated a

---

correct, such a critique of religion could be applied only to late forms of religiosity such as those of post-Vedic India or of Judeo-Christianity—that is, religions in which the element of "other-worldness" plays an important role. Alienation and estrangement of man from the earth are unknown, and, moreover, inconceivable, in all religions of the cosmic type, "primitive" as well as oriental; in this case (that is to say, in the overwhelming majority of religions known to history) the religious life consists exactly in exalting the solidarity of man with life and nature.

revolutionary aesthetic but also formulated a technique by which they hoped to *change* the human condition. A number of these "exercises" (for examples, the effort to obtain a "mode of existence" that participates in both the waking and sleeping states or the effort to realize the "coexistence of the conscious and the unconscious") recall certain Yogic or Zen practices. Moreover, one deciphers in the early *élan* of sur-realism, and notably in the poems and theoretical manifestos of André Breton, a nostalgia for the "primordial totality," the desire to effect *in concreto* the coincidence of opposites, the hope of being able to annul history in order to begin anew with the original power and purity—nostalgia and hopes rather familiar to historians of religions.

Moreover, all the modern artistic movements seek, con-sciously or unconsciously, the destruction of the traditional aesthetic universes, the reduction of "forms" to elementary, germinal, larval states in the hope of re-creating "fresh worlds"; in other words these movements seek to abolish the history of art and to reintegrate the auroral moment when man saw the world "for the first time." It is unnecessary to mention how all this should interest the historian of religions familiar with the rather well-known mythological system that involves the symbolic destruction and re-creation of the uni-verse in order periodically to begin anew a "pure" existence in a fresh, strong, and fertile world.

It is not a question of developing close correspondences here between the modern artistic experiments and certain behaviors, symbolisms, and beliefs familiar to historians of religions. For a generation already, especially in the United States, critics have utilized historico-religious documents in the interpretation of literary works. We have stressed else-where[8] the interest in symbolisms and rituals of initiation shown by literary critics; indeed, they have grasped the im-portance of this religious complex for the elucidation of the secret message of certain works. To be sure, it is not a matter of homologous phenomena; the pattern of initiation survives in literature in relation to the structure of an imaginary uni-

[8] *L'Initiation,* to appear in a forthcoming *Supplement* to *Numen.*

verse, while the historian of religions has to do with lived experiences and traditional institutions. But the fact that the pattern of initiation persists in the imaginary universes of modern man—in literature, dreams, and day-dreams—invites the historian of religions to meditate more attentively on the value of his own documents.

In brief, the History of Religions affirms itself as both a "pedagogy," in the strong sense of that term, for it is susceptible of changing man, and a source of creation of "cultural values," whatever may be the expression of these values, historiographic, philosophic, or artistic. It is to be expected that the assumption of this function by the History of Religions will be suspected, if not frankly contested, by the scientists as well as by the theologians. The former are suspicious of any effort to revalorize religion. Satisfied with the vertiginous secularization of Western societies, the scientists are inclined to suspect obscurantism or nostalgia in authors who see in the different forms of religion something other than superstition, ignorance, or, at the most, psychological behavior, social institutions, rudimentary ideologies, fortunately left behind by the progress of scientific thought and the triumph of technology. Such a suspicion does not belong exclusively to the scientists in the strict sense of the terms; it is equally shared by a large number of sociologists, anthropologists, and social scientists who conduct themselves, not as humanists, but as naturalists with respect to their object of study. But it is necessary to accept such resistance gracefully; it is inevitable in any culture that can still develop in complete freedom.

As for the theologians, their hesitations are explained by various reasons. On the one hand, they are rather suspicious of historico-religious hermeneutics that might encourage syncretism or religious dilettantism or, worse yet, raise doubts about the uniqueness of the Judeo-Christian revelation. On the other hand, the History of Religions envisages, in the end, cultural *creation* and the *modification* of man. The humanist culture poses an embarrassing problem for the theologians and for Christians in general: What do Athens and Jerusalem have in common? We do not intend to discuss here this problem that still obsesses certain theologies. But it would be futile to ignore the fact that nearly all the contemporary philosophies and ideologies recognize that man's specific mode of being in the universe inevitably forces him to be a creator of culture. Whatever the point of departure for an analysis that seeks a definition of man, whether one utilizes the psychological, sociological, or existentialist approach, or some criterion borrowed from classical philosophies, one comes, explicitly or implicitly, to characterize man as a creator of culture (i.e., language, institutions, techniques, arts, etc.). And all the methods of liberation of man—economic, political, psychological—are justified by their final goal: to deliver man from his chains or his complexes in order to open him to the world of the spirit and to render him *culturally creative*. Moreover, for the unbelievers or the irreligious all that a theologian, indeed, simply a Christian, considers heterogeneous in the sphere of culture—the mystery of faith, the sacramental life, etc.—is included in the sphere of "cultural creations." And one cannot deny the character of "cultural facts," at least to the *historical expressions* of the Christian religious experience. Many contemporary theologians have already accepted the presuppositions of the sociology of religion and are ready to accept the inevitability of technology. The fact that there are some theologies of culture indicates the direction in which contemporary theological thought is moving.[9]

But for the historian of religions the problem is posed differently, although not necessarily in contradiction with the theologies of culture. The historian of religions knows that what one calls "profane culture" is a comparatively recent manifestation in the history of the spirit. In the beginning, every cultural creation—tools, institutions, arts, ideologies, etc.—was a religious expression or had a religious justification or source. This is not always evident to a non-specialist, par-

---

[9] The recent "anticultural" crises should not impress us too much. Contempt for or the rejection of culture constitutes dialectical moments in the history of the mind.

ticularly because he is used to conceiving "religion" according to the forms familiar in Western societies or in the great Asian religions. It is conceded that dance, poetry, or wisdom were, in their beginning, religious; one has difficulty in imagining that alimentation or sexuality, an essential work (hunting, fishing, agriculture, etc.), the tools employed, or a habitation, equally participate in the sacred. And yet, one of the embarrassing difficulties for the historian of religions is that the nearer he approaches to "origins," the greater becomes the number of "religious facts." This is so much so that in certain cases (for example, in archaic or prehistoric societies) one asks himself what is *not* or has not once been "sacred" or connected with the sacred.

It would be useless, because ineffectual, to appeal to some reductionist principle and to demystify the behavior and ideologies of *homo religiosus* by showing, for example, that it is a matter of projections of the unconscious, or of screens raised for social, economic, political, or other reasons. Here we touch a rather thorny problem that comes again to each generation with new force. We shall not try to discuss it in a few lines, especially as we have already discussed it in several earlier publications.[10] Let us recall, however, a single example. In a number of traditional archaic cultures the village, temple, or house is considered to be located at the "Center of the World." There is no sense in trying to "demystify" such a belief by drawing the attention of the reader to the fact that there exists no Center of the World and that, in any case, the the multiplicity of such centers is an absurd notion because it is self-contradictory. On the contrary, it is only by taking this belief seriously, by trying to clarify all its cosmological, ritual, and social implications, that one succeeds in comprehending the existential situation of a man who believes that he is at the Center of the World. All his behavior, his understanding of the world, the values he accords to life and to his own existence, arise and become articulated in a

[10] Cf., for example, *Images et symboles* (Paris, 1952), pp. 13 ff. (*Images and Symbols* [New York, 1961], pp. 9 ff.); *Mythes, rêves et mystères* (Paris, 1957), pp. 10 ff., 156 ff. (*Myths, Dreams and Mysteries* [New York, 1960], pp. 13 ff., 106 ff.); *Méphistophélès et l'Androgyne*, pp. 194 ff.

"system" on the basis of this belief that his house or his village is situated near the *axis mundi*.

We have cited this example in order to recall that demystification does not serve hermeneutics. Consequently, whatever may be the reason for which human activities in the most distant past were charged with a religious value, the important thing for the historian of religions remains the fact that these activities *have had* religious values. This means to say that the historian of religions recognizes a spiritual unity subjacent to the history of humanity; in other terms, in studying the Australians, Vedic Indians, or whatever other ethnic group or cultural system, the historian of religions does not have a sense of moving in a world radically "foreign" to him. Certainly, the unity of the human species is accepted *de facto* in other disciplines, for example, linguistics, anthropology, sociology. But the historian of religions has the privilege of grasping this unity at the highest levels—or the deepest—and such an experience is susceptible of enriching and changing him. Today history is becoming truly universal for the first time, and so culture is in the process of becoming "planetary." The history of many from paleolithic to present times is destined to occupy the center of humanist education, whatever the local or national interpretations. The History of Religions can play an essential role in this effort toward a *planétisation* of culture; it can contribute to the elaboration of a universal type of culture.

Certainly, all this will not come tomorrow. But the History of Religions will be able to play this role only if the historians of religions become conscious of their responsibility, in other words, if they break free of the inferiority complexes, timidity, and immobility of the last fifty years. To remind historians of religions that they are supposed to contribute creatively to culture, that they do not have the right to produce only *Beiträge* but also some *cultural values* does not mean to say that one invites them to make facile syntheses and hasty generalizations. It is on the example of an E. Rohde, a Pettazzoni, a Van der Leeuw that one ought to meditate and not on that of some successful journalist. But it is the attitude of the historian of religions vis-à-vis his own discipline that ought to change if he wants to hope for an early renewal of this discipline. In the measure that the historians of religions will not attempt to integrate their researches in the living stream of contemporary culture, the "generalizations" and "syntheses" will be made by dilettantes, amateurs, journalists. Or, what is no happier, instead of a creative hermeneutics in the perspective of the History of Religions, we shall continue to submit to the audacious and irrelevant interpretations of religious realities made by psychologists, sociologists, or devotees of various reductionist ideologies. And for one or two generations yet we shall read books in which the religious realities will be explained in terms of infantile traumatisms, social organization, class conflict, and so on. Certainly such books, including those produced by dilettantes as well as those written by reductionists of various kinds, will continue to appear, and probably with the same success. But the cultural milieu will not be the same if, beside this production, appear some responsible books signed by historians of religions. (This on the condition, understandably, that these books of synthesis are not improvised, at the demand of an editor, as happens sometimes even with very respectable scholars. Obviously, "synthesis," like "analysis," is not amenable to improvisation.)

It seems to me difficult to believe that, living in a historical moment like ours, the historians of religions will not take account of the creative possibilities of their discipline. How to assimilate *culturally* the spiritual universes that Africa, Oceania, Southeast Asia open to us? All these spiritual universes have a religious origin and structure. If one does not approach them in the perspective of the History of Religions, they will disappear as spiritual universes; they will be reduced to *facts* about social organizations, economic regimes, epochs of precolonial and colonial history, etc. In other words, they will not be grasped as spiritual creations; they will not enrich Western and world culture—they will serve to augment the number, already terrifying, of *documents* classified in archives, awaiting electronic computers to take them in charge.

It may be, of course, that this time also the historians of religions will sin through an excessive timidity and leave to other disciplines the task of interpreting these spiritual universes (alas! already changing vertiginously, perhaps even disappearing). It may be also that, for various reasons, the historians of religions will prefer to remain in the subordinate situation that they have previously accepted. In this case we must expect a slow but irrevocable process of decomposition, which will end in the disappearance of the History of Religions as an autonomous discipline. Thus, in one or two generations, we shall have some Latinist "specialists" in the history of Roman religion, Indianist "specialists" in one of the Indian religions, and so on. In other words, the History of Religions will be endlessly fragmented and the fragments reabsorbed in the different "philologies," which today still serve it as documentary sources nourishing its own hermeneutics.

As for the problems of more general interest—for example, myth, ritual, religious symbolism, conceptions of death, initiation, etc.—they will be treated by sociologists, anthropologists, philosophers (as was done, moreover, from the beginnings of our studies, although never exclusively). But this leads us to say that the problems that preoccupy the historians of religions today *will not in themselves disappear;* it is to say only that they will be studied in other perspectives, with different methods, and in the pursual of different objectives. The void left by the disappearance of the History of Religions as an autonomous discipline will not be filled. But the gravity of our responsibility will remain the same.

Symbol, Myth, and the Biblical Revelation

Avery Dulles, S.J.

Avery Dulles, S.J., finds himself at odds both with the "demythologizers" who hold that the Bible must be purged of mythical and symbolic elements if its message is to be communicated to modern man and with the literalist conservatives who claim that the Bible contains no myth. Defining myth as "a symbolic narrative which deals with events attributed to superhuman, personalized agencies," Father Dulles presents a closely reasoned discussion of the value and significance of myth, with particular reference to the Bible. He concludes that while "faith can never be bound to a single set of images," the historical experience of the people of God as set down in the Old and New Testaments remains normative, and that "Scripture, even in its imagery, pertains to the patrimony which God has permanently entrusted to the Church for its study, contemplation, consolation, and guidance." And though each age requires new, secondary images for purposes of evangelization, "they are ultimately controlled by the primary sources from which they stem." Associate Professor of Fundamental Theology at Woodstock College—from whose publication, *Theological Studies*, his essay is taken (March 1966)[*]—Father Dulles is the author of *Apologetics and the Biblical Christ, Introductory Metaphysics*, and *A Testimonial to Grace*.

IF REVELATION were a collection of eternal and necessary truths concerning God, the soul, and immortality—as some rationalists contended—the proper style of theological speech would not differ from that of philosophy. If the stuff of revelation were common historical facts—as some

[*] Woodstock College, Woodstock, Md. 21163.

positivists seemed inclined to think—theology could speak the language of ordinary history. But revelation has to do with the hidden God and the ways in which He calls man into union with Himself. Its doctrine is, therefore, sacred doctrine; its history, sacred history. At every point the subject matter of theology touches on mystery. And how can mystery be expressed? Unlike historical or abstract truth, mystery cannot be described or positively defined. It can only be evoked. Religious language must contrive to point beyond itself and to summon up, in some fashion, the gracious experience of the mystery with which it deals.[1]

The Bible employs a great variety of literary forms. It is a small library containing historical records, poetic effusions, theological meditations, dramatic dialogues, hortatory epistles, etc. But in practically every biblical book we find exceptionally vivid and imaginative speech. The inspired imagery of the Bible may surely be reckoned as one of the main sources of its spiritual power. The biblical images astonish our expectations, grip our attention, challenge our receptivity, haunt our memory, stir our affections, and transform our attitudes. While the Bible is not lacking in doctrine, its language suggests far more about God and His ways with man than it conveys by express concepts. From the crude anthropomorphisms of Genesis to the luxuriant visions of the Apocalypse, the Bible proves itself a treasure house of vivid and majestic symbolism.

This very wealth of symbolism, however, is sometimes considered to be a stumbling block for modern man. Some are of the opinion that the "mythopoeic" idiom of the Bible has had its day, and that the educated man of the twentieth century must be given a religion in statements which he can clearly analyze and verify. Others maintain that while symbolism as such is a constant feature of religious communication, the symbols of the Bible are outmoded. The biblical imagery, emanating from a type of pastoral and patriarchal

[1] Cf. K. Rahner, "Was ist eine dogmatische Aussage?" *Schriften zur Theologie* 5 (Einsiedeln, 1952) 72–74. I. T. Ramsey has shown the inadequacy of observational language in the territory of faith; cf. his *Religious Language* (London, 1957).

society which has vanished in most parts of the globe, is said to be beyond the grasp of modern man. Still others, more attached to what they revere as the divinely given sources, feel that the Bible has lost none of its power, provided it be properly studied and expounded. The main obstacles to Christian communication, according to these conservatives, come not from the language of Scripture but from the human philosophical categories into which the Christian message has all too often been transposed. A return to biblical language, it is contended, could spark a great revival of Christian faith and devotion.

In view of these difficult but urgent questions, considerable attention is currently focused on the question of symbol and myth in the Bible. What role does each of these actually play in the canonical writings? Are the biblical images themselves canonical—in the sense of pertaining to the substance of the revelation—or are they expendable? If they are expendable, should we try to devise new myths and symbols to take the place of those which are no longer appropriate? Or should we seek to "demythologize" the Bible by setting forth the Christian message in a language purged of mythical and symbolic elements? The following pages, without claiming to solve these thorny problems, will perhaps throw light on a proper approach to them.

The Role of Symbol in the Bible

It would be tedious to begin with a long investigation of the exact nature of religious symbolism.[2] Very briefly, we may say that a symbol is a type of sign. It is a word, gesture, picture, statue, or some other type of reality which can be made present to the senses or the imagination, and which points to a reality behind itself. But this other reality is one which cannot be precisely described or defined; it is not

[2] For a full treatment with extensive bibliography, see S. Wisse, *Das religiöse Symbol* (Essen, 1963). In English, valuable contributions by Tillich and others may be found in F. E. Johnson (ed.), *Religious Symbolism* (New York, 1955).

knowable, at least with the same richness and power, except in and through the symbol. The symbol has power to evoke more than it can clearly represent because it addresses itself not simply to the senses and the abstractive intelligence, but to the entire human psyche. It works on the imagination, the will, and the emotions, and thus elicits a response from the whole man. Symbols, therefore, have an existential power which is lacking to purely conventional or conceptual signs. Symbols are of vast importance not simply for cognitive purposes but also for the integration of the human personality, for the cohesion of human societies, and for the corporate life of religious groups. A religion without symbolism would be unthinkable.

Symbols may be found in the natural world, in the events of history, and in the inventions of art and literature. The Bible abounds in literary symbolism, thanks to its poetic and vivid style; but, more fundamentally, it is symbolic because it has to do with symbolic realities, especially with symbolic historical events.

The central theme of both Testaments is quite evidently the great series of mighty deeds by which God manifested His mercy, His loving power, and His enduring fidelity toward the people of His choice. These deeds may be called God's gestures in history, and like human gestures they are symbolic. The divine deed par excellence is the miracle. A miracle, according to the biblical conception, is a sign-event in which a properly attuned religious consciousness can recognize, so to speak, the handwriting of God. For those who have eyes to see and ears to hear, the miracles are eloquent. Like Caesar's wounds, they have tongues of their own.[3] They reveal, with compelling realism and vividness, what Paul calls the "philanthropy of God our Saviour" (Tit 3:5).

Quite apart from particular miracles—the true value of which has unfortunately been obscured by the opportunistic

---

[3] Cf. the famous words of Augustine concerning the miracles of Christ: "Interrogemus ipsa miracula, quid nobis loquantur de Christo; habent enim, si intelligantur, linguam suam. Nam quia ipse Christus Verbum Dei est, etiam factum Verbi verbum nobis est" (*In evang. Ioh.* 24, 1 [*Corpus christianorum, series latina* 36, 244]).

apologetics of a rationalistic age—the entire history of Israel constitutes, one may say, an immense continuing deed of God and stands as an everlasting reminder of God's justice and mercy. The individual operations of God which punctuate this history—such as the crossing of the Red Sea, the manna in the desert, the entry into the Promised Land, and the return of the exiles from Babylon—are heavily charged with symbolic overtones, magnificently brought out by the figurative and hyperbolic language of the inspired accounts. Viewed in connection with their New Testament fulfilment, these events take on a fuller and more abiding significance.

In the New Testament the Incarnate Word is the absolute, unsurpassable earthly embodiment of God, and hence the supreme religious symbol. But for Christ to be effectively a symbol for us, He must be manifested for what He is. Jesus' mighty deeds, His symbolic actions (such as the cleansing of the Temple or the Eucharistic action at the Last Supper), His total self-oblation on Calvary, and God's acceptance of that sacrifice in the Resurrection and Ascension—all these events symbolically disclose various aspects of His person and mission. In Christ and the Church the religious symbolism of the Old Testament was "recapitulated"—in the rich sense given to the term by Irenaeus—and fulfilled beyond all expectation.

If we wish to fathom the true nature of symbol, we could not do better than to ponder a central Christian reality, such as the Cross. Here, in a simple and easily imagined figure, we have a vast wealth of meaning that speaks straight to the human heart. The Cross, as Susanne Langer has pointed out, evokes a whole gamut of related significances:

Many symbols—not only words, but other forms—may be said to be "charged" with meanings. They have many symbolic and signific functions, and these functions have been integrated into a complex so that they are all apt to be sympathetically invoked with any chosen one. The cross is such a "charged" symbol: the actual instrument of Christ's death, hence a symbol of suffering; first laid on his shoulders, an actual burden, as well as an actual product of human handiwork, and on both grounds a symbol of his accepted moral burden; also an ancient symbol of the four zodiac points, with a cosmic connotation; a "natural" symbol of cross-roads (we still use it on our highways as a warning before an intersection), and therefore of decision, crisis, choice; also of *being crossed*, i.e. of frustration, adversity, fate; and finally, to the artistic eye a cross is the figure of a man. All these and many other meanings lie dormant in that simple, familiar, significant shape. No wonder that it is a magical form! It is charged with meanings, all human and emotional and vaguely cosmic, so that they have become integrated into a connotation of the whole religious drama—sin, suffering, and redemption. . . .[4]

For reasons such as these, the Cross performs in an eminent way what all symbolism tends to do: it binds up the shattered, alienated existence of individuals and gives meaning and direction where these previously seemed to be absent. It also serves to bring men together into solidarity with one another. Christians of all ages and nations are welded into a community by their common allegiance to the standard of the Cross.

Thus far we have been speaking of the symbolic realities which form the substance of the biblical message. If we turn now to the language of Scripture, we immediately note that it is highly figurative and frequently poetic. The sacred writers quarry their images from many sources. Sometimes they build on the natural symbolic capacities of elemental realities such as fire, water, sun, bread, wine, and the like. Other images they take over from the social institutions of Israel. Thus, they speak of God as Father, King, Judge, Shepherd, Vinedresser, and Spouse. And all these images, once they have imbedded themselves in the literature and thinking of Israel, begin to take on a history of their own, parallel to that of the people. As Austin Farrer has observed,[5] calamities such as the collapse of the Davidic monarchy, the destruction of the Temple, and the Babylonian captivity providentially served to purify the images, to detach them from their terrestrial moorings, and in this way to give them a higher and more universal

---

[4] Susanne K. Langer, *Philosophy in a New Key* (Cambridge, Mass., 1942) pp. 284 f.
[5] *The Glass of Vision* (Westminster, Eng., 1948) esp. chap. 8.

spiritual meaning. To give one example: it was necessary for the Davidic monarchy to be irrevocably overthrown before the term "Son of David" could be an apt designation for the kind of Messiah Jesus was to be.

The literary imagery of the Old Testament was taken up with added power in the New. Christ described His own status in terms of the Old Testament figures. The parables which He preached are replete with Old Testament reminiscences. The Johannine Gospel, the most symbolic of the four, is built about dominant images such as the Good Shepherd, the True Vine, the Manna, the Living Water, and the Light of the World. Such symbols, as C. H. Dodd remarks, "retire behind the realities for which they stand, and derive their significance from the background of thought in which they had already served as symbols for religious conceptions."[6] The same is true in varying degrees of the other New Testament writings. The most highly figurative of all is, of course, the Apocalypse, which writes of heaven and things to come— that is, as Austin Farrer puts it, "of a realm which has no shape at all but that which the images give it."[7]

The abundance of symbolism in the Bible is not a matter of whim or accident. The language of everyday prose would be incapable of mediating the loving approach of the all-holy God with comparable warmth and efficacy. The inexhaustible riches which theologians and men of prayer have been able to find in the Bible would seem to be intimately bound up with its inspired symbolism; for every symbol, by reason of its concreteness and polyvalence, defies exhaustive translation into the abstract language of doctrinal discourse.[8]

The coexistence in Scripture of symbolic realities and symbolic language poses an obvious problem for the exegete. In many instances it is most difficult to ascertain whether the biblical writers intend to report an actually symbolic event or have supplied the symbolism in order to convey some theo-

---

[6] *The Interpretation of the Fourth Gospel* (Cambridge, Eng., 1958) p. 137.
[7] *A Rebirth of Images* (Westminster, Eng., 1949) p. 17.
[8] Pius XII taught that Scripture as well as tradition "tot tantosque continet thesauros veritatis, ut numquam reapse exhauriatur" (*Humani generis* [1950]; cf. Denzinger-Schönmetzer, *Enchiridion symbolorum* [32nd ed.; Freiburg, 1963] no. 3886).

logical insight. The infancy narratives of Matthew and Luke, because of their peculiarly literary genre (generally classified as midrashic), are a case in point. It may eventually be agreed that some of the incidents in these narratives are not, in the modern sense, historical events; but one cannot lay it down as a general principle that symbolism in a narrative is evidence against its historical realism. On the contrary, the central mysteries of the Christian faith derive much of their symbolic value from their historical reality. The Cross, for example, is a compelling symbol of our redemption precisely because the Son of God was truly crucified. And the Resurrection is a symbol of our new life in Christ because it vividly declares what God has actually done for us. Some modern interpreters, especially outside the Catholic Church, are too ready to let the symbolism of language do service for the symbolism of actual deeds. Such an attitude is ultimately at odds with the realism of the Incarnation; it is more congenial to ancient Gnosticism than to normative Christianity.

Myth: Its Nature

As a form of symbolic thought and expression, myth plays a central role in many, if not all, religions. Our consideration of Christian symbolism, therefore, raises inevitably the problem of Christian mythology. Can it be admitted that myth has a function in revelation, in the inspired Scriptures, in the Christian religion? These questions are large and divisive. In order to approach them fruitfully, we must form some approximate idea of what the term "myth" means or should mean in such contexts. The very meaning of the term is much disputed, and the diversity of opinion on the questions just posed is largely due to this variety of definitions.

For some writers, practically any numinous symbol may be characterized as myth. If myth is whatever points up the permanent spiritual dimension of events, thus linking them with their divine ground, it is obvious that any religion, including Christianity, must have its mythology. John Knox, working with a very wide concept of myth, says that if modern man cannot accept myth, religion is no longer a possibility.[9]

But the problem of myth is more acutely posed if one defines myth, as most do, in a narrower sense. Brevard S. Childs, in an important study,[10] distinguishes among several current meanings. First, there is the view of the so-called "mythical school" of Old Testament critics (Eichhorn, Gabler, and G. L. Bauer), for whom myth is a primitive form of thinking in which unexplainable events are attributed to the direct intervention of deities. Secondly, there is the Form-Critical definition, held by the Grimm brothers, W. Wundt, and H. Gunkel, who look on myth as any story in which the active persons are gods. But neither of these two definitions is satisfactory. The first rests upon the unspoken rationalistic assumption that only a primitive mind could attribute anything to an interposition of divine power. The second definition is too exclusively literary and fails to do justice to the numinous and cultic dimensions normally associated with myth. A fanciful story told merely to entertain the imagination, even if some of its characters were deities, would not appear to deserve the name of myth.

It seems best, therefore, to arrive at our definition of myth —as Prof. Childs proposes—by a phenomenological method, taking advantage of the findings of modern ethnology and the history of religions. John L. McKenzie, in a recently published article,[11] gives a very helpful synthesis, lining up some of the principal characteristics of myth, at least as found in the religious literature of the ancient Near East. Relying on studies such as this, one may list the following traits as characteristically mythical.

1) Myth is a communal possession. In most cases myths have their origin in a very distant past and are folk creations. If a modern author deliberately constructs a myth, this can

[9] *Myth and Truth: An Essay on the Language of Faith* (Charlottesville, 1964) p. 28. For a similar view, see B. H. Throckmorton, Jr., *The New Testament and Mythology* (Philadelphia, 1959) pp. 94–105.

[10] *Myth and Reality in the Old Testament* (Naperville, 1960) pp. 13–16.

[11] "Myth and the Old Testament," in *Myths and Realities: Studies in Biblical Theology* (Milwaukee, 1963) pp. 182–200, 266–68.

only be an imitation of the ancient anonymous myths which have been handed down in tradition. And it will not really obtain currency as myth unless it is accepted by a community as a symbol and carrier of its concrete form of life. It must be, as Wellek and Warren put it, endorsed by the "consent of the faithful."[12]

2) Like other symbols, a myth is a figurative representation of a reality which eludes precise description or definition. But in contrast to the rather sophisticated symbolism of parable and allegory, mythical symbolism involves a minimum of critical reflection. The myth-maker thinks and speaks quite naively, without any effort to determine the extent to which his story corresponds to, and falls short of, the reality to which it points.

3) Myth deals with a numinous order of reality behind the appearances of the phenomenal world. If there is an animistic stage of religious evolution, in which men divinize the objects of nature themselves, this stage deserves to be called premythical. The properly mythical phase presupposes that man has learned to make some distinction between nature and its transcendent ground.[13] Only when this insight has been achieved does man look to the actions of the gods as offering an explanation of what is experienced in the world.

4) The numinous presence which myth discerns behind the world of phenomena is portrayed in personal terms. This does not mean that the god or gods are clearly recognized as being persons. Myth, being essentially vague and closely bound to imaginative thought, would be incapable of conveying a definite judgment about whether the transcendent is ultimately personal. But the forces behind the world are at least depicted as if they were persons.

In a wider sense, the concept of myth can be extended to include impersonal agencies, provided these are hypostatized. In this looser usage, one may speak of the myth of inevitable progress or the myth of democracy. But since the personal

[12] R. Wellek and A. Warren, *Theory of Literature* (New York, 1942) p. 196; a similar point is made by J. Knox, *op. cit.*, p. 24.
[13] P. Tillich, "Mythus," *Die Religion in Geschichte und Gegenwart* 4 (2nd ed., 1930) 370; J. Sløk, "Mythus," *ibid.* 4 (3rd ed., 1960) 1264.

reference is lacking, we do not have myth in the strict sense. If a force such as progress is portrayed as a god or goddess, this can only be by the merest artifice.[14]

5) The transcendent figures of the mythical world are represented as taking part in activities on a cosmic scale, which exert a permanent causal influence on earthly happenings. Each particular myth aims to account for a whole series of recurring phenomena, such as the rhythm of the seasons, the variations of weather, the alternation of night and day. To all such events one may apply what McKenzie says of the fertility gods: "The gods of fertility are not merely symbols of natural forces; the succession of phenomena depends on the perpetual life-death cycle on a cosmic scale, and these gods make the cycle."[15]

6) The cosmic event is expressed in the form of a story, a drama which unfolds in a dimension of duration quite removed from time as we experience it. As Eliade says, "mythic or sacred time is qualitatively different from profane time, from the continuous and irreversible time of our profane existence. . . . The myth takes man out of his own time— his individual, chronological, 'historic' time—and projects him, symbolically at least, into the Great Time, into a paradoxical instant which cannot be measured because it does not consist of duration."[16] Through cultic action the mythical events are brought to bear upon particular earthly situations.

The time dimension proper to myth is of great importance in distinguishing myth not only from static types of symbolism (such as a skull or a flag) but also from legends, tales, and sacred history. Legends or sagas are imaginary divinatory amplifications of events which are located in history. Tales take place in an indefinite time, "once upon a time," but not in a distinct species of time which causally underlies the time we experience on earth. Sacred history, as we shall see,

---

[14] In his polemic against Bultmann, Barth insists on the permanence of myth in the modern world—a point he proceeds to exemplify by referring to "the myth of the twentieth century, the Marxist myth, the myth of the Christian West, etc." But are these properly myths? Cf. H. W. Bartsch (ed.), *Kerygma and Myth* 2 (London, 1962) 109.

[15] McKenzie, *art. cit.*, p. 190.

[16] M. Eliade, *Images and Symbols* (New York, 1961) pp. 57–58.

unfolds in the dimension of irreversible, earthly time, and is therefore not mythical.

7) The stories of myth are not told for their own sake. As we have already indicated, they deal with matters of intense concern to man. Thanks to mythical symbolism, as Eliade says, "man does not feel himself 'isolated' in the cosmos. . . . He 'opens out' into a world which, thanks to a symbol, proves 'familiar.' "[17] This existential import gives myths their religious value and their holding power. But myths vary in the immediacy with which they are connected with the present concerns of man. This will appear from any of the standard classifications of myth by reason of their content. Following Tillich,[18] we may break down myths into categories such as (a) theogonic, (b) cosmogonic and cosmological, (c) anthropological, (d) soteriological, and (e) eschatological. All these areas are capable of being treated mythically insofar as realities within them are attributed to actions of the gods described in the form of symbolic narrative.

A final question about the nature of myth may now be raised. Is it necessarily polytheistic or does the notion of myth prescind from the alternatives of polytheism and monotheism? Of itself, myth is not a doctrine but a mode of thinking and expression. It might seem, then, that a man could think mythically about one god as well as about many. But the content of myth cannot surpass the capacities of mythical representation. Since the rhythms of nature are apparently manifold and mutually opposed, myth can hardly look upon the divine ground as being other than multiple. For the same reason, this ground will be viewed as closely involved with the forces of nature, and as having some kind of successive duration, ambiguously related to time as we know it. Of itself, myth cannot criticize or rise above these limitations in its own mode of representation.

In summary, then, we may conclude that myth, at least in the sense in which we shall use the term, is a particular

[17] Id., "Methodological Remarks on the Study of Religious Symbolism," in The History of Religions: Essays in Methodology (Chicago, 1959) p. 103.
[18] Art. cit., col. 366.

type of symbol. It is a symbolic narrative which deals with events attributed to superhuman, personalized agencies. These events, unfolding in a time above that of our experience, are conceived as having a profound influence on the typical occurrences familiar to us. Through the recital and cultic re-enactment of the myths which it accepts, a community feels itself delivered from the grip of cosmic forces and, on occasion, brought into union with the divine. Not all these elements, of course, will be equally prominent in every instance. There are borderline cases which it is hard to classify as myth or legend or simple tale. Some authors may wish to give a wider or narrower meaning to the term "myth" than ours. But the description given in the preceding paragraphs is not arbitrary; it has a solid basis in the usage of many acknowledged authorities and commends itself by its relative clarity.

The Abiding Value of Myth

From the Enlightenment until the twentieth century, myth was generally characterized as a primitive mode of thought, practically devoid of value as an approach to truth. This point of view is reflected in the definition in the Oxford English Dictionary: "A purely fictitious narrative usually involving supernatural persons, actions, or events, and embodying some popular idea concerning natural or historical phenomena." The assumption behind all such definitions is that while primitive, prelogical men may have taken myths seriously, modern man goes to them only for entertainment or relaxation. The myth in itself says something false. If it contains a hidden grain of truth, this can and should be restated in strictly rational terms.

Modern studies in fields such as depth psychology and the history of religions have brought about a far-reaching rehabilitation of myth. It is rather commonly regarded today as a distinct mode of knowledge which can never be adequately reduced to rational discourse. Some contemporary thinkers, under the influence of a Kantian epistemology, stress chiefly the value of myth in the subjective order. Cassirer, for instance, considers that it registers states of soul which cannot be otherwise expressed.[19] For Jung, the study of myths affords new insights into the structure of the human psyche, inasmuch as myths have their source in the archetypes of the collective unconscious, and never cease to emerge from it, at least in the forms of dreams and fantasies.[20]

A second group of modern thinkers who defend the permanent validity of myth are known as "symbolico-realists." They prefer to stress the transsubjective content revealed by mythical symbols. Eliade, for instance, has explained at length how the myths of polarity and reintegration in many religious traditions—for example the myth of androgyny—disclose the structure of the divine as *coincidentia oppositorum,* thus lending support to the whole tradition of Christion negative theology from Pseudo-Dionysius to Nicholas of Cusa.[21] Tillich, building on the religious philosophy of Schelling, agrees that myths, as a source of knowledge, have independent value. Symbols concerning divine figures and actions, he holds, are uniquely apt for relating man to the object of his ultimate concern, which is the proper domain of religious faith.[22]

While he looks on myth as an abiding religious category, which can never be simply left behind, Tillich acknowledges that in a certain sense we live in a postmythical age. Once critical thought has been applied to religious questions, mythical portrayals of the gods as involved in the flux and multiplicity of natural phenomena are seen to be inadequate. The divine is grasped as unconditionally transcendent. But in the postmythical period the myth survives, according to Tillich, as a symbol or pointer to the divine. It is no longer taken

---

[19] Cassirer's philosophy of myth is found in several works, most importantly in *The Philosophy of Symbolic Forms* 2: *Mythical Thought* (New Haven, 1955).

[20] For an exposition and critique, see R. Hostie, *Du mythe à la religion: La psychologie analytique de C. G. Jung* (Bruges, 1955).

[21] *Patterns in Comparative Religion* (New York, 1958) pp. 416–26.

[22] P. Tillich, *The Dynamics of Faith* (New York, 1957) p. 49. Tillich's doctrine of myth has been fully analyzed in P. Barthel, *Interprétation du langage mythique et théologie biblique* (Leiden, 1963) pp. 152–98.

literally, but is understood to be, precisely, a myth. In being recognized as such, it is in a certain sense demythologized; it becomes what Tillich likes to call a "broken myth." Thereafter both myth and critical thinking coexist, Tillich affirms, in a state of correlation or dialectical tension. Neither succeeds in completely eliminating the other.

Many authors object that a myth, once it has been "elucidated into a symbol," no longer remains a myth in the true sense of the term.[23] Others maintain that it remains a myth properly so called, for it is still accepted as an element of community tradition which in some mysterious way answers to the deeper aspects of experience.[24] Tillich's term "broken myth" seems to combine what is valid in both these approaches. While the application of critical thinking represents a real advance over the merely mythical mode of conception, it does not fully displace the latter. Even for modern Western man, Greek myths such as those of Prometheus, Oedipus, and Sisyphus, although clearly distinguished from historical events, have not lost their psychic power. They continue to speak to the depths of our existence and help to reintegrate us with ourselves and our universe. If this be true even of pagan myths, we must consider seriously whether there cannot be such a thing as Judeo-Christian mythology.

The very term will seem shocking to those who look upon religion exclusively as revelation, and upon revelation as a collection of dogmas set forth in strict propositional language. But if religion is a dialogue between man and God, and if revelation is the whole process by which God draws near to man and manifests His presence, one must keep open, at least provisionally, the possibility that the divine presence might be apprehended and registered in mythical thought and expression. Without prejudice to the dogmatic content of revelation, which is certainly not mythical in the sense described above, it seems possible to hold that the doctrines are sometimes surrounded by a penumbra of thinking and

[23] So, for example, G. Miegge in *Gospel and Myth in the Thought of Rudolf Bultmann* (London, 1960) pp. 118–19.
[24] J. Knox, *op. cit.*, p. 78.

speech which deserves to be called mythical. If myth is ever a bearer of revelation, we should expect to find that this is true in the Holy Scriptures.

Myth in the Bible: A Priori Considerations

Catholics and conservative Protestants have often expressed the view that myth can have no place in revelation or in the Bible. Billot, for instance, wrote that since myth is a product of popular credulity or is invented by the learned to foster popular credulity, God could not inspire such a thing.[25] Benoit, in the French edition of his *La prophétie* (1947), after observing that it is not for us to decide antecedently what literary forms are or are not worthy of God, adds in a footnote: "There is nevertheless one type which must a priori be excluded from the Bible as unworthy of God: this is 'myth'—for it introduces error and fiction into the very essence of religious speculations about the divinity."[26]

As a partial explanation for these negative judgments, it may be pointed out that these authors and the Church documents to which they appeal[27] presuppose the "rationalistic" notion of myth which was popularized by the "mythical school" already mentioned. But it is also doubtless true that

[25] L. Billot, S.J., *De inspiratione sacrae Scripturae* (4th ed.; Rome, 1929) p. 155.

[26] "Il y a toutefois un genre qu'on doit exclure *a priori* de la Bible comme 'indigne' de Dieu: c'est le 'mythe,' parce qu'il introduit l'erreur et la fiction dans l'essence même des spéculations religieuses sur la Divinité" (in P. Synave, O.P., and P. Benoit, O.P., *La prophétie: Somme théologique, 2a-2ae, qq. 171-78* [Tournai, 1947] p. 369, n. 1). But note that in the English translation (*Prophecy and Inspiration* [New York, 1961]), made with some additions and corrections by the author, this is modified to read (p. 161): ". . . any kind of 'myth' which would introduce error or fiction into the very essence of religious speculations about the Deity." Among the manualists, Vosté and Chr. Pesch, like Billot, flatly assert that myths are excluded from the inspired books. Nicolau (in *Sacrae theologiae summa* 1 [2nd ed.; Madrid, 1952] p. 1055 [Part 4, no. 188]) holds that myth as such cannot be present in the Bible, but that myths may be cited or used as literary ornaments by the biblical authors. Bea (*De Scripturae sacrae inspiratione* [2nd ed.; Rome, 1935] no. 89) says that it may not be affirmed a priori that God cannot teach men even by myth, "dummodo curet ut haec genera ut talia cognosci possint et verbis non necessario ascribatur veritas proprio sensu historica."

[27] *Pius IX, Syllabus* (*DS* 2907/1707) and Decree of the Biblical Commission of 1909 (*EB* [4th ed.] 325).

Catholic authors until very recently took it too much for granted that revelation occurred through objective historical events whose meaning was determinately given, prior to any intervention of the human mind. If we hold that God made Himself known not simply through historical happenings "which impinge from above upon Israel and to which she subsequently adds subjective reflection," but rather through "the total experience of Israel," the question of myth presents itself in an entirely new light.[28] Like other creative expressions of the Israelite spirit, myths might well serve as building blocks of the great temple which was to receive its capping stone in Christ. We believe, therefore, that myths cannot be excluded on principle from the Bible on the ground that they are "fabula religiosa falsa" (Nicolau, no. 188), but that the question should be resolved a posteriori. We should examine what is actually to be found in the biblical books, conducting this search in the light of the notion of myth we have derived from comparative religion and ethnology.

Myth in the Old Testament

At first sight it would seem that myth bulks large in the Old Testament. Competent scholars are practically unanimous in recognizing in many sections of the Old Testament, especially in Genesis, reminiscences of myths which can likewise be found in Sumerian, Accadian, and Canaanite literature.[29] The stories of the formation of the world, the Garden of Eden, the Flood, and the Tower of Babel—to cite several well-known examples—would seem to be adaptations of primitive myths such as we find in other cultures. But once we allow the presence of *mythical elements* in the Bible, the question still remains intact: Are they still *myths* as they appear on the pages of Scripture?

[28] The phrases quoted are from B. S. Childs (*op. cit.*, p. 102), who is criticizing certain Protestant views of *Heilsgeschichte*.

[29] For a convenient summary, cf. H. Cazelles, "Mythe et l'A.T.," *Dict. de la Bible, Supplément* 6, 246–61. Also, more briefly, T. H. Gaster in *Interpreter's Dictionary of the Bible* 3, 481–87.

From the beginning of her existence as a people, the Israelites had an overriding conception of Yahweh which cannot be written off as myth. As McKenzie says, myth when left to its own resources remains imprisoned in the order of shifting phenomena; it merely retells the story of the phenomenal world on a larger scale, and is incapable of attaining the divine in its transcendence.[30] Since the time of Gunkel it has been a commonplace that Israel was not favorable soil for myths, since they link the divine with nature in a way contrary to that of the Bible and are basically incapable of overcoming polytheism.[31] As distinct from all the mythical gods, Yahweh is constantly portrayed by the Israelites as unique, free, and totally sovereign over every other power in heaven and on earth.

Closely linked with the absolute sovereignty of Yahweh is the fact that the Bible disavows all nature religion. Barth is fundamentally right in holding that the Bible deals from first to last with God's historical action. Not everything in the Bible is history in the modern and technical understanding of the term; much of it is rather saga, i.e., a poetic and divinatory elaboration on history.[32] But saga, like history, claims to deal with unique and unrepeatable events, whereas myth does not intend to be, but merely pretends to be, history.[33] The creation account in Genesis, far from falling in the same category as the Babylonian cosmogonies, may be viewed as a polemic against them. According to Barth, it asserts precisely what myth cannot grasp, namely, the transcendent and creative act whereby God gave the universe an absolute beginning.[34]

The central faith of Israel undoubtedly rests not upon mythological construction but upon a privileged religious experience giving the people and its religious leaders a singularly vivid knowledge of Yahweh as Lord of the universe. This insight issued in firm doctrinal affirmations, in exclusive

[30] *Art. cit.*, p. 291.
[31] H. Gunkel, "Mythus und Mythologie im A.T.," *Die Religion in Geschichte und Gegenwart* 4 (2nd ed., 1930) 381. Also G. Stählin, art. "Mythos," in G. Kittel, *Theologisches Wörterbuch zum Neuen Testament* 4, 787.
[32] Karl Barth, *Church Dogmatics* 3/1 (Edinburgh, 1938) 83.
[33] *Ibid.* 1/1 (Edinburgh, 1936) 376.
[34] *Ibid.* 3/1, 84–90.

claims, and in a demand for total commitment—responses in no way required by a myth, which can coexist quite contentedly beside its own contrary.[35]

Since their essential faith was nourished by something quite different from myth, it is not surprising that the Israelites produced no mythology of their own. They did, however, borrow from the mythologies of the surrounding peoples, and in some cases subjected these to a process of demythologizing which is at best relatively complete. For example, in various references to the creation, we find allusions to mighty struggles between Yahweh and mysterious monsters such as Leviathan and Rahab (e.g., Ps 73/74, Ps 88/89, Is 27, Job 9, Job 20).[36] What have we here if not a mythical representation—not false but not fully translated into doctrinal terms—of the ceaseless conflict between Yahweh and the powers of evil? In other passages, such as the mention of the sexual intercourse between the sons of God and the daughters of men (Gn 6:4 ff.), the myths seem to have been only lightly retouched and to remain, as Childs points out, in partial tension with the fundamental faith of Israel.[37]

In the later portions of the Old Testament the mythological elements are subjected to stricter control. The prophets use mythological themes with considerable detachment and deliberation to suggest the quality of events which had not been revealed to them in detail. Especially is this true of the accounts of the creation and final consummation. Dodd gives a good explanation:

These first and last things can be spoken of only in symbols. They lie, obviously, outside the order of time and space to which all factual statements refer. They are not events (as the historian knows events), but realities of a suprahistorical order. In referring to them the Biblical writers make free use of mythology.[38]

---

[35] This point is well made by H. Fries, "Mythos und Offenbarung," in J. Feiner *et al.* (ed.), *Fragen der Theologie heute* (Einsiedeln, 1957) p. 39.
[36] J. L. McKenzie has assembled a collection of *OT* passages of this type in THEOLOGICAL STUDIES 11 (1950) 275–82. For his present judgment on their mythical character, see *art. cit.*, (supra n. 11) p. 193.
[37] *Op. cit.*, chap. 3.
[38] C. H. Dodd, *The Bible Today* (paperback ed.; Cambridge, Eng., 1961) p. 112. O. Cullmann, who likewise labels the biblical descriptions of the prehistory and posthistory as myth, draws a very sharp opposition between myth and history; cf. *Christ and Time* (Philadelphia, 1950) pp. 94–96.

The entire process, which leads from the earliest traditions of Genesis to the latest contributions of the postexilic prophets, may be characterized as a continual process of demythologizing.[39] The primitive pagan myths, which gave concrete expression to man's longing for divine deliverance from the hostile powers, are gradually answered by divine revelation. As the answer is heard and assimilated, the myths are progressively purified, broken, and sublimated. But for the fulness of the answer, we must look beyond the Old Testament.

Myth in the New Testament

The question of myth in the New Testament has been the subject of lively controversy in recent years and requires some special treatment, even in so brief a survey as we are attempting. The New Testament itself uses the term "myth" in a definitely pejorative sense. On four occasions in the Pauline pastoral epistles, *mythos* is denounced as contrary to revealed truth and sound doctrine.[40] 2 Peter, moreover, vehemently declares that the Christian faith is founded on solidly attested facts, vouched for by eyewitnesses, and is therefore totally unlike "cunningly devised myths (*mythois*)" (2 Pt 1:16). But the very fact that the New Testament writers, toward the close of the first century, are obliged to warn the faithful so insistently against following myths, and to remind them that the gospel itself is no myth, implies that there was enough similarity so that some Christians were confusing the two. If the gospel is so closely related to myth, we may well ask whether myth did not in fact gain some foothold in the New Testament.

Since the early nineteenth century, various scholars have argued that the New Testament is heavily infected with myth. To simplify a complex chapter in the history of modern theology, we may content ourselves with a brief sketch of three main "mythicizing" positions.

1) The first great movement in this direction was influ-

[39] H. Cazelles, *art. cit.,* col. 260–61.
[40] 1 Tim 1:4; 4:6 f.; 2 Tim 4:3 f.; Tit 1:14. The two references to myth in the *OT* "deuterocanonicals" are no more complimentary: Sir 20:19, Bar 3:23.

enced on the one hand by the rationalistic Old Testament critics (G. L. Bauer and others), and on the other hand by the idealistic philosophy of Hegel in particular. David Friedrich Strauss, the most eminent representative of this movement, maintained that the central truth of Christianity— namely, the idea of God-manhood—initially emerged in mythical form, which was the only way in which the men of the day were capable of accepting such a lofty idea. Strauss's conception of myth, substantially taken over from the "mythical school," included every kind of intrusion of religious ideas into historical narration. Adapting Christianity to the *Zeitgeist* of the modern age, as he understood it, Strauss systematically rejected miracles and supernatural revelation.[41] Some of his successors in the Hegelian school, outstripping even Strauss in their mythomania, went so far as to deny even the historical existence of Jesus.

2) Early in the twentieth century, and especially in the 1920s, the history-of-religions school gave a new account of the mythical elements in the New Testament.[42] They maintained that great numbers of the early Christians were converts from the Hellenistic mystery religions, which consequently exerted a decisive influence upon their understanding of their new faith. For many of these former pagans, the mystery god simply acquired a new name, Jesus of Nazareth. Thus, the Christian doctrine of the resurrection of Jesus owed much to the pagan myths of gods who died and rose; the sacraments of baptism and the Eucharist were Christian counterparts of what had previously been practiced in the worship of Attis, Serapis, and other deities.

3) The most recent champion of the mythical view of the New Testament is Rudolf Bultmann. In a series of writings which go back to the 1920s—and especially in a controversial article published in 1941[43]—he has argued that the New

---

[41] Strauss's conception of myth has been studied by C. Hartlich and W. Sachs, *Der Ursprung des Mythosbegriffes in der modernen Bibelwissenschaft* (Tübingen, 1952) chap. 5, and by P. Barthel, *op. cit.*, pp. 36–42.

[42] On the views of R. Reitzenstein and W. Bousset, see S. Neill, *The Interpretation of the New Testament, 1861–1961* (Oxford, 1964) pp. 160–65.

[43] "New Testament and Mythology," in *Kerygma and Myth* (London, 1953) pp. 1–44. This essay does little more than restate, in more programmatic form, the essential content of his article in *RGG* 4 (2nd ed., 1930) 390–94, reprinted without change in the 3rd ed.: 4, 1278–82.

Testament is thoroughly imbued with myth, notably in the three crucial areas of cosmology, eschatology, and Christology.

The cosmology, he maintains, is mythical, since the New Testament writers accept a three-decker view of the universe, in which the earthly realm is subject to constant incursions from numinous powers who inhabit the heavens above and the underworld below. The course of history is largely shaped by the incessant struggle between the spirits of light and darkness, who seek to wrest it to their own ends. In this supernatural dualism Bultmann finds traces of Iranian mythology.

As regards eschatology, the early Christians, according to Bultmann, took over the contemporary Jewish ideas concerning the coming drama of the end-time. This was to be ushered in by the advent of the Anti-christ and a season of great tribulation. Then the Messiah would appear in glory, the dead would be recalled to bodily life, the nations would be judged, and the elect admitted to the heavenly banquet.

In the realm of Christology, Bultmann finds that the figure of Jesus was heavily overlaid with Jewish mythical expectations concerning the Messiah, the Son of Man, and the Suffering Servant. Even more significantly, the Christology of Paul and John, he holds, was influenced by the Gnostic myth of the primal man (*Urmensch*), which seems to have been Iranian in origin but was widely current by that time in the Near East.

In developing his thesis, Bultmann contends that the New Testament ideas of the incarnation and virginal conception of Jesus, His miracles, His bodily resurrection and ascension, are all mythical. This mythology has become a grave obstacle to the preaching of the gospel, for modern man can no longer understand or accept it. Bultmann himself proposes a fascinating existential reinterpretation of Christianity. The Church, he maintains, must summon man to decision and authentic existence. But this summons can be issued without invoking those elements of the New Testament which Bultmann, in his existential reinterpretation, discards as mythical.

To attempt any general critique of Strauss, of the *religionsgeschichtliche Schule,* or of Bultmann would take us far beyond the scope of this essay. The only question which concerns us is whether they have shown that the New Testament is to a great extent shot through with myth.

In the first place, it may be noted that both Strauss and Bultmann use the term "myth" in a very wide sense, to include practically everything they themselves reject. For Strauss, it embraces all allegedly supernatural events, much that we should call legend, and even poetic passages. For Bultmann, every assertion that God is active in the physical world is forthwith dismissed as mythical; so also everything betraying a prescientific approach to physics, medicine, or astronomy. By bracketing under a single term such radically diverse materials, these authors have tended to confuse the discussion.

Proceeding from a carefully considered notion of myth not unlike that adopted in this paper, Heinrich Schlier has written a very helpful essay on myth in the New Testament.[44] He lists three possible sources from which such myths might conceivably have originated: (*a*) contemporary Jewish apocalyptic, which sometimes made use of symbolic schemata to depict the unfolding of celestial events; (*b*) the Gnostic myth of the primal man, the redeemed Redeemer, which may have been current in the Mediterranean world at this time; (*c*) the Hellenistic and Oriental mystery religions with their dying and rising gods—although these are scarcely known to us except from post-Christian sources which afford no direct evidence for the period which concerns us.

As regards the apocalyptic elements, we may concede, with Schlier, that the New Testament borrows ideograms and terminology from the apocalyptic passages in Isaiah, Daniel, and other Old Testament prophets, as well as from the further development of these forms in intertestamental Jewish apocalyptic. The Synoptic Gospels, Paul, 2 Peter, and the

[44] "Das N.T. und der Mythus," *Hochland* 48 (1956) 201–12. For a concurring view, see H. Fries, "Entmythologisierung und theologische Wahrheit," in H. Vorgrimler (ed.), *Gott in Welt* 1 (Freiburg, 1964) 366–91, esp. pp. 380–91.

Apocalypse freely make use of such stereotyped imagery in referring to the eschatological events which will bring time to a close. When they speak of the days when the sun will lose its brightness, when the last trumpet will be sounded, when the elect, both living and dead, will be summoned to sit at the Messianic banquet, they are surely aware of the limitations of human language in dealing with such matters. They would no doubt be hard pressed to draw a precise line between their own doctrinal affirmations and the symbolic imagery in which these are clad. But are they using myth? The doctrinal context of these passages, their reference to a determinate future, and, above all, the conscious employment of sophisticated literary forms differentiate these apocalyptic scenes from myths in the strict sense we have adopted. The mythical elements have been taken up into an expression of eschatological faith. To the extent that critical thought has not completely penetrated the primitive imagery, we may admit the existence of a certain "mythical residue" in these passages; but there are no grounds for dismissing the whole New Testament teaching concerning the end-time as myth.

The other two ostensible sources of myth are somewhat problematical. Part of the difficulty comes from our lack of knowledge as to the forms which Gnostic speculation and the Hellenistic mystery cults had assumed by the first century. It seems probable that there were myths about, not unlike those known to us from the second and third centuries. We cannot antecedently deny that such myths may have influenced the New Testament writers.

At least it is clear that the Gospel was not radically mythicized. Nowhere in the New Testament do we find a full-blown mythical tale; we find only fragments and suggestions of myth. The faith of the community is evidently built upon a particular historical person, His actual death at some moment of worldly history, and His actual resurrection, the nonoccurrence of which would reduce the Christian religion to an empty tale (cf. 1 Cor 15:14). The events and the interpretation which faith set upon them may be judged true or false, but they do not share in the radical ambiguity of myth, which hovers in a twilight zone between truth and falsehood, between time and eternity.

Some would say that these events are historicized myth. But this term is, I think, inept. It implies that the history of salvation, as set forth in the New Testament, belongs in the same category as stories about Greek and Hindu gods. This is to confuse the deliberate affirmations of Christian faith with the hazy dreams of a far less demanding type of religion. The central message of the gospel, which concerns the supreme intervention of God into the course of human history, is far removed from myth. But the good news had to be set forth in a way that would reach the whole man, including the very depths of human consciousness. Symbolic and even mythical forms of expression could, therefore, serve as vehicles for communicating the gospel. There is no need to deny that Christian believers in the first century, or even in the twentieth, have often thought and spoken about the contents of their faith in a somewhat mythical style. Something of the tension between *logos* and *mythos* which we have already noted in the Old Testament remains in the New, even after the Logos has Himself appeared on earth.

To identify the precise passages in which mythical thinking survives is a matter of detailed exegesis which would go beyond the limits of this article. The New Testament scholar might consider, for example, whether there is not a mythical component in the Q–narrative of the temptation of Jesus in the desert. Perhaps this scene comes as close to anything in the Gospels to verifying the notion of myth proposed earlier in this article. But its collocation in the life of a historical individual, together with the heavy doctrinal and typological emphasis, prevents us from speaking, even here, of myth pure and simple.

Because of the power of myth to speak to man in the depths of his existence, it is quite intelligible that the apostles may have used mythical language in order to bring home to their hearers, and even to themselves, the full significance of the Christian kerygma. No one doubts that, in their preaching to the Jews, they exploited to the full all the Old Testament themes which seemed to fit their purpose. They applied to Jesus with sovereign liberty whatever the Old Testament had to say about the Messianic King, the Son of Man, the Son of God, or the Suffering Servant. In addressing pagans or converts from paganism, they might be expected to adopt similar techniques, explaining the gospel in terms of the religious thought characteristic of the Gentiles (cf. Acts 17:23).

It is presently controverted among New Testament scholars to what extent Paul and John were influenced by Gnosticism and the mystery religions. Without attempting to solve this disputed question, we may say that such influences should not be ruled out on a priori grounds. If the Gnostic myth of the redeemed Redeemer seemed to illustrate well the meaning of Christ's death and resurrection in its cosmic and heavenly dimensions, there is no reason to think that Paul would not have exploited it in the service of the exalted Christology which we find in Colossians and Ephesians. So too, in his efforts to bring the Hellenistic communities to appreciate the wonderful effects of baptism and the Eucharist, Paul could have consciously borrowed from the language of the mystery religions.

Christ, in the perspectives of faith, appears as an answer to the hopes and prayers of all mankind, pagans as well as Jews. If Messianic prophecy expressed the hopes and longings of Israel, myth was the vehicle in which the Gentiles set forth their deepest anxieties and presentiments. "In daring to take over the language of myth," Schlier asserts, "the New Testament shows that Jesus Christ is the end not only of the Law, but of myth besides."[45] In this connection we may recall the remark of Harnack: "In Christ the primal figure (*Urbild*) of all the myths has become history."[46]

This process of restating the Christian message in language influenced by pagan myth and mystery—the first beginnings of which may be indistinctly discerned in the New Testament

---

[45] *Art. cit.*, p. 212.
[46] *Die Entstehung der christlichen Theologie und des christlichen Dogmas* (1927) p. 16; quoted by G. Miegge, *op. cit.*, p. 106.

itself—was to be carried much further, perhaps even too far, in the following centuries. Christian art and poetry did not hesitate to depict Christ in the form of Hermes, Orpheus, and Odysseus, and to apply to Him, the true Sun of Justice, what the pagan myths had undeservedly attributed to the sun-god Helios. The reasons for such procedures are apparent from the words which Clement of Alexandria addressed to the cultured pagans of his day: "Come, I will show you the Word and the mysteries of the Word, and I will give you understanding of them by means of images familiar to you."[47]

Permanent Value of the Biblical Symbolism

The boldness with which the early Christians transposed the gospel into new patterns of thought is highly instructive. At the beginning of this essay we raised the question, to which we may return in closing, whether the traditional Christian symbolism is not obsolete. The example of the early Christians themselves suggests that the symbolism may be changed; faith can never be bound to a single set of images. The overwhelming realities of revelation are such that they can never be contained within a single set of terms. Those who wished to evangelize and catechize in the Greek-speaking world found the terminology of Judeo-Christianity provincial and unintelligible. They abandoned titles such as "Son of Man," which was almost meaningless to Gentile Christians, and treated the title "Christ" almost as if it were a proper name. Their boldness should be an encouragement to the contemporary Christian who feels that his idiom has become strange to the secular mentality of our day.

Does this mean that the biblical symbolism is outmoded? The question cannot be answered by a simple yes or no. A balanced attitude must steer clear of both archaism and modernism. Archaism would treat beginnings as if they were final; it would take the fundamentalistic position that the

---

[47] *Protrepticus* 12, 119, 1 (*GCS* 1, 84). H. Rahner, in his *Greek Myths and Christian Mystery* (London, 1963), splendidly develops this theme from patristic sources.

Church can use no terms, images, or concepts not positively authorized by the Bible; it would practically convert preaching into Bible-reading.

The modernist extreme would say that the Church is not bound to her own origins, that she can devise new ways of thinking and speaking without having to justify them by an appeal to the past.

In a balanced view, the historical experience of the people of God, as enshrined in the Old and New Testaments, is recognized as perpetually normative. Foundations are given once for all; they cannot be replaced. Christianity, as a historical revelation, must always look back to its origins and develop in continuity with them. Scripture, even in its imagery, pertains to the patrimony which God has permanently entrusted to the Church for its study, contemplation, consolation, and guidance, "that the man of God may be made perfect, equipped for every good work" (2 Tim 3:17).

It will, of course, be objected that the symbols of the Bible are based on a very naive and archaic world picture. But are they for that reason less valid? The ancient cosmology, which pictures the divine abode as above and the underworld below, while it is scientifically obsolete, retains much of its power as symbol. The picture of a God high above us corresponds well with the Christian doctrine of His transcendence. So likewise, the simple relationships of pastoral and patriarchal life, which supply so many of the biblical images, have close counterparts in ordinary human experience. Eliade can therefore say:

We may even wonder whether the accessibility of Christianity may not be attributable in great measure to its symbolism, whether the universal Images that it takes up in its turn have not considerably facilitated the diffusion of its message. For, to the non-Christian, one question occurs first of all: how can a local history —that of the Jewish people and of the first Judaeo-Christian communities—how can this claim to have become the pattern for all divine manifestation in concrete, historical time? I believe we have pointed to the answer: this sacred history, although in the eyes of an alien observer it looks like a local history, is also an exemplary history, because it takes up and perfects these transtemporal Images.[48]

It seems clear, on the other hand, that the biblical images do not furnish sufficient materials for evangelizing the increasingly secular and urban world in which we live. It is therefore urgent, as Pope John XXIII declared, to restate the Christian message in "the literary forms of modern thought." But the challenge is not new. At no time in her history has the Church been content to reproduce mechanically the symbols of the Bible. It continually forges new ciphers to convey more adequately that which, in its full reality, bursts the bonds of any human language.

Abundant examples of the incessant creativity of the Christian imagination could be found in the visual arts or in poets such as Dante and Milton. To adduce but one example, we may note how the medieval artists, relying on the bestiaries of the time, depicted Christ as a pelican, feeding its young with its own blood. The image helped to bring home to medieval man what was already implied in the biblical images, which attribute our redemption to the blood of Christ, freely shed for our sake, and which represent Him as inviting us to drink of the blood of the Son of Man.

In a thriving Christianity the creation of secondary images of this sort goes on apace. At times they may even seem to overshadow the biblical imagery, somewhat as in New Testament times the symbol of the heavenly Lord assumed priority over the older symbol of the Son of Man. But the new images, devised for the needs of a particular culture, are never completely new. They look back to the great ideas and symbols in Scripture. Like new doctrines, they are ultimately controlled by the primary sources from which they stem.

There is no need to minimize the problem of bridging the cultural gap between biblical times and our emerging technopolitan civilization. But it would be a mistake, I suggest, to concede too quickly that the biblical images should be cast aside. If some of them are less immediately available for

[48] *Images and Symbols*, pp. 168 f.

popular preaching, they can continue to nourish the thought of the preachers themselves. Remaining in historical and spiritual continuity with the people of God in biblical times, the Church will not wish to shelve the memory of the experiences by which God originally manifested Himself to the prophets and apostles. The biblical symbolism which enshrines these experiences will always remain a primary object of study and meditation. And it is doubtful that the faithful will ever cease to look upon God as their Father and Lord, or upon Jesus as the Good Shepherd and the Lamb of God. These inspired symbols form part of the patrimony by which the minds, imaginations, and emotions of the Christian people are to be formed and educated.

On the Meaning of "God":
Transcendence Without Mythology

Gordon D. Kaufman

Can "God-talk" have cognitive meaningfulness even granting the premises of "secular man," even when the traditional mythological dualism dividing "earth" and "heaven" is abandoned? Gordon D. Kaufman answers this question in the affirmative, even as he qualifies his affirmation by taking into account the limits placed on God-talk as a consequence of eschewing illegitimate mythology in favor of experiential reality. Though not purporting to offer a full-blown doctrine of God, Dr. Kaufman's essay—from the *Harvard Theological Review* (April 1966)*— is truly a "think piece" which argues persuasively that only on the basis of revelation is genuine knowledge of God possible. Of Mennonite background, Dr. Kaufman since 1963 has been professor of Theology at Harvard Divinity School. In addition to numerous articles in theological journals, he has written two books, *Relativism, Knowledge and Faith,* and *The Context of Decision.*

MANY have observed that modern man, more than the man of any other age, lives in a world from which God is absent, a genuinely secular world. Our forefathers had a sense of God's continuous providential guidance of history as a whole and of their individual destinies in particular; they found their lives meaningful because they were lived within the context of God's purposes, each man having his own unique place and task. But such meaning as most men of our time find is the this-worldly humanly-created meaning emergent from ordinary social intercourse and/or cultural

* Harvard University Divinity School, Cambridge, Mass. 02138. Copyright © 1966 by the President and Fellows of Harvard College.

activity. For some this loss of a transcendent source and purpose has reduced human life to meaninglessness and absurdity, a pointless and empty burden simply to be endured (Beckett); others react with bitterness and revulsion (Sartre); still others seem to find sufficient satisfaction in their daily round of activities, punctuated occasionally by aesthetic experience or unusual excitement, not to miss or lament the dimensions of depth and transcendence and mystery in which previous generations found their lives ensconced. But in any case the radical "eclipse of God" (Buber) or even the final irretrievable "death of God" (Nietzsche) appears to be the most momentous theological fact of our age. Given this cultural context, it is little wonder that linguistic analysts find it dubious whether the word "God" has any genuinely specifiable meaning,[1] and theological writers, in a desperate attempt to rescue the Christian faith from what appears to be its certain demise, seek wholly "secular" interpretations which go so far as to dispense with the word and idea of "God" entirely.[2]

I

The problem with the concept of "God" arises out of the fundamental metaphysical-cosmological dualism found in the Bible (as well as in traditional metaphysics) and in virtually all Western religious thought.[3] This is the division of reality into "earth" and "heaven"—that which is accessible to us in and through our experience and in some measure under our control, and that beyond our experience and not directly open to our knowledge or manipulation. The latter "world" is, if anything, more real and more significant than the ex-

---

[1] For a summary of the discussion see F. Ferré, *Language, Logic and God* (New York, Harper, 1961), and also W. T. Blackstone, *The Problem of Religious Knowledge* (Englewood Cliffs [N.J.], Prentice-Hall, 1963).

[2] Cf., e.g., Paul van Buren, *The Secular Meaning of the Gospel* (New York, Macmillan, 1963).

[3] Karl Barth, who supposes himself not to be engaged in metaphysical or cosmological "speculations," nevertheless makes a considerable point of the essential duality of the world in the Christian view. Cf. *Church Dogmatics* (Edinburgh, T. & T. Clark, 1936–1962), III/1, 17 ff.; III/3, 369 ff.; etc.

perienced world, since it is God's own abiding place (whence he directs the affairs of the cosmos) and man's ultimate home. In the Bible this dualism is expressed in full-blown mythological terms. Heaven is a kind of "place" or "world" in certain respects like the places found in the world of experience; it is peopled by "heavenly beings" and even a "heavenly court" visualized in analogy with earthly persons and political structures; and God is the absolute monarch ruling the cosmos in a way analogous to an Oriental despot. Some writers, e.g., Bultmann, have supposed that if it were possible for Christian thinking to rid itself of this somewhat crude and unbelievable mythological machinery, faith in God would once more become a live option for contemporary man. But the difficulty is much deeper than that, for this elaborate and fantastic mythological imagery is simply a naive and embellished expression of a more fundamental problem: the religious presupposition of a reality other than or "beyond" this world, the assumption that *the eminent reality with which we have to do—God—is somehow "out there"* (or "up there" or "down there" or "in there"—it does not matter) *beyond the given realities of our experience.*

For the purposes of his "demythologizing" program Bultmann defines mythology as "the use of imagery to express the otherworldly in terms of this world and the divine in terms of human life, the other side in terms of this side."[4] But this leaves unquestioned the most problematic feature of mythological thinking: that there *is* an "otherworldly" or "other side" at all, which, in contrast with the "human," is to be viewed as "divine." Attempting to resolve the problem of myth by cutting away most of the minor mythological realities (demons, angels, and other supernatural and superpersonal powers), but continuing to speak of an "exalted Christ," of the "Word of God" as something which comes *to* man from some "beyond," and of "acts of God" which *transform* men and history, is to miss entirely the central problem posed by mythological language. For that problem does not arise

[4] *Kerygma and Myth,* ed. H. W. Bartsch (London, S.P.C.K., 1953), 10, n. 2.

from the mere picturing of another *world* ("heaven," "super-nature") over against our world, in imagery drawn from within our world; the problem is whether there is *any significant reality at all* "above" or "beyond" or "below" the world which we know in our experience, or whether life is to be understood simply in this-worldly, i.e., secular, terms. De-mythologizing which fails to come to terms with the ultimate metaphysical-cosmological dualism expressed in the mythology, and in fact at the root, of all Western religious thinking, is not seriously facing up to the problem of the irrelevance of Christian faith and the Christian church in contemporary life

Men of other ages found it necessary to create and believe elaborate mythologies and metaphysics of the "beyond" in order to understand their world and themselves. Contemporary men in contrast—partially freed by scientific advance from the ignorance which mythological explanations attempted to fill, and through technological advance increasingly able to control forces which were to earlier generations simply mystery—find it more and more unnecessary and even ridiculous to make this dualistic assumption. They have learned in recent centuries that those claims to knowledge of reality which have warrant in this-worldly experience lead to prediction and control of their world, while speech about some "other world" or "supernatural reality" appears to be without warrant or significant effect, a merely traditional and probably superstitious usage. The authority of church and Bible no longer suffices to sustain the dualistic position; indeed, it is precisely the dubiousness to many moderns of the metaphysical dualism which these "authorities" so unquestioningly take for granted that can be credited in part for their obviously waning significance in modern life. We seem thus faced with two options. The dualism can be given up without remainder as an unjustifiable metaphysical vestige from previous stages of civilization[5]—and it is difficult to see how anything recog-

---

[5] Auguste Comte more than a century ago, of course, already took this position, and he has proved to be the prophet of modern man in this respect.

nizably Christian would remain if one took this course without some qualifications. Or else we must find a way in the present situation to restate (in terms not simply presupposing the old dualistic mythology) the contention that the ultimate reality with which man has to do is somehow "beyond" that which is directly given in experience. That is, we must seek to show in terms meaningful for our own time how it is possible and why it is significant to speak not only of this world but of "God." It is to this latter alternative that the present paper is directed.[6]

[6] It should be observed that the present paper is concerned with the question of the *meaning* rather than the *truth* of statements containing the word "God." No attempt will be made here to prove either that God does or does not exist, that is, that the word "God" does or does not actually refer to a reality. Questions of that sort can be faced only if we already know what we mean when we use the word "God"—the issue to which this paper is directed. (It should be evident that—certain "neo-orthodox" theologians to the contrary notwithstanding—prior discussion of the meaning of "God" is just as important for "Christian faith" as for "philosophy of religion," for it is meaningless to speak of "what God has done" or "what God has revealed" if it is doubtful whether the word "God" itself has any referential meaning.) It is my contention that the underlying assumption both of theists and a-theists is that "God-language" *presupposes* the validity of what I have above called the mythological-cosmological dualism between this world and another world, the holy and the secular, the eternal and the temporal, the absolute and the relative. Believers find themselves defending one or another of the several forms of this dualism; unbelievers (as well as many believers, if the truth be admitted) find the whole dualistic conception without sufficient warrant and possibly even a ludicrous vestige of earlier stages of culture. The question of the meaning and significance of speaking about God at all thus tends to get decided not in its own terms but on the basis of a prior attitude taken up toward the dualism of this world and the other. The purpose of the present paper is to show that the meaning of the word "God," even in its reference to the "transcendent," can be developed and understood entirely in terms of this-worldly (i.e., "secular") experiences and conceptions—that is, in terms fully comprehensible and significant to the most "modern" of men—and that therefore the whole issue of a presupposed cosmological dualism, so problematic for modern man, can be bypassed. In English the word "God" is understood by some to designate a mere psychological projection of a father-image and by others to indicate the Father of Jesus Christ and the ultimate reality with which we have to do. Since we are here attempting to uncover the basis on which significant conversation between such diverse points of view may proceed, and are not trying to prejudice the case for one or the other of these alternatives, it is evident that our delineation of meaning will need to have great flexibility. Doubtless to believers the present analysis may seem to concede too much to psychological reductionism; to unbelievers, too much to outgrown superstition. However, my intention is to favor neither view—that would be to argue the question of *truth* not *meaning*—but to provide a framework of meaning within which each can take up his position and arguments without prejudice, and within which, therefore, genuinely significant conversation between them can once again proceed.

II

We may begin our investigation by asking about the purpose or intention of "God-language." What function does the word "God" perform in religious and theological speech? That is, which experiences or problems *in this world* seem to require some people to talk about extramundane reality? And why do they think such an odd extrapolation or postulation is necessary? When one puts the question this way, the first thing to be observed is that the question about God-language has been transformed from a strictly logical to a quasi-historical form. The problem to which we shall initially address ourselves is not the abstract and general problem of proving to any rational mind the meaningfulness and even truth of the concept of "God"; it is, rather, the concrete problem of locating the context and situation in which the word "God" is used and found appropriate and meaningful. Clearly, only if this latter task is performed first can the former be undertaken with any hope of significant outcome. Indeed, it may turn out that this word or its context has a peculiar character which makes impossible such general logical justification.

In connection with what sorts of questions or problems, then, has speech about God or another world emerged and been used? The answer is not far to seek. Such speech appears within the context of man's sense of limitation, finitude, guilt and sin, on the one hand, and his question about the meaning or value or significance of himself, his life, and his world, on the other.[7]

On the one hand, man knows himself to be limited in many respects: God (or the gods, angels, demons, etc.) is seen as the reality which is the final limit to his being and power. This is the experiential dimension of the claim that God is creator, sovereign, lord of the world, etc.: men experience themselves as "thrown" into a world (Heidegger) not of their

[7] The emphases of biblical faith on salvation, deliverance, succor, abundant life, forgiveness, resurrection, atonement, eternal life, etc. all have this double reference, negatively to man's inadequacy and need, and positively to man's meaningful destiny and fulfillment.

own making and ultimately not under their control; they look forward to an end, death, which they may be able to defer slightly but which they can never avoid; they are hemmed in on all sides and determined by their peculiar aptitudes, temperaments, and interests, by the position in society and history into which they have been born, by circumstances of all sorts completely out of their control. The details of the analysis and elaboration of this awareness of limitation and weakness will of course differ widely in different cultures and traditions, and the way in which the limiting factor(s)—God —is understood will vary accordingly, but the basic *fact* of man's finiteness is rooted in man's actual situation as a particular limited being in the world. When in the course of evolution man emerged to full consciousness and self-consciousness, it was inevitable that he would also become conscious of, and seek modes of interpretation of, this his finitude. The earliest forms of such interpretation were highly mythological and are no longer acceptable or meaningful to many moderns. But the problem which gave rise to those views remains, and talk about God in the contemporary context must be understood as a modern way of seeking to speak about these same issues. In this respect the idea of God functions as a *limiting concept*, i.e., a concept which does not primarily have content in its own right drawn directly out of a specific experience but which refers to that which we do *not* know but which is the ultimate limit of all our experiences. While ancient man spoke with some confidence in his knowledge of this reality *beyond the limits* of his world —and it is just this which makes his thought "mythological" or "gnostic," and dubious to many today—most moderns are somewhat more fastidious and restrict themselves to positive affirmation about only what falls *this side* of the limits.[8] But

---

[8] In this respect modern man appears to be more heir of the skeptical than the metaphysical tradition in philosophy. One remembers, for example, the speech of Hume's Philo at the end of Part 8 of the *Dialogues Concerning Natural Religion:* "All religious systems, it is confessed, are subject to great and insuperable difficulties. Each disputant triumphs in his turn, while he carries on an offensive war, and exposes the absurdities, barbarities, and pernicious tenets of his antagonist. But all of them, on the whole, prepare a complete triumph for the *sceptic,* who tells them that no system ought

it must be observed that we, like ancient men, are also involved in a certain duality here, i.e., between what is in fact concretely experienced, and the limit(s) of all experience and knowledge.

On the other hand, as a being who lives in a world of symbolic meanings (i.e., who is a linguistic being) and values (i.e., who is a deciding and acting being, making choices between alternatives), man asks about the meaning and value of his own existence. His conscious experience and thought is made possible by his ability symbolically to compare and contrast the fragments and pieces of experience with each other through the creation of words and symbols and thus to build up a symbolical and ordered world of increasingly comprehensive wholes. His action in and measure of control over his world is made possible by his learning to create and define standards or criteria for evaluating alternatives before him, and by his learning to discriminate with increasing precision between the realities of his experience in terms of these norms. It is only natural, then, that he should ask about the meaning of his own existence within this structured world in which he finds himself, and the value of himself and his activity in the midst of all these other valued realities. This question becomes especially urgent in the light of his ultimate limitation and powerlessness, which seem to suggest that no lasting meaning or value can be placed on his being; certainly he by himself could not be its adequate source or ground. Once more, then, answer to this question could be found only *beyond the limits* of human possibilities and knowledge. Here again the mythologies of earlier generations were able to provide concrete answers. In the "other world," the world "beyond the grave," the inequities and injustices of this life are made right (doctrines of karma and the judg-

---

ever to be embraced with regard to such subjects: for this plain reason that no absurdity ought to be assented to with regard to any subject. A total suspense of judgment is here our only reasonable resource. And if every attack, as is commonly observed, and no defence among theologians is successful, how complete must be *his* victory who remains always, with all mankind, on the offensive, and has himself no fixed station or abiding city which he is ever, on any occasion, obliged to defend?"

ment of God, of heaven and of hell) and the value and meaning of human existence is assured. Though such affirmations could hardly be made simply on the basis of this-worldly experience, the religious myths provided a *gnosis* of the "beyond" (i.e., of God's nature and will, or of the ultimate order of things) which gave adequate assurance. In contrast, contemporary man finds it exceedingly difficult to speak with any confidence at all about that which is *beyond* the limits of his world, although the duality (between what is accessible to us and some ultimate limit) may be acknowledged.

It is in the context of these questions and problems about man's finitude and the significance of his existence in the light of this finitude that the meaning and use of the word "God" should be understood. That is, our speech about this Other arises because certain features of experience force us up against the limit(s) of all possible knowledge and experience. If there were no experiences within the world which brought us in this way up against the Limit of our world—if there were no point at which man sensed his finitude—then there would be no justification whatsoever for the use of "God-language."[9] This means that any persons (positivists?) who by temperament or training either do not often find themselves forced up against these limits or do not choose to reflect on them when they are will find speech about God seeming useless or empty. Since it is in relation to this particular context of problems and experience and language that "God" has meaning or justifiable use, its significance or validity cannot be demonstrated to anyone who either refuses to acknowledge the legitimacy of the context or any substantial interest in it. In this sense, the problem of the meaning and importance of theological speech depends upon matters of temperament and history. But, though not everyone will acknowledge the significance of questions about the Limit, to those who do, such questions will appear to be of universal import; for every man (whether he acknowledges it or not and whether he is interested in this or not) stands under and

---

[9] The highly complex character of this "experience" of finitude will be briefly analyzed below in Section IV.

within the limits here under consideration. It is not unimportant to raise the question, then, about the degree to which one's understanding of the issues here involved depends on the traditions which seem to him significant as well as the climactic historical occurrences in his own life.

III

We must now examine further the content of the term "God." Though the fact of ultimate limitations on our being and meaning provides the context within which religious language arises and has meaning, it is clear that more is intended by that language than simply the bare and abstract notion of Limit. It is not surprising that primitive man, in confronting this situation, created imagery (in analogy with certain concrete powers within his experience) by means of which the power of the ultimate Limit could be conceived; and so the mythological "other world" appeared as the home of the mysterious powers that invaded and controlled this world. Our modern problem with theological language arises out of the fact that we no longer find it justifiable or meaningful to speak of this other world and the powers which inhabit it. Even when, in more sophisticated interpretations, the plethora of mythological powers supposedly controlling human destiny is reduced to one—God (or, as in a contemporary highly bloodless form, "being-itself")—we are dubious of the claims to knowledge. And that for a rather obvious reason: if it is really the *limits* of our experience and knowledge with which we are here dealing, by what right can anyone speak of the nature or even the existence of reality beyond those limits? Here sheer agnosticism would seem to be not merely prudent but the only honest course as well.

Inasmuch as theological language often claims or pretends to speak of that *beyond* the limits of the humanly experienceable—even, upon occasion, claiming to know on the basis of "revelation" about the inner workings of the divine being(s) —it is not surprising that such talk seems highly dubious and even sheer nonsense to many. Limit means *limit*. And it is both deceitful and inconsistent on the one hand to justify talk about God on the ground of our limitedness, and then, on the other, to transcend those limits in order to spell out in some detail the structure of the reality that lies beyond them. Insofar as theological language is involved in this sort of self-contradiction and self-delusion, it very rightly has fallen into ill repute. If the experiential base which justifies the very use of theological terms is man's awareness of his own finitude, then the fact of that finitude must be consistently adhered to in that language; and the too easy transcending of finitude implicit in every form of mythology must be renounced. Because the awareness of the "boundary situation" (Jaspers) within which man lives was first expressed in mythological forms which themselves implicitly ignored that boundary,[10] it has been extremely difficult to discern clearly the experiential base which justifies theological language. Consequently it has been supposed, both within the theological community and without, that theology deals primarily in otherworldly realities. From this common assumption the religious have proudly drawn the conclusion that they have been granted a secret *gnosis* denied others, while the worldly supposed that theology dealt simply in old wives' tales and other superstitions about some "other world" which the imagination of man has fabricated out of whole cloth. Neither side was able to focus clearly on the actual base *in concrete experience* from which theological work proceeds, thus giving an interpretation of religious language which could justify its use to contemporary secular man. It is clear that if we have located correctly the experiential context of speech about God, the theological vocabulary will have to be rebuilt from the ground up with a much more sensitive ear to the epistemological

[10] It may be observed in passing that, despite all his strictures to the contrary, Jaspers also really allows his alleged "boundary situations" to be surpassable under certain circumstances in the experience of what he calls "transcendence" (see, e.g., *Philosophie* [Berlin, Springer Verlag, 1948, 2nd ed.], 44 ff., 470, 675 ff.). In the respect and degree to which this is the case his conception and analysis of finitude represents one more attempt to deny its real meaning, and my more drastic interpretation of the "boundary situation" should not be confused with his. (For similar criticism, see also Karl Barth's analysis in *Church Dogmatics*, III/2, 109–21.)

consequences *for theology itself* of the fundamental religious situation of limitedness.[11]

It is not possible to undertake that project in any detail in this paper. The most that can be done is to analyze briefly the complex character of the awareness of our finitude and the special understanding of that awareness implicit in the use of the word "God." It must be clear, of course, just what I am attempting here. I am not seeking to develop a full-blown doctrine of God on the basis of a kind of natural theology of human finitude. Rather, I am trying to define with some precision the sort of "God-talk" which is justifiable and responsible from that base, as well as the limitations which must be imposed on theological speech when one seeks to avoid presupposing the traditional—and illegitimate! in the modern view—mythology of two worlds. (If someone wishes to live and speak within that mythological framework, of course that is his business. I am here concerned with searching out the meaning which theological language can have for those of us who no longer find warrant for or meaning in that dualism.)

We begin then with a somewhat different duality than that of two-world thinking: the duality of experience and its Limit(s). Such content of the term "God" as derives from an alleged *gnosis* of some "other world," transmitted by mythological traditions, may not be admitted to consideration here, for our interest is in defining the meaning which the awareness of our finitude as such permits and requires.

IV

What kind of conception is this notion of ultimate Limit? Some existentialist literature seems to suggest that there is a particular immediate experience involved here which is to be contrasted with other experiences of lesser limits. I do not

---

[11] It goes without saying that my repeated use of such terms as "finite," "limit," etc. is meant simply to *characterize* man; the respects in which man's finitude might be either "good" or "evil" is not considered. The usage is intended as neutral description.

think this is a very careful reading of the matter. All that we ever experience directly are particular events of suffering, death (of others), joy, peace, etc. It is only in *reflection upon these* and the attempt to *understand ourselves in the light of these happenings* that we become aware of our limitedness on all sides. Along with this awareness of our being hemmed in, powerful emotions of terror, despair, revulsion, anxiety, and the like, are often—perhaps always—generated, and this total intellectual-emotional complex may then be called the "experience of finitude" or awareness of the "boundary situation," or something of the sort. But it must be observed that this "experience" of radical contingency is not an *immediate* awareness of restriction, as when one butts one's head directly against a stone wall; it depends rather upon a generalization from such occasional immediate experiences of limitation to the total situation of the self. The self, in this way perceived as hemmed in on all sides, comes to a new and deeper awareness of its nature and powers: it is *finite,* master neither of itself nor of its world. Thus, the so-called experience of finitude or contingency, however powerful the emotions which accompany and deepen and reinforce it, has an intellectual root, and it is possible only because man is a reflective being. (Dogs also die, but this does not lead them to despair over canine life, because they, presumably, are unable to anticipate their own death imaginatively and reflect on its meaning.) As we shall see below, the peculiar character of this complex experience—being rooted in particular simple experiences of restriction, but apprehended as referring to the contingency of the self (and of man generally) in every moment, man's boundedness on all sides—enables it to be the experiential ground both of theological conceptions and of nontheistic metaphysical schemas as well.

It is with the aid of concepts such as *limit* that the generalizing movement of consciousness from particular immediate experiences of restriction to the total situation of the self is made. This term, originally applying to physical boundary lines (e.g., between fields or nations), here becomes used metaphorically to designate the self's awareness of being circumscribed or hemmed in. How is such restriction and limitation to be conceived? The imagery built into the notion of limit by its physical origins reminds us that every *actual* limit or boundary which marks off and restricts *real being* (in contrast to, for example, a mathematical limit or similar abstract "limiting idea") must itself be conceived *as a reality, as having some kind of substance and structure.*[12] Thus, a city wall is made of earth and stones, a fence of wire and posts, etc. It is important to observe here, however, that only because we can examine the wall or fence from all sides, test it in various ways, and the like—that is, only because the limit is not an ultimate or absolute limit but can be surpassed—is it possible for us to know the stuff of which it consists. If we could not in any way *get beyond* the limit we were examining, we would have no means of directly discovering its nature but would have to construct the conception of it imaginatively out of elements more fully known in our experience.

Consider, for example, the situation of a man imprisoned in a cell outside of which he has never been and from which he absolutely cannot escape. If he seeks to conceive the restricting walls of his room—with their resistance to his efforts to push through them, their hardness and solidity and color—as (material) realities, he will be able to do so only in analogy with the experienceable (material) objects *within* the room. Thus, his conclusion that the walls are composed of some sort of *thickness* of material substance, however plausible, in fact presupposes an interpretation of that which is *beyond* what is directly experienceable by him, namely, the bare surface of the walls. The conception of the ultimate

[12] I do not think the notion of a mathematical limit, which is always approached asymptotically but never actually reached, can serve as a root conception for the notion of *metaphysical limit* with which we are here working. For the awareness of finitude is not purely conceptual or hypothetical; it is an awareness of *my actual being* as here (in this time and place) rather than there, as restricted in this particular concrete way by aptitudes, interests, and training, as one which must and shall in fact die. It is the awareness of *my being limited* that we are here dealing with and thus in some sense an actual "encounter" with that which *limits me.* The notion of an asymptotic approach to a limit is simply not applicable, and we must revert to the physical experiences of limitation for models for our concept.

limit of his movements is constructed imaginatively out of elements derived from objects within his experience that partially restrict and limit him; for the stuff or structure of the walls themselves—that "behind" their surfaces—cannot be directly known, though the restrictingness of the walls is, of course, directly experienced.

The same point about the way in which the notion of the ultimate Limit is conceived by analogy with certain relative limits known within experience may be made with reference to another illustration, the ancient image of the "end of the world"—a kind of final edge of a bottomless abyss beyond which it is impossible to go. In this case it is obvious that what is *beyond the Limit* is being imagined rather precisely in terms of the intramundane experience of dangerous cliffs and other places from which one might fall to his destruction. Even the abstract notion of limit itself, we may now recall, was drawn originally from the experience of (relative) physical boundaries; only by analogical extension of its meaning could it be applied to the self in such a way that the sense of being completely circumscribed and confined—the awareness underlying the concept of finitude—could develop.[13] It is hardly surprising, then, that when we seek to conceive this Limit concretely, as restricting and constricting our actual being, images and notions drawn from concrete intramundane experiences of limitation provide the material making up the conception. Certain characteristics of known finite limits are abstracted from their context, and built by analogy into the notion of the ultimate Limit. Our problem, now, is to discern what experiences provide the images and what restrictions must be laid down governing their use in this way.

Let us recall what it is that is being limited here and see how its limits are in fact experienced. It is not property or a

---

[13] In view of this complex structure of the concept of limit—it being derived from the experience of relative limits which can be surpassed, and then extended to the notion of ultimate Limit which cannot—we should really not be surprised that men of all ages have supposed they actually knew something of that beyond the Limit, and that they expressed this in what I have above designated as mythological thinking. The duality of conscious finite being and Limit very easily, and almost naturally, goes over into the dualism of this world and the other world. These facts also throw light on the roots and meaning of Kant's first antinomy.

nation or even the world with which we are here concerned, but the self. The self's awareness of being restricted on all sides, rendering problematic the very meaning of its existence, gives rise to the question: *What* is it that in this way hems us in? How is this *ultimate* Limit, of which we are aware in the "experience of finitude," to be conceived? There appear to be four fundamental types of limiting experience, and these supply models with the aid of which the ultimate Limit can be conceived. The first two are relatively simple: a) selves experience external *physical* limitation and restriction upon their activities through the resistance of material objects over against them; b) they experience from within the *organic* limitation of their own powers, especially in illness, weakness, failure, exhaustion, etc. The other two are somewhat more complex: c) they experience the external *personal* limitation of other selves engaged in activities and programs running counter to their own—i.e., the clash of wills, decisions, and purposes—but precisely because matters of volition and intention are subjective, this experience is neither simply internal nor external but is interpersonal and social; d) they experience the *normative* constraints and restrictions upon them expressed in such distinctions as true-false, real-illusory, good-bad, right-wrong, beautiful-ugly, etc., which distinctions, though felt subjectively and from within, appear to the self not to be its own spontaneous creations but to impinge upon it with categorical demands and claims.

The self is restricted in its actual willing and acting, in its formulation of projects and its attempts to actualize them, in each of these quite different ways. Each is the basis for a peculiar experience of the nature of limitation which cannot be reduced to any of the others. Thus, for example, it is not possible to understand the sense of being at cross purposes with and thus restricted by another person, in terms simply of the concept of *physical* resistance or limitation, any more than the experience of utter weakness in connection with a severe illness can be comprehended with categories derived from the concept of logical necessity. Though these four modes of experienced limitation may sometimes be confused with each other and often (or perhaps always) are experienced in complex interconnection with each other, they are obviously distinct and separate. In each case the *limiter* is conceived in somewhat different terms so as to be appropriate to that of the self which is actually restricted. Thus, material objects impose physical restrictions, and physiological deficiencies limit our organic capacities; other active wills are responsible for personal constraints, while values and ideals impinge with normative force. In a situation such as imprisonment I experience physical restriction (the prison walls), but am also aware of the personal constraint of other wills (those who built the prison and put me in it), and perhaps of organic deterioration (increasing weakness due to poor food, lack of exercise, etc.). Each restriction is involved with the others and with the concrete situation of imprisonment, and some (e.g., the physical restrictions) may be the result of others (the conflict of wills) and essential to the effective realization of those others; but none of the limiters can be reduced to any of the others. Escape from prison will not dissolve the conflict of wills, and personal reconciliation will not correct malnutrition. In each case the specific limiter restricting the self must be dealt with appropriately to its own nature.

If we turn now from this identification of the variety of finite limiters to the problem of understanding the ultimate Limit, it will be clear that there are a number of possibilities. The ultimate Limit could be understood on analogy with any one of the types of finite limiter, or through some combination of several of them; but there is no way of grasping the nature of the ultimate Limit simply and purely in its own terms. For, in the first place, if this is really the *Limit* beyond which we can never move at all, then by definition there could be no way for us directly to apprehend its character; at best we could experience and know its "surface," that is, its mere impingement as such, its limitingness, a quite abstract notion. But the ultimate Limit—being that which is apprehended as the *real* and *effective* restriction on our being and movement (no mere "empty idea")—is grasped as concrete actuality impinging on us, i.e., not merely abstractly but as having some concrete character or nature. Moreover, in the second place, as the preceding analysis has shown, awareness of the ultimate Limit is no fifth entirely distinct type of direct and immediate experience of limitation; on the contrary, this awareness arises only mediately through complex acts which generalize the immediate and particular experiences of constraints upon the self into the "experience of finitude."[14] It is out of this complex experience that the question about an ultimate Limit over against the self first arises and it is within this context that any apprehension or conception of the ultimate Limit will emerge.[15] Insofar as its character or nature is explicitly conceived at all, it will evidently be understood then, with the aid of one or more of the actually experienced finite limiters (the experiences of which are the only concrete sorts of limitation we know), and will be interpreted in terms of implications derived from that (or those) image(s).

[14] It will be observed that, though in many respects my position resembles Schleiermacher's, at this point I am setting myself against his contention that we have a specific and unique sense of absolute dependence as such (cf. *The Christian Faith* [Edinburgh, T. & T. Clark, 1928], § 3–5).

[15] It might be helpful to summarize here the various phases of the complex process through which, according to this analysis, the conception of an ultimate Limit is formulated: (1) there must be particular concrete experiences of limitation (of the several types described); (2) the self must be sufficiently mature and reflective to be able to move from consciousness of these particular experiences to a more general concept of limitation or finitude; (3) the awareness of the significance that it is *I* who am in this inescapable way hemmed in must arise, together with the powerful emotions which contribute to the "experience of finitude"; (4) this awareness of my own radical contingency may then give rise to the question about *what* it is which so confines and limits me; (5) the ultimate Limit may then be conceived in terms of one (or possibly some combination) of the four types of finite limiter. It should not be thought that the complexity of this process in any way prejudices the legitimacy of the question (4) or the possible truth of the answer (5). For it is certainly conceivable that we are limited ultimately by some (one) reality, and, if so, that only through some such complex process could we—all our knowledge being rooted in experiences of the finite—come to know it. As we shall see below, if the ultimate Limit were personal (as the notion of "God" suggests), we would expect him to be known through complex mediatorial processes in any case (as is a finite person), and there would seem to be no reason why these processes could not include the sort here suggested (cf. note 25, below). On the other hand, it must also be admitted that there seems to be no compelling necessity to move from step (3) in the above process through (4) and (5). One could claim (positivistically), if one chose to do so, that the only *what* which limits me are the four types of finite limiter as experienced in (1), and that there is no reason to suppose there is some one reality beyond and behind these which is the *ultimate Limiter*. The fact that the present analysis of the consciousness of finitude lends itself to such varied sorts of interpretation is no shortcoming: it means, rather, that significantly different perspectives—from positivism to a variety of types of metaphysics and Christian theology—can enter into common discourse with the aid of this framework, and this is precisely what we are seeking to make possible with this analysis (see note 6, above).

Moreover, since there is no possible way to prove the special appropriateness of any one or combination of the finite limiters to perform this function (again, that would presuppose a direct knowledge of the nature of the absolute Limit, which, as we have seen, is not available), it is evident that any particular concrete conception of the ultimate Limit may be quite arbitrary.[16] Despite this difficulty we cannot avoid conceiving the Limit as concrete, for if it is apprehended at all, it must be apprehended as that which in fact constricts and constrains the actual concrete self.

Any of the types of finite limiter could serve as the model in terms of which a conception of the ultimate Limit might be developed, but difficulties arise when any one of them is used exclusively. Thus, when physical limitation is taken as the fundamental analogy, a materialistic world-view results and man's being is understood as simply a function of the physical universe. This is a common enough view and has much to commend it, notably the obvious dependence of all man's functions on his physical being. However, it is very difficult to see how the other types of limiter are to be understood simply in physical terms. This problem is often dealt with in modern times through some conception of emergent evolution, but the problems here are immense and probably insoluble for a purely materialistic point of view. Hence one may be led, as with Whitehead or Bergson, to seek a resolution of the difficulties with some sort of organicism or vitalism. Yet it is difficult to see how the notion of organic limitation is really of much help in developing a conception of the world which does justice to the other limiters. Similar problems arise with the various forms of idealism which take normative limitation to be the most fundamental.

However, our objective here is not to resolve these difficult problems of metaphysics but rather to examine the grounds for speech about God when the traditional mytho-

---

[16] It is, of course, better that we be aware of these peculiar difficulties in the conception with which we are dealing here than, in ignorance, simply refuse to face the question at all. In this respect Kant, who saw that we could never resolve the antinomies and problems of metaphysics but who also saw that we could never cease struggling with these issues (see, e.g., *The Critique of Pure Reason*, A849/B877–A851/B879), was much wiser than many of his latter-day (positivistic, existentialistic, and fideistic) followers.

logical dualism is given up. The ultimate experiential ground for such speech should now be evident. Talk about God appears when the ultimate Limit is understood on analogy with the experience of *personal limiting* as known in the intercourse and interaction of personal wills. In this respect religious faith opts for one particular metaphysical alternative from among the several available. However, this metaphysical decision is not of mere speculative interest, for the option involved is active will, that over against which a self can live in interaction and intercourse and communion. The other options understand the ultimate Limit in terms of an image of dead being or passive structure (as a quasi-physical limiter or like certain aspects of a normative limiter), or else as a vital but unconscious and certainly purposeless force (like an organic limiter and/or certain other features of a normative limiter). Though each of these significantly interprets certain dimensions of our experience, none of them comes directly to grips with our distinctive experience as persons in communities, as conscious, active, deciding, purposing beings living in a symbolical world which provides the context and the possibility for continuous communication and intercourse with others. The interpretation of the ultimate Limit in terms of this social level and dimension of our experience—which, however dependent it may be on the others in many respects, is the presupposition of our having any experience (properly so called)—is the metaphysical prerogative of theistic religion and defines its peculiar character. The religious attractiveness of this metaphysics—in that the ultimate context of human existence is here seen as personal and purposive volitional activity and not dead matter or unfeeling logical structure or unconscious vital power—makes theism relevant to the existential problems of the person in a way unmatched by any of the other metaphysical alternatives.[17] Hence, it very naturally appears as the essential ideological dimension of most

[17] If in this paper I were seeking an argument for the truth of theism, instead of limiting myself to an analysis of the experiential bases for—and thus the root meaning of—the word "God," it would be necessary and appropriate to expand and develop some of the implications of these sentences. (See also note 19, below.)

religious faith. But precisely this same attractiveness makes theistic belief seem so dubious to many, in that the powerful desire of man to find genuine purpose and meaning in his life here seems too easily and happily fulfilled. The intrinsic anthropomorphism of this perspective thus makes it at once suspect and seductive. (This, of course, really does not bear directly on the question of its actual truth, since *all* the metaphysical alternatives conceive the ultimate Limit with the aid of a more or less arbitrarily chosen finite model.)

V

When a personal limiter is the analogical basis for understanding the ultimate Limit, a doctrine of God results. The ultimate Limit is then conceived in quasi-personal terms to be understood most decisively with notions drawn originally from the language used to deal with interpersonal experience. It is clear that this conception is the one operative in the biblical tradition where God is spoken of as lord, father, judge, king, etc., and he is said to love and hate, to make covenants with his people, to perform "mighty acts," to be characterized by mercy, forgiveness, faithfulness, patience, wisdom, and the like—all terms drawn from the linguistic region of interpersonal discourse. Moreover, the biblical God is understood not to be accessible to man's every beck and call; he is not some structure or reality immanent in human experience and thus directly available to man. On the contrary, he resides in lofty transcendence, whence he acts in complete freedom to change the course of history or to reveal himself to his people through his prophets. Now it is clear that this image of inaccessible transcendence and freedom made known and effective through explicit acts of communication and power—through words and deeds—is built up analogically from the model of the hiddenness and transcendence and freedom of the finite self, who also can (in some significant measure) hide himself from his fellows and remain inaccessible, except as he chooses to manifest himself through acts and words.[18] Though other terminology and images are also found in the biblical materials, there can be no doubt that personalistic language and conceptions most decisively shape the biblical view of the ultimate Limit.

I contended earlier in this paper, however, that the biblical and Christian traditions appear determined in large part by a metaphysical-cosmological dualism characteristic of mythology and no longer meaningful to many moderns. Moreover, it has often been held that precisely the anthropomorphic image of God as personal is an especially crude example of the mythological thinking of primitive man and therefore to be regarded as only symbolic or picture language, of significance in worship or prayer but not adequate for precise theological or philosophical work. We must now ask, therefore, how far a personalistic conception of God is essentially bound up with an inadequate mythology, how far it may be an independent and justifiable interpretation of the ultimate Limit.

It should be evident that to conceive the ultimate Limit personalistically is formally neither more nor less mythological than to conceive it on analogy with any of the other types of finite limiter. Each has its own peculiar appropriateness to certain dimensions of the self's experience of limitation, and each has difficulty in interpreting the other dimensions. With respect to the experience of limitation itself, then, no reason for preferring any of the four to the others can be given.[19] Moreover, inasmuch as it is necessary to grasp the ultimate Limit in terms of *some* model if it is to be adequately conceived at all, the attempt to grasp it personalistically should not be rejected as mythological (in the dubious sense of

[18] For a full discussion of this claim that genuine transcendence is intrinsically a personalistic notion and can be consistently developed only in connection with a personalistic conception of God, see my paper on "Two Models of Transcendence," published in *The Heritage of Christian Thought, Essays in Honor of Robert L. Calhoun,* ed. R. E. Cushman and E. Grislis (New York, Harper & Row, 1965).

[19] It might be noted here, however, that inasmuch as the personalistic model involves the notion of a self whose active center is *beyond* that which is directly experienced, the latter being conceived as the vehicle or medium of the self's action or revelation (see below), there is a certain flexibility and breadth in theism enabling it to deal with the considerable diversity of types of finite limiter somewhat more easily, perhaps, than can other kinds of metaphysics.

claiming unwarranted knowledge of that *beyond* the Limit) in any way not also applicable to every other attempt to apprehend and understand our finitude.

In a manner not characteristic of the other finite limiters, however, the personalistic image lends itself to a reopening of the question not only of the Limit, but of what is beyond it. For (as we noted above) it interprets man's relationship to that which ultimately limits him as being like his relationship to the finite selves with which he is in interaction. Such selves over against me always transcend in their subjectivity and freedom what is directly accessible to me in my experience (i.e., their bodies) even though they "come to me" and communicate with me in and through this physical dimension of their being that is open to my view. What I directly experience of the other, strictly speaking, are the external physical sights and sounds which he makes, not the deciding, acting, purposing center of the self—though I have no doubt these externalities are not *merely* physical phenomena but are the outward and visible expression of inner thought, purpose, intention. Thus I do not speak merely of "sights and sounds" but of the "sights and sounds which *he* makes" in *his* attempt to act or to communicate. In my interaction with other persons I presuppose a reality (the active center of the self) *beyond* that which I immediately perceive, a reality encountered by me and known to me not simply in physiologically-based perception (though that is of course also involved) but in and through the language which we jointly speak.[20] It is in the act of communication that we discover that the other is more than merely physical being, is a conscious self; it is in the experience of speaking and hearing that we come to know the *personal* hidden behind and in the merely physical.[21] This is the most powerful experience we have of *transcendence of the given* on the finite level, the awareness

[20] To avoid confusion in this already very complex analysis, I shall use the term "encounter" to designate the linguistic-experiential ground of our knowledge of other selves, reserving the more general term "experience" for the sensory-perceptual foundations of our knowledge of physical objects (including the bodies of persons qua their purely physical character).

[21] For a more linguistically oriented treatment of these problems which comes to fundamentally similar conclusions on the basis of careful analysis of personalistic modes of speech, see Stuart Hampshire, *Thought and Action* (New York, Viking Press, 1960).

of genuine activity and reality *beyond* and *behind* what is directly open to our view.

When this type of complex interrelationship is used to interpret the ultimate Limit, it is clear that an active reality (or "self") beyond the Limit—beyond what is directly experienceable as such—will be implied. A self in its active center is never directly open to view, but is known only as he reveals himself in communication and communion. Likewise, on this model God cannot be identified with what is accessible to or within our experience, not even with the ultimate Limit of our experience; rather this Limit must be grasped as the *medium* through which God encounters us (as noises and gestures are media for finite selves), God himself being conceived as the dynamic acting reality beyond the Limit.[22] In this way a certain reference to reality beyond the Limit of our experience is intrinsic to the personalistic image, and therefore such reference need not depend upon nor involve a reversion to mythology. It must be emphasized, however, that reference of this sort to transcendent reality is justifiable only when the ultimate Limit is understood in terms of a personal limiter; for only in the interaction with other

---

[22] In an early paper Paul Tillich seemed to be taking a position close to the analysis of this essay. "The non-symbolic element in all religious knowledge is the experience of the unconditioned as the boundary, ground, and abyss of everything conditioned. This experience is the boundary-experience of human reason and therefore expressible in negative-rational terms. But the unconditioned is not God. God is the affirmative concept pointing beyond the boundary of the negative-rational terms and therefore itself a positive-symbolic term" ("Symbol and Knowledge," *Journal of Liberal Religion* [1940], II, 203). Tillich, however, failed to refine his analysis and develop his insight. Thus, the peculiar character of "boundary experiences" remains unanalyzed here, and the "boundary" can even be interpreted in terms of such positive images as the (almost hypostatized) "unconditioned" or "ground"; this blurs its radical character as the ultimate unsurpassable Limit. Again (similarly to my analysis), "God" is distinguished from "the unconditioned" as "a positive-symbolic term" pointing beyond the ultimate boundary, but Tillich fails to see (either here or anywhere else in his writings) that this is because of the peculiar character of the transcendence known only in interpersonal relations and is thus intrinsically connected with the personalistic overtones of the term "God." In his later writings, where Tillich apparently gives up the view that the "non-symbolic element in all religious knowledge" is a special experience and holds instead that we can make at least one nonsymbolic *statement* about God (see, e.g., *Systematic Theology* [Chicago, University of Chicago Press, 1951], I, 238 ff.), there remains little resemblance to the view I am trying to develop in the present essay.

selves do we encounter an active reality which comes to us from beyond what is accessible in experience. Organic, physical, and normative limiters can all be interpreted exhaustively in terms of what is given in and to experience (though it is not essential to do so), and it is mythology, therefore, if one speaks of a transcendent extra-experiential reality on the basis of one of those models; a personal limiter alone necessarily and intrinsically involves genuine transcendence.[23]

Correlative with this reference to a locus of reality beyond the Limit there must be a conception of revelation. We know the transcendent reality of other selves only as they act toward and communicate with us, as they reveal to us their reality and character and purposes in word and deed. So also, only if we are prepared to acknowledge some genuine encounter with God through his own actions directed toward us, is it appropriate to speak of the ultimate Limit in personalistic terms, i.e., with "God"-language. By definition we could know nothing of any personal being beyond the Limit of our experience if that being did not in some way manifest himself to us through our experience or its Limit.[24] Once again, the organic, physical, and normative analogies for understanding the ultimate Limit require no doctrine of revelation, nor is any appropriate to them. This is the mode of knowledge characteristic of interpersonal communion, and it is when such encounters are taken as the model for understanding the Limit of all experience that the category of revelation is required.[25] Thus, to speak of God acting or God revealing

[23] For further discussion, see my paper cited in note 18.

[24] Since, according to the present analysis, every *positive* doctrine of God must rest on revelation, it should be clear both a) why no real doctrine of God appears in this paper (no concrete revelation being expounded here), and b) that the present analysis of "limit" is not to be confused with the "negative way" *to* God.

[25] It will be observed that, according to the analysis presented in this paper, the "encounter" with God actually rests on a double mediation, whereas our encounters with finite selves involve only the single mediation (of noises, visible gestures, etc.) discussed in the text: a) the ultimate Limit is not immediately experienced, but is known only through the mediation provided by reflection on and generalization of particular experiences of limitation (cf. note 15, above); b) the "selfhood" or "nature" of God is not immediately experienced or directly encountered, but is known through the mediation of the ultimate Limit. This does not mean, however, that an "encounter" with God is really the product of a rather long chain of some-

himself is not necessarily to make a mythological statement presupposing an unjustified and unjustifiable metaphysical-cosmological dualism; such forms of conceptualization and speech are necessary if and whenever a personal limiter is taken as the model for grasping the ultimate Limit.

VI

Most attempts to locate the experiential referent or basis for the term "God" heretofore have accepted the framework of what I here called metaphysical or mythological dualism and then tried to justify it in terms of some sort of direct "experience of God," or "apprehension of the infinite," or something similar. For those who had such experiences or intuitions, these analyses doubtless had meaning and significance; but for others of a more secular or this-worldly temperament or turn of mind, this seemed to be nothing more than paying rather extravagant "metaphysical compliments" to certain dimensions of experience. The present analysis

what dubious inferences and no encounter with a reality at all. Rather, as the encounter with other selves makes clear, such communication through media is the mode in which realities transcending the reach of our immediate experience are known to us. In such an encounter, of course, I do not attend directly to the mediating processes (the noises the other is making); rather, I am conscious of *him,* of the speaker. Insofar as I must attend to his *words,* consciously, in bewilderment about their meaning, making deliberate inferences, the process of communication is halting and ineffective. Only if I can and do "leap beyond" the media to the self who is mediated through these words is there significant encounter with the other. In most of our intercourse with others precisely this leap is made in the most natural fashion; this is why we say we *know* the other *person,* and not merely the noises he makes. In a similar way, God is never directly "experienced," but is "encountered" (as is appropriate to his transcendence) only in and through media. (The *double* mediation involved in this case, in contrast with finite selves, is appropriate to the fact that this is *God,* and not merely some intramundane reality, of which we are here speaking.) If the media are the focus of attention here, of course the encounter with God will seem problematic and unreal; as with a finite self, only if and when a "leap beyond" the media (although through the media) occurs will the encounter with God be felt as genuine, i.e., only then could men properly speak of *God* being encountered. Theologically such moments were referred to as "revelation," i.e., God's self-manifestation. It is only because men have believed these to have occurred to themselves, or others, that talk about "encounters" with God—and thus talk about "God"—has appeared and continues to be sustained in human discourse. *Faith,* we can now see, is that stance in which the "experience" of the ultimate Limit is apprehended as the medium of the encounter with God (see below, section VI); *unfaith* is that attitude which, unable to "leap beyond" the ultimate Limit, finds itself always attending instead to the mere Limit as such.

does not rest on the assumed validity of some esoteric experience of the other world or the supernatural or even the "numinous" (Otto). On the contrary, I have claimed that the experiential root of the notion of God is simply the awareness of Limit or finitude (known in some form by every man). In and of itself this awareness does not presuppose or imply some "infinite" or "unconditional" being. Indeed, only when it is grasped and interpreted in concrete personalistic terms does the Limit become understood as the expression of a being transcending our world, i.e., of an active God.[26] Thus, the constitutive *experience* underlying the word "God" is that of limitation; the constitutive *image* which gives the term its peculiar transcendent reference is personalistic. These fused into one in the concretely religious apprehension of our finitude provide us with the root referent for the word.

This double rootage accounts for the fact that, on the one hand, the presence or action of God is sometimes said to be immediately "experienced" or "known," and, accordingly, doctrines of religious experience are developed. On the other hand, it is often maintained that the knowledge of God rests on "faith" or "belief," and that he cannot be experienced directly at all. If, as I am arguing, the most we could be said to experience directly here is our bare finitude as such—and even this is a very complex sort of "experience" which is never apprehended concretely apart from the image of one or another of the finite limiters used analogically—then the truth in both claims can be understood: the encounter with God will involve both the "experience" of our finitude and the faith-interpretation through which this limitedness is apprehended as due to an active will over against us. Since in the actual encounter with God these two elements so interpenetrate each other as not to be separately distinguishable,[27] there is little wonder that conflicting views about the relative

---

[26] It might be argued that it is no accident that such impersonal philosophical notions as "infinite" or "unconditional" reality, "being itself," the bare notion of "transcendence," etc., appear always as demythologized or depersonalized versions of the more anthropomorphic god(s) of a religious tradition, and that in their impersonal (sometimes called "superpersonal") form they are in fact denying the vital root on which their very life and meaning depend.

[27] See note 25, above.

importance of "experience" and "faith" appear. The faith interpretation, of course, is shaped by the concrete historical tradition within which one stands. If one stands within the Christian tradition, which knows of a loving and powerful Creator, it is hardly surprising that he will tend to see the course and destiny of his own being—i.e., its limits on all sides—as determined by the activity of God: God's mercy and benevolence toward him will be felt in that which seems good in life; his judgment and wrath, in the painful and constrictive.[28]

I conclude, therefore, that God-language is not necessarily hopelessly mythological and old-fashioned, but that, if carefully defined and restricted, it has a genuine basis in our awareness and knowledge of the Limit. This of course does not mean that the door is opened wide again for the well-structured "other world" of much traditional Christian thought. We have found it possible and legitimate to speak only of the reality which ultimately limits us on all sides—i.e., God—in this way. Of the existence beyond the Limit of finite beings alongside God—angels, demons, supernatural powers of all sorts, or the departed spirits of the dead—we know nothing and can know nothing. There is no warrant in the present analysis, then, for reintroducing the "mythological world-view" in any form at all.[29] Since historically Christian

[28] If we have correctly identified the experiential elements underlying the term "God," the doctrine of God must always deal in some fashion with the notion of transcendent reality (even if only to refer it to some "depth" in everything that is) and with the way in which this transcendence is known to us (i.e., with "revelation"). However, such highly problematic negative notions as "infinite" and "unconditional"—probably rooted ultimately in "mystical" experience of the "supernatural"—would perhaps not need to be given the constitutive role in a doctrine of God which they have so often played in the past (though they might well have a certain secondary and interpretative role to play); and the meaning of the doctrine would not in that way be placed so completely out of reach of those whose direct experience seems to them limited to the finite and contingent.

[29] It should perhaps be observed that my contention that such a doctrine of God would not be mythological rests on a distinction between "mythological" and "analogical." A *mythological* doctrine of God *begins in* and *presupposes* what I have called the cosmological dualism of "this world" and "another world," "this side" and "the other side." For such a presupposition there seems little warrant. An *analogical* doctrine of God makes no such presupposition, but results when (the experience of) finitude is understood in personalistic terms. Thus, an analogical doctrine, being experientially rooted, can be carefully disciplined and controlled methodologically; with

theology grew out of and accepted rather uncritically the cosmological dualism underlying and expressed in that world-view, and in many details seems still to presuppose it, it is necessary to think through the whole of the Christian perspective afresh, sifting out all mythological elements to arrive at what of Christian faith modern, this-worldly man can affirm. Only when this winnowing has been performed will we be in a position to see whether the essentials of Christian belief in fact depend on the acceptance of a mythology meaningless and even ridiculous to moderns, or whether Christian faith can be a live issue in our secular culture.

I have tried in this paper to show that there is some justification for continuing to speak of a personal God even though the mythological framework characteristic of earlier speech of this sort be completely given up. This of course in no way can or should be construed as a kind of proof of the existence of such a God. As we have seen, there are other ways of conceiving the ultimate Limit which may in some respects seem more credible. All that I have attempted here is to show that "God-language" has its roots in concrete (secular) experience and that its cognitive meaningfulness can be defended, even granting the premises of "secular man"; whether it is *true* or not is another question. Our analysis has brought us into a position from which we can see what would be required if the truth of this claim were to be affirmed, however. Only on the ground that God had in fact revealed himself could it be claimed he exists; only if there were and is some sort of movement from beyond the Limit to us, making known to us through the medium of the Limit the reality of that which lies beyond, could we be in a position to speak of such reality at all; only if God actually "spoke" to man could we know there is a God. It is of course

---

mythology the rootage is so vague and legendary that strict methodological control is almost impossible. For the position I am taking here, only if the Christian *doctrine of God* itself—worked out in strict accord with the foundations of theological knowledge as sketched in this paper—were to require the re-introduction of certain features of the otherwise discarded mythical world-view, would it be justifiable to reinstate them. But this is as it should be: Christian faith is first of all faith in *God*—and all else that must be said theologically should follow from this premise.

the Christian claim that God has acted to reveal himself and continues to do so. Whether that claim is true or not—and the grounds on which one might decide its truth—cannot be taken up in this paper; a full systematic theology would be required to deal with it. This paper should have made clear, however, that genuine knowledge of God could not be affirmed on any other basis than such revelation, and that the Christian claim is, therefore, directly relevant to the general philosophical question of God's existence.

Talk about Religious Talk
Various Approaches to the Nature of Religious Language

Jerry H. Gill

Definitely a "comer," Jerry H. Gill, who completed his doctorate in philosophy at Duke University in 1966, has already published articles in half a dozen major theological journals and is the author of a forthcoming book on the thought of language-analyst Ian T. Ramsay. Himself a specialist on religious language, Dr. Gill in this essay—reprinted from the *Scottish Journal of Theology* (March 1966)*— takes note of the increasing number of theological responses to developments in analytical philosophy and endeavors to classify them. He finds three primary approaches among religious thinkers: to view religious language as autonomous, or unique; to view it as having a manifold structure, neither totally autonomous nor totally dependent on empirical and logical criteria; and to view it as essentially related to ordinary empirical experience. While Gill is least sympathetic with the first of these approaches and most sympathetic with the last, he subjects all three to incisive critical scrutiny. Dr. Gill is a member of the Philosophy department of Southwestern University at Memphis.

THE RESPONSE of the theological world to contemporary developments in empirical and language philosophy is beginning to take on a more definite and active form. Books and articles are now appearing which deal with everything from the semantics of the Old Testament[1] and the

* Oliver and Boyd Ltd., Tweeddale Court, Edinburgh 1, Scotland.

[1] James Barr, *The Semantics of Biblical Language* (Clarendon Press, Oxford, 1961).

Church Fathers[2] to parallels between language analysis and Karl Barth's theology.[3] In addition, anthologies in the philosophy of religion are now including a section on "The Nature of Religious Language."[4]

As the quantity and quality of this response increase there arises a need for a survey and classification of the various approaches of which it is composed. It is the purpose of this article to provide such a survey, and to make some evaluational comments and suggestions. It should be mentioned at the outset that it is impossible completely to classify approaches; and yet there are similarities and dissimilarities among these approaches which enable one to point out "family resemblances."

Obviously, such a survey cannot come close to being exhaustive, but certain tendencies can be noted. Moreover, an effort will be made to classify the various approaches according to a continuum. Those that are dealt with first tend towards maintaining the autonomy of religious language, while those that are discussed further along in the article would prefer to relate religious language to empirical experience. In between there are those who would advocate something similar to an eclectic view.

Religious Language as Autonomous

Of the many religious thinkers who could be lined up at this end of the continuum, space will only permit a discussion of two; the late William F. Zuurdeeg of McCormick Theological Seminary, and the late Michael Foster of Oxford University. Theologians such as Karl Barth and William Hordern also bear certain positive relations to this approach.

Perhaps the clearest statement of Zuurdeeg's thinking on this subject is to be found in his article in the July 1961 issue

---

[2] Samauel Laeuchli, *The Language of Faith* (Abingdon Press, Nashville, 1962).

[3] Bernard Ramm, "Karl Barth and Analytic Philosophy," *The Christian Century*, 11th April, 1962.

[4] McGregor and Robb, *Readings in Religious Philosophy* (Houghton Mifflin Co., Boston, 1962).

of *The Journal of Bible and Religion* entitled "Implications of Analytical Philosophy for Theology." Zuurdeeg divides his discussion into two main parts which deal with the advantages and disadvantages of analytical philosophy for theology. On the whole this is a knowledgable, clear, and stimulating presentation. There are, however, several serious questions that arise in connexion with his position. These will be taken up after a brief summary of the article.

In his section on the advantages of analytical philosophy, Zuurdeeg mentions first the new clarity that has resulted from the contemporary distinction between science, philosophy, and axiology. The history of western thought has always been plagued by the frustrating confusion of these three areas of experience. Questions concerning make-up of the solar system, as well as questions concerning human values, have historically been answered by the philosopher without even making a distinction between them. The break of modern philosophy from ancient philosophy, beginning with F. Bacon and R. Descartes, went along with the scientific revolution and pretty much divided science and philosophy. The revolution of twentieth-century philosophy has provided the break between philosophy and axiology, since analytic philosophers classify aesthetic, ethical, and religious language as emotive and/or non-factual. Philosophy's main concern now is with language, its structure (syntactics) and its referential aspects (semantics).

This new approach to philosophy is an advantage for theology, according to Zuurdeeg, because its disentangles religious language from philosophical problems.

The recognition that Christian faith and its theology are other languages than science and philosophy helps to clear the atmosphere. Of course, this means that now the difficult problem arises of how we are to understand the various relationships between the language of theology and those of science, philosophy, and historical investigation. Here is a task for the philosophy of religion: to make clear what these relations actually are.[5]

[5] Willem F. Zuurdeeg, "Implications of Analytical Philosophy for Theology," *The Journal of Bible and Religion*, July 1961, p. 206.

The problem and the task mentioned in the latter part of this quotation will be taken up shortly. Suffice it to say at this point that Zuurdeeg has here correctly nailed down the crucial issue which this whole "autonomous" approach raises.

The second advantage of this approach to philosophy is that:

The analytical claim that philosophy should drop religious and moral language implies the conclusion that it does not belong to the business of philosophy to construct or justify metaphysical or theological systems.[6]

At long last religion and theology can be rescued from the dominance of philosophy and the ensuing responsibility to build and defend giant intellectual systems. The whole history of philosophy prior to the twentieth century is replete with thinkers who attempt to synthesise philosophy and religion, to the embarrassment and detriment of both. Plato, Aristotle, Plotinus, Augustine, Aquinas, Kant, and Hegel all were guilty of this to some degree.

The analytic approach to philosophy, together with the existential approach, has served notice that neither philosophy nor theology can be the other's handmaid. Hume and his followers, such as Schlick, Russell, and Wittgenstein, together with Kierkegaard and his counterparts, such as Nietzsche and Sartre, all stand agreed that system-building is not the task of philosophy nor theology. Moreover, religion need not depend upon philosophy and logic for its justification. The following excerpt from Zuurdeeg's article will make his thoughts on the matter quite clear.

How can we think of justifying Him who has revealed Himself in One who was a stumbling-block to the Jews and folly to the Gentiles? How can we feel obliged to erect an impressive and respectable structure of thought around Him who had no form nor comeliness? If we look for a theology which honours such a God and such a Lord, we arrive, not at a well fitting system of thought, but at a stumbling attempt to set forth and interpret that which it has pleased our Lord God to disclose and communicate in his revelation. Of course, that which has been disclosed and com-

6 Ibid., p. 206.

municated by God escapes clear classification and analysis. Although revelation is not unrelated to propositional truth, it is much more than that. It is above all God giving himself to us in Jesus Christ. Hence, while Christian "truth" can be uttered to a certain extent in human words, this propositional aspect is not its most important element. Truth has to do, in the first place, with encountering God in Jesus Christ. Truth is our relationship with God in Christ. Christ is Truth. It is amazing nonsense to think that we can justify this Truth by philosophy.[7]

The first disadvantage of analytical philosophy which Zuurdeeg mentions is its exclusive use of logical analysis when attempting to come to grips with the meaning and truth of all languages. According to Zuurdeeg, logical analysis is appropriate when one is dealing with the languages of mathematics and empirical science, but highly inappropriate in connexion with the languages of poetry, ethics, and religion. These latter are existential in nature (or "convictional" as Zuurdeeg says elsewhere[8]) and thus cannot be submitted to the same type of analysis as mathematics and science. In fact, Zuurdeeg clearly implies that the languages of ethics and religion can only be submitted to a type of analysis which is a-logical. Such an analysis does not result in the discovery or construction of rules for these languages. His most straightforward expression of this point of view is where he says:

I must protest vehemently against the notion that language of Christian faith consists of propositions which can be analysed by means of logic. If it does not make sense to a philosopher to attempt a logical analysis of persons, how much sense will it make to a theologian to try to do so with the Lord God? Exactly in the way that man is man-who-speaks, so God is God-who-speaks. Can we offer a logical analysis of the Creator of Heaven and Earth? Shall we discard the doctrine of the Trinity simply because the language in which it is expressed is logically inconsistent?[9]

Just prior to this passage Zuurdeeg admits that he may not fully understand Wittgenstein's use of the analytical approach to language, and that consequently his argument may be based

[7] Ibid., p. 208.
[8] Zuurdeeg, *An Analytical Philosophy of Religion* (Abingdon Press, 1961).
[9] Zuurdeeg, op. cit., p. 209.

on a misinterpretation. Shortly I hope to suggest that this is a very imminent possibility.

Zuurdeeg's second criticism of the analytical approach to philosophy is its lack of response to "the challenge of existentialist philosophy." He feels that existentialism deals with relationships between beings which are non-rational, and that analytic philosophy has failed to address itself to these non-rational relationships. Moreover, since these relationships are basic to human existence and experience, to ignore them may well be to commit philosophical suicide.

Just two comments about this last point. First, although I agree that analytic philosophers have often become esoteric and remiss in failing to face up to existential issues, the same criticism can be made of many of the existentialist philosophers. Anyone who has ground his way through Heidegger's and Jaspers' rarified vocabulary may well wonder what all this has to do with real life situations. Moreover, which existentialists are facing up to the challenge of analytical philosophy and its stress on clarity and precision? The appeal to respond to challenges cuts both ways.

Secondly, Zuurdeeg and the existentialists are clearly right when they maintain that man's basic relationships are non-rational. But to conclude from this that the description of these relationships can be non-rational is to invite confusion. But more of this later.

Another exponent of this general approach to the nature of religious language is Michael Foster. Foster's views come out clearly in his article entitled "Contemporary British Philosophy and Christian Belief" which appeared in the fall 1960 edition of *The Christian Scholar*.[10] After tracing the development of logical empiricism and linguistic analysis in Britain, Foster directs his attention to the question of the implications of contemporary philosophy and Christian faith for each other. He thinks that the implications of the latter for the former form the basic question for the Christian, and thus focuses his discussion in this area.

Foster's main complaint concerning contemporary em-

---

[10] For a more complete exposition of Foster's position see his book *Mystery and Philosophy* (S.C.M. Press, London, 1957).

pirical philosophy is its "demand for clarity" and its "assumption" that this demand can always be met.[11] He maintains that such a procedure smacks of rationalism and the ambition of human dominion over experience. The end result of such an approach, according to Foster, is the denial of the possibility of saying anything that is not clear; which is in essence the denial of revelation. Such a conclusion not only puts contemporary philosophy at odds with the Greek tradition in the history of philosophy, but causes it to stand in direct conflict with Christian faith and biblical theology.

In the final section of his article, Foster offers an alternative conception of philosophy in general and Christian philosophy in particular. The essential element of this alternative is the concept of a philosophy based on revelation. Foster states that he does not mean *natural* revelation, but rather a type of revelation which recognises that its world view is an interpretation and invites others to view the world from this new vantage point.[12]

There are two aspects of Foster's suggestion which call for special notation. First, he is objecting to the use of logic and reason as the criteria for understanding and evaluating religious language. Thus, reason does not fulfil a revelatory, nor an evaluatory function in religious experience and communication.

Secondly, Foster stresses the importance of the mysterious aspect of revelation. The following paragraph indicates his point of view.

Revelation is of mystery, but mystery revealed is not eliminated, but remains mysterious. It remains object of wonder, which is dispelled when mystery is eliminated. There is no method by which revelation can be commanded: it is [in the Bible] not a thing to be procured from God by any technique. That is to say, it is not subject to human mastery.[13]

Both of these aspects of Foster's thought indicate why he is classified along with Zuurdeeg as one who maintains the autonomy of religious language.

[11] *The Christian Scholar*, Fall 1960, p. 194.
[12] Ibid., p. 197.
[13] Ibid., p. 196.

By way of evaluation of the foregoing position, at least three basic questions need to be raised. First, if the languages of theology and religion are held to be autonomous, or to use Zuurdeeg's terminology, *sui generis*,[14] and are thus independent of logical analysis and evaluation, what criterion is to be used in determining their meaning? Zuurdeeg mentions (in the quotation above) that it is the task of the philosophy of religion "to make clear" what the relationships are between the languages of history, science, and theology. But does he actually do this? Does he even suggest what standards or rules one should employ in determining the meaning of religious and theological expressions?

On the contrary, Zuurdeeg actually says that there can be no rules governing the religious use of such terms as "Christ" and "salvation."[15] What I am getting at in this objection is simply that we do have rules for how these and other religious terms are used, and it is the indirect learning of these rules and usages that enable us to think and speak religiously. Certainly the term "Christ" functions in ways that are similar to those of other nouns. Moreover, some uses of this term are not accepted, such as "Christ is not interested in men." It would seem that the whole point of referring to God's revelation in the Incarnation as "the Word of God" implies an inter-subjective communication which man is meant to understand, and which is capable of verification.

As has been indicated, Zuurdeeg thinks that since personal and religious experiences are not by nature rational, they cannot be subjected to rational analysis. This, I would like to suggest, is pure confusion. Basic facts, situations, and relationships are neither rational nor irrational; they just are. But human talk about, and descriptions of, such entities must either follow some rules or be judged meaningless for the simple reason that it fails to communicate; which, after all, is the purpose of language. Zuurdeeg and, I should add, others who hold this position talk as if there were some other type of analysis than "logical" analysis. Unfortunately, they never

[14] Op. cit., p. 20.
[15] Ibid., p. 209.

seem to indicate how such analysis would proceed. Indeed, any attempt to indicate such a procedure by means of language would, of necessity, involve logic. It would seem that "non-logical analysis" is devoid of any meaning whatsoever.

Secondly, and along the same line, I cannot help but think that Foster's fear of logic as an attempt to "master" experience in general, and revelation in particular, rests upon a basic misunderstanding of the nature of logic. The laws of logic are essentially a set of rules governing the use of symbols, and by means of which these symbols become effective for communication. The only ultimate justification (?) that can be given for their use is that they facilitate communication; assuming, of course, that one has something to say.

Now to say, as Foster does, that the demand for clarity is out of place in religious language is, in effect, to say that religious language does not attempt to communicate—and thus is not a language. If a person utters symbols which have an established use in a way which does not follow that use, and if that person does not offer another use by means of which his utterances can be understood, then he cannot be said to be talking at all. This would seem to be the ultimate result of viewing religious language as autonomous.

Thirdly, this suggested autonomy involves the rejection of logical criteria as the means of justifying and evaluating the claims of religious language. In a passage already quoted Zuurdeeg asks: "How can we think of justifying Him who has revealed Himself in One who was a stumbling-block to the Jews and folly to the Gentiles?" And he answers by saying: "Truth has to do, in the first place, with encountering God in Jesus Christ. Truth is our relationship with God in Christ. Christ is truth. It is amazing nonsense to think that we can justify this truth by philosophy."

It is not my intention to disagree with these statements. It is my intention to suggest that if such statements are to have any meaning, and in addition any truth-value, there must be some criteria by which to judge them. Logic certainly is not the only criterion, but it just as certainly is a necessary one. The whole business of encountering God has to be cognised in some sense even to be an experience, let alone to be appreciated and substantiated.

The foregoing remarks are applicable to Foster's position in a slightly different way. To be perfectly honest, I simply am unable to understand what Foster means in the paragraph quoted above. It appears that he wants to have it both ways with revelation; revelation reveals a mystery and revelation does not reveal a mystery. The only way that this can make sense, as I see it, is to equivocate on the meaning of the term "reveal" so that one can say "revelation *points out* mystery, but does not *fully explain* mystery." But is this what is meant by Christian revelation? If all that God's communication to man is meant to do is point out mystery, what need has the Church for doctrine, creeds, etc., and more important, wherein lies the hope of salvation? Does not the Christian faith involve the communication of a solution, as well as a mystery? Foster and other existentialist theologians write as if man's redemption comes from appreciating mystery, whereas the biblical approach would seem to indicate that such appreciation is only the beginning of the redemptive process. "The fear of the Lord is the beginning of wisdom."

The approach which would set religious language off as autonomous proceeds from the worthy motive of safeguarding it from rationalism; but such safety comes at the expense of disrelating religious language from experience by eliminating any inter-subjective criterion of meaning and truth. Is it too much to suggest that this is too high a price to pay? I think not.

Religious Language as Manifold

An approach to the question concerning the nature of religious language which would seem to have more to commend itself is that approach which views religious language as having a manifold structure. Such language is not totally autonomous, nor totally dependent on empirical and logical criteria, but is some of each, according to the various aspects of its structure and purpose. Among the writers who take this approach, Frederick Ferré and John McIntyre are representative, if not exemplary, and I will endeavour to delineate their views at this time.

Ferré's book, *Language, Logic, and God,* is undoubtedly the clearest and most thorough presentation of his position.[16] This book provides a fine survey of many of the approaches to the meaning and verification of religious and theological talk, and concludes with a thesis chapter entitled "The Manifold Logic of Theism." Ferré begins this chapter by stating that:

Three factors are present in every "signification-situation" (as we shall call the situation wherein language purports to signify a "fact" of some kind, a state of affairs, or "something that is the case"): first, there is the factor of the language itself, the presence of marks or sounds which serve to signify; second, there is the factor of the language-using agent, or interpreter, for whom the language signifies something; and third, there is the factor of the "something" referred to, the content signified.[17]

He proceeds to emphasise the necessity of studying all three of these aspects of religious language in order to obtain a full understanding of its nature. Many of the shortcomings within the various contemporary approaches to religious language can be traced to a restricted focus on any one of these three factors, which Ferré designates "syntactic, interpretic, and semantic" respectively.

According to Ferré, religious language is essentially autonomous in its syntactic function, due to its use of both formal and "informal" logic. Certainly there are logical connectives which have the same function in religious talk as in other modes of expression, but there are also instances in which religious talk seems to have "its own logic."

If, on an unpleasant day, I describe the weather by saying "It's raining and it's not," I am uttering a formal contradiction, but it may be the best possible characterisation of the day. If it is, it will not be so merely because I use a form of words which seems

16 See also his article "Is Language About God Fraudulent?" in *The Scottish Journal of Theology,* December 1959.
17 Ferré, F., *Language, Logic, and God* (Harper, New York, 1961), p. 146.

to contradict itself but because the expression I use acts as an incentive to increased conceptual precision. Perhaps the English language is not yet equipped to indicate the more-than-drizzling but less-than-sprinkling condition of the atmosphere. The subject-matter demands an increase in vocabulary, a more careful act of attention to what is the case. Again, "She's pretty and she's not," "He's likable and he's not" serve to suggest that further refinement of our concepts of "pretty" or "likable" is needed before an adequate non-paradoxical statement about him or her will be in order. Likewise the apparent contradiction "God is involved in change and he is not" is an indication that further investigation of our concepts of "involvement" and "change" are in order so that we may discover more precisely their logical powers for the inferences which, in theology, hinge on them.[18]

This passage is followed by another in which Ferré implies that these seemingly odd uses of language in a religious way serve to point up the complexity of the subject matter of religion, and should, therefore, eventually be replaced by statements which possess rational coherence while remaining true to the nature of religious experience.

Ferré divides his discussion of the interpretic function of religious talk into two parts. There is the effect the talk has on the listener ("passive") and the purpose of the user of the language ("active"). After pointing out that the former is important from the psychological and sociological standpoint, and that it is in need of much further study, the author directs his attention to the latter which bears more centrally on theology and philosophy.

Language is a human tool which is so closely bound up with the thought-life and experience of the user that it can never be properly understood apart from a serious study of the purpose and experience of those who speak. Religious language is no different in this respect, and for this reason involves an element of autonomy at this point also. The richness and significance of religious talk can only be appreciated from within the community of those who share the same experiences and purposes in verbal expression.

The matter of sharing experiences directs our attention to the semantic function of theological language. In some sense

[18] Ibid., p. 153.

religious talk is meant to refer to states of affairs which exist outside of individual feelings and concepts. These so-called "metaphysical facts" which serve as the referents of much of religious language are "not the same kind of facts which are discussed in the language of the empirical sciences" (p. 160). Ferré gives the main reasons for drawing this distinction.

First, metaphysical facts are not subject to the rigorous experimentation and prediction-fulfilment that scientific facts are. There simply is no clearly established method for verification of religious language and experience. Yet, "metaphysical facts" are not to be written off as empirical facts viewed through an attitude of worship.

Secondly, this type of fact to which religious talk refers is not "given" in a purely objective fashion, but has its existence within a conceptual system. "A metaphysical fact, therefore, is a concept which plays a key role within the system, without which the system would founder."[19] This situation is not entirely unique to metaphysical facts, however, since even scientific facts can be shown to depend upon a broader conceptual system for their meaning and verification.

Given this situation, Ferré suggests that there are, nevertheless, definite criteria which are relevant to the evaluation of these conceptual, metaphysical systems and thus their metaphysical facts as well. He mentions consistence and coherence as "internal" criteria and applicability to experience as an "external" standard. The more universality of experiential applicability a system possesses the more valuable it is.

Ferré concludes his discussion of "the manifold logic of theism" by raising and answering the question, "In what respect can theological statements claim to be *true* to reality?" His answer suggests that that conceptual system, based on certain key model thought structures and concepts, which is able to synthesise and illuminate our total experience to the greatest degree can be said to be "true to reality." Although there are many such systems, the theist is convinced that theism does the best job in this regard.[20]

In his article which was mentioned earlier, Ferré stresses

19 Ibid., p. 161.
20 Ibid., p. 165.

the necessity of a third type of meaning to complement the usual dichotomy between "cognitive" and "emotive" meaning. He designates this type of meaning as "responsive" meaning and says it is communicated by symbols which

> touch many of our most basic drives and experiences. They can reflect a pattern or organisation of these depth-experiences and, if responded to affirmatively, can mould one's total response to his world: implicitly embodying a scale of values, an emphasis of outlook, a dominance of drive which provides a distinctive "stance" or "posture" towards the normal flow as well as the great crises of life. Such great symbols may be called "organising images."[21]

These symbols or images which carry responsive meaning are evaluated by such criteria as "appropriateness," "ringing true," and "resultant quality of life." It never seems to occur to Ferré that such criteria are notorious for failing to provide any kind of agreement either with regard to meaning or truth-value. I fail to see how this type of standard can be sufficient, but we will return to this matter shortly.

Another attempt to point up the complexity of religious language is found in the thought of John McIntyre. He discusses the more traditional view of the nature of religious language, namely that religious talk is *analogical*. McIntyre deals with four expressions of this viewpoint, beginning with Thomas Aquinas as interpreted by Thomas de Vio Cajetanus, and mentioning J. C. McClelland's Reformed view, Karl Barth's contemporary view, and concluding with the views of some philosophers. It is obvious that the author is very impressed with the insights provided by this approach, in spite of its various limitations, which he so clearly points out.

Two of the more important points which McIntyre thinks need to be made about analogy as used in theology are: (1) There are two basic types of analogy, analogy of attribution which draws attention to attributes which two entities or situations have in common, and analogy of proportionality which draws attention to the similarities of function or relationship which exist between two sets of entities. McIntyre is con-

[21] Ferré, op. cit., p. 354.

vinced that both of these types, and perhaps others, will need to be employed in coming to grips with the nature of religious language. These two types of analogy also differ in that the former (attribution) is based on an external relation between the primary and the secondary uses of the analogical term, while the latter (proportionality) is based on a similarity of inherent relations between the term and its contexts. (2) As J. S. Mill pointed out, analogical description must not be taken as final, but should, rather, be considered both as a helpful beginning point and as an indication that a more rigorous description needs to be developed.

As McIntyre says,

We must firmly remember that *all* of our knowledge of God cannot be analogical; otherwise we would not know that it was so. We have to have non-analogical knowledge with which to compare analogical and by which to judge its accuracy. Here J. S. Mill's word becomes extremely relevant: theological inquiry must accept as its goal the reduction of the area of analogical affirmation. We must not err by seeking to impose upon analogy any too rigid structure. Otherwise it ceases to be analogy and becomes univocity. For this reason, we must keep an open mind on the many analogies with which contemporary biblical exposition and dogmatic assertion operate. But this is not to say that one analogy is as good as any other. The philosophers have helped us to see that analogies must be carefully scrutinised for positive and negative content, and graded accordingly. But ultimately analogies establish themselves not by their conformity to the rubrics of medieval or modern logic, or yet to the requirements of an anti-metaphysical metaphysic, but by the living relation in which they stand to the living Word of God, to the worshipping and obedient community, and to the salvation of God's children.[22]

Obviously the most important value of this manifold approach is that it is sensitive to the many and varied uses of religious language. As such it is in a position to avoid the criticism of being oversimplified. Moreover, it is appreciative of the complex nature of religious talk and realises that much

[22] McIntyre, John, "Analogy," *Scottish Journal of Theology,* March 1959, p. 20.

of it is closely related to ordinary language, and thus must be governed by the same rules and standards.

Still, there is a tendency even within this view to suggest that in some sense religious language is autonomous and must be understood and evaluated by special methods. Ferré talks of "metaphysical facts" and McIntyre seems to favour an analogical interpretation of religious language. Both of these modes of thought imply that in some sense religious language is generically distinct from ordinary and empirical language, and thus seems to be immune to evaluation by the usual canons of understanding and evaluation at certain key points.

One is hard pressed to make much sense out of Ferré's notion of "metaphysical facts." On the one hand theological statements are said to refer to a state of affairs or to reality,[23] and on the other "are not the same kind of facts" as those of the sciences.[24] To add to the confusion, Ferré fails to give a single example of a "metaphysical fact." If one says that there are different kinds of facts, he ought to say how he is able to distinguish between them. "Every difference ought to make a difference." A descriptive analogy is legitimate, as long as one gives some criterion for distinguishing between the two factors which are being compared. This Ferré has not done. By the use of the phrase "metaphysical fact," Ferré seems to indicate that he wants to eat his cake and have it at the same time. Such facts describe reality, but the usual canons of meaning and verification do not apply to them.

This ambivalence shows up again in his suggestions for establishing criteria for meaning and truth for theological language. Both in his book and in the aforementioned article, Ferré suggests internal consistency and external applicability as such criteria. There is nothing intrinsically wrong with these suggestions, provided he is prepared to indicate the specific meaning of these concepts. I find him especially vague in regard to the concept of "external applicability." In a very general way he seems to mean the ability of a particular metaphysical interpretation of the existential aspects of human experience to produce a new quality of life.

[23] Ferré, op. cit., p. 159.
[24] Ibid., p. 160.

Two brief remarks are in order at this point. (1) This is a valid suggestion, but I wonder if it is so far removed from the usual interpretation of the "correspondence theory of truth"? Ferré seems to ask for new criteria and then reverts to an expansion of the old ones. (2) Is such a "pragmatic" criterion sufficient? Ferré says nothing about the importance of external applicability to historical fact, for instance. Is a metaphysical construct which produces newness of life all that is necessary as a standard of truth? I think not.

McIntyre manifests a somewhat more versatile approach than Ferré, although their views are essentially similar. His reminder concerning the necessity of non-analogical language and knowledge by means of which we interpret and evaluate the analogical is well taken. So is his warning with regard to being insensitive to the complex and unique structure of various uses of analogy, both in scriptural and theological contexts.

I am puzzled, however, by McIntyre's final statement in the above-quoted passage, with which he concludes his analysis of analogy. Here again we can see an implication that religious language is autonomous in relation to the traditional and modern criteria of truth. He seems to be calling attention to the additional requirement that religious analogies, and thus religious language, must effectively relate to the essential existential qualities of human religious experience. This may be so, but why is this any more of an "ultimate" criterion than the others? Indeed, would it be possible to meet this criterion without also meeting the others? It seems to me that McIntyre's final remark would be more appropriate as a proclamation than as part of analysis. At any rate, he introduces concepts at the very close of his analysis which only serve to confuse the very fine insights made earlier.

Religious Language as Empirical

In moving one step further away from the position which views religious talk as autonomous, or unique, one comes to an attempt to understand religious language in terms of recent developments in contemporary empirical philosophy.

Both Ian T. Ramsey and John Hick are concerned to relate religious talk and belief to ordinary language and empirical assertions. They are aware that religious language has many functions, but they are convinced that a, if not the, primary function is to convey information about states of affairs.

Ramsey's position is expressed in detail in his book *Religious Language,* but its major thrust comes out clearly in an article entitled "Contemporary Empiricism" in the fall 1960 issue of *The Christian Scholar.* After outlining the two major themes of contemporary language philosophy—the interest in meaning and the concern with language—Ramsey concludes with "two suggestions of importance for reflection about the Christian faith," and he entitles this section "The Empirical Anchor of Theology."

His first suggestion is that "we must contrive to show the kind of situation which illuminates theological discourse. . . . We must make plain the empirical anchorage of theological assertions. . . ."[25] Ramsey goes on to point out that although religious language cannot be fully understood in terms of statements dealing with public and observable activity alone, there must be a vital relation between the two or else the former will become so autonomous as to render itself esoteric and irrelevant.

The author under discussion rejects the attempts which have been made to protect theological discourse by appealing to Wittgenstein's statement that "every sentence has its own logic" as a gross oversimplification of Wittgenstein's point of view.[26] Such "logical segregation" renders religious talk irrelevant to the man in the street, and thereby contradicts its very reason for existence.

Theological assertions must have a logical context which extends to, and is continuous with, those assertions of ordinary language for which sense experience is directly relevant. From such straightforward assertions, theological assertions must not be logically

---

[25] Ramsey, I. T., "Contemporary Empiricism," *The Christian Scholar,* Fall 1960, p. 181.
[26] For a direct application of Wittgenstein's approach see "Wittgenstein and Religious Language," *Theology Today,* April 1964.

segregated: for that would mean that they were pointless and, in contrast to the only language which has an agreed meaning, meaningless.[27]

We can, according to Ramsey, get close to the empirical heart of religious and theological language if we follow Wittgenstein's theme that language is only understood in connexion with the actions, or "forms of life" which comprise its context and purpose. Such a study will reveal what Ramsey calls "disclosure situations" wherein we become aware of our own self-identity, for example. Although this awareness may be considered "subjective," it arises out of experiences and situations which are objective in nature. Self-awareness does not come about originally by means of introspection (à la Descartes), but rather indirectly by means of objective physical and social experiences.

As I understand Ramsey's suggestion, he is pleading for a "broadening" of empiricism so as to include such disclosures as objective experiences which, while being more complex, are nonetheless valid and valuable entities of empirical study. His approach sounds somewhat like a half-way house between logical empiricism and existentialism. Needless to say, if such a synthesis could be worked out, it would be very welcome on the contemporary scene.

Ramsey's second suggestion is to "give to our theology a logical structure peculiar enough to ground it in the kind of situation I have just called a disclosure."[28] Such a programme will certainly lead to a good number of reforms in theological expression. Each expression needs to be examined thoroughly, both with regard to its individual context and its variety of uses and functions. We must avoid being misled by the *grammatical similarities* between statements such as, "My soul is immortal" and "My flowers are everlasting" (or "My flowers are red"), into overlooking their basic *logical dissimilarities*.

Ramsey summarizes his twofold proposal with the following paragraph:

[27] Op. cit., p. 181.
[28] Ibid., p. 183.

Here then, if the empirical possibility of disclosures be allowed, is an approach both sympathetic to, and benefiting from, contemporary empirical insights, while being of real value to theology. It is an approach which forces on theology no systematic metaphysics. Rather it goes to theology interested in the whole range of theological discourse, and its only aim is to map the logical relations exhibited by this discourse, so that we may see more clearly, more reliably, less ambiguously, how it performs the task which its initiators gave it when they theologised about their religion.[29]

Professor John Hick represents another attempt to see theological and religious talk as essentially empirical. His article, "Theology and Verification," which appeared in the April 1960 issue of *Theology Today,* is his most recent effort at clarifying this position. The most complete presentation of Hick's approach, however, is to be found in his book *Faith and Knowledge.*

Part One of Hick's book is devoted to the analysis of the use, and thus the meaning, of the two key terms in religious epistemology—"knowledge" and "belief." In this analysis Hick aligns himself with the empiricist position which distinguishes between logical (analytic) and empirical (synthetic) knowledge, and limits the former as having nothing to do with the existence or non-existence of states-of-affairs or entities. Matters of fact are known through experience alone.[30] "Belief" is found to have several basic characteristics, namely, entertainment of the proposition, assent to the proposition, disposition to act on the proposition, and an emotion of conviction to defend the proposition.

In Part Two of his book, Hick outlines and evaluates three influential approaches to the nature of religious knowledge. He takes up the "voluntarist," the "moral order," and the "illative sense" theories in that order. Although Hick criticises each of these theories as essentially wrong, he does think each has a contribution to make.

Part Three Hick calls "the central section of the book," for it is here that he sets forth his theory concerning the nature

29 Ibid., p. 183.
30 Hick, John, *Fraith and Knowledge* (Cornell University Press, Ithaca, New York, 1957), p. 21.

of religious knowledge and its relation to the empirical structure of human knowledge in general. In the chapter on "The Nature of Faith" two key concepts are developed by way of elucidating the structure of human cognition. "Significance" is used to designate the fact that our minds play an active part in selecting and organising our experience. In a way our minds do function according to "categories" (similar to Kant's conception) which form the very structure or precondition of thought. Significance is motivated primarily by practical simplicity. The "givenness" of significance is closely related to the act of "interpretation" by means of which we, consciously or unconsciously, give a total interpretation to the whole of experience.

Hick's thinking is that there are three levels of human experience, each involving significance and interpretation. The physical world (nature) comes in on us with a given structure and we respond and relate to this significance in ways which indicate our interpretation of it. We can view the physical world as real or as a dream. Growing up out of physical relations is our awareness of the moral world (man), which also has a given structure to which we respond in an act of interpretation. We can take moral responsibility seriously or we can ignore it. Finally, growing up out of human relations is our awareness of the religious world (God), which also has a given significance which we interpret. God exists or He does not.

The major difference between these levels of experience is that each involves an increasing degree of interpretive freedom. The physical level presses in with such forcefulness that its reality can only be questioned philosophically, not pragmatically. The moral level is not nearly so forceful, and thus is capable of being pragmatically denied. Thirdly, the religious level is even less forceful, and often goes completely unnoticed by many people. The reason God remains in the background and does not "force Himself upon us" is that He desires to leave the decision to relate one's self to God up to the individual. Such indirect revelation is necessary to the development of an inter-personal relationship.[31]

[31] Ibid., chap. 8, "Faith and Freedom."

I have developed Hick's viewpoint on religious knowledge at some length because only with it as a background can the real significance of his empirical interpretation of religious language be appreciated. Chapter Seven, "The Logic of Faith," concerns itself with the problem of verification of religious statements. This, of course, raises the question of what kind of statements they are. After concluding that, although they are essentially empirical, they are not verified in terms of probabilities, Hick develops his own theory.

He begins by accepting the empiricist maxim that the meaningfulness of a proposition is dependent on its asserting a state-of-affairs which is open to confirmation or dis-confirmation.

Applying this principle to theology, the questions are asked of the theist: How do you suppose the present state of the universe to differ from the state in which it would be if there were no God? What do you *deny* by your assertion that there is a God? What does the theistic assertion allege to exist or to happen or to happen thus, which might conceivably fail to exist or occur or which might occur otherwise? At what point, in short, does it lay itself open to confirmation or refutation?[32]

Although theistic assertions generally fit this pattern, there is an oddness about those that claim the reality of life after death.

The logical peculiarity of the claim is that it is open to confirmation but not to refutation. There can be conclusive evidence for it if it be true, but there cannot be conclusive evidence against it if it be untrue. For if we survive bodily death we shall (presumably) know that we have survived it, but if we do not survive death we shall not know that we have not survived it. The verification situation is thus asymmetrical. However, the religious doctrine at least is open to verification and is accordingly meaningful. Its eschatological prediction assures its status as an assertion.[33]

It is this concept of "eschatological verification" which Hick feels fulfils the basic requirement of meaningfulness for theological language. Not only are statements dealing with life

[32] Ibid., p. 147.
[33] Ibid., p. 150.

after death open to validation in this manner, but statements concerning the existence and nature of God, and the divinity of Christ would seem to be verifiable in this way also.

Hick points out that, although the new quality of life experienced by believers in theism cannot, *per se,* be used as evidence for the confirmation of theistic assertions, there is an important connection between these assertions and practical living:

This alleged future experience of heaven cannot of course be appealed to as evidence for theism as a present interpretation; but it does render the choice between theism and naturalism a real and not a merely empty or verbal choice. When we now add that the alternative interpretations are such as to render different plans and policies appropriate now, the difference between them is seen to be not only epistemically real but also of immediate practical importance.[34]

These same themes are emphasised by Hick in his article in *Theology Today,* which he concludes with the following words:

My concern here is not to seek to establish the religious facts, but rather to establish that there are such things as religious facts, and in particular that the existence or non-existence of the God of the New Testament is a matter of fact, and claims as such eventual experiential verification.[35]

There are several questions that can be raised by way of evaluating the empirical approach to the nature of religious language. The biggest weakness, in my way of thinking, of Ramsey's view is the lack of explicitness. Just what is the exact nature of a "disclosure"? How does this concept fit into epistemological experience? Nor do I fully understand exactly how this concept fits into the structure of theological discourse. I realise that Ramsey has taken definite steps to make these matters explicit in recent publications,[36] but a good deal of work remains to be done.

[34] Ibid., p. 152.
[35] Hick, J., "Theology and Verification," *Theology Today,* April 1960.
[36] See especially his *Models and Mystery* (Oxford, 1964) which goes a long way to meeting these difficulties.

With regard to Hick's approach, I am not entirely satisfied with his handling of the relation of probabilities to religious knowledge. How can one call himself an empiricist, talk of evidence and verification, and still maintain that probabilities play no part in religious knowledge? If one interpretation of the whole experience results in a more coherent and inclusive explanation of all the aspects of that experience, it would seem appropriate to say that that interpretation has the highest probability of being true. Hick deals with both the traditional and the informal conceptions of probability, but does not explore the possibility of conceiving of probability as a relation of an explanation to evidence. The nature of probability is a very key issue in contemporary philosophy of science, and its developments and implications for religious knowledge deserve our attention.[37]

In addition, I cannot help but feel that Hick's definition of Christian theism in terms of "eschatological verification" should be broadened to include what might be called "pragmatic verification." Certainly Christ's teachings included assertions about the reality of a transcendent and personal God, and about an after-life. But they also included assertions about the reality of an experience with God in this life which would yield a life of joy, peace, love, and purpose. These assertions are open to verification and refutation also. In both cases the assertions are equally empirical, so this suggestion does not obviate Hick's basic approach.[38]

A Final Note

As may be surmised from the foregoing survey, I am more impressed with those approaches which stress the manifold and empirical aspects of religious language. Religious discourse clearly has certain unique and complex characteristics,

[37] See R. Carnap, *Logical Foundations of Probability* (University of Chicago Press); and E. Nagel, "Principles of the Theory of Probability," *International Encyclopedia of Unified Science*, University of Chicago Press.

[38] My own approach to a "Christian empiricism" is outlined in the June 1963 issue of *The Scottish Journal of Theology* under the title "The Possibility of Apologetics."

and much work needs to be done to uncover their logic. At the same time, much of religious talk is composed of factual assertions, and is subject to empirical verification. It would seem that the most light can be brought into this whole area by analyses which focus on this aspect of religious talk. In the words of I. T. Ramsey, whose work impresses me the most,

. . . contemporary empiricism, broadened to include "disclosures," introduces a more generous account of rationality, endeavours to map mystery, and displays a deliberate concern for the empirical basis of the Christian faith as expressed in its language of Bible, doctrine, and liturgy knit with appropriate activity. We may recall that contemporary empiricism began in protest against neo-Hegelianism. It may even yet revitalise "theological thinking" as it has revolutionised philosophy.[39]

[39] Ramsey, op. cit., p. 184.

Language and Understanding

Heinrich Ott

To be found in *New Theology No. 1* (1964) is an article by Dean Robert C. Johnson of Yale Divinity School titled "Who Is Heinrich Ott?"—an article introducing the thirty-three-year-old Swiss theologian who had lately succeeded Karl Barth as professor of Systematic Theology at the University of Basel. At that time Ott was little known in the United States, and his appointment to the chair vacated by the eminent Professor Barth occasioned puzzlement, even perturbation, in some quarters. Since then Ott has lectured in this country, and the manifest high caliber of his scholarly work has served to allay all doubts. The article that follows is an example of that work; it first appeared in *Theologische Forschung 31 Kerygma und Mythos VI-2* (published by Herbert Reich Evangelischer Verlag, Hamburg-Bergstedt, West Germany), and was translated by doctoral candidate Thomas Dean for reprinting in *Union Seminary Quarterly Review* (March 1966).* Drawing on philosopher Martin Heidegger's analysis of language, Ott in this essay demonstrates how the complex problem of language and understanding is also the problem of hermeneutics, of effective, intelligible communication of the Christian faith. Recommended for further acquaintance with Ott's thought is his 1965 volume *Theology and Preaching*.

RUDOLF BULTMANN's outstanding contribution is to have confronted us with the problem of understanding so clearly and insistently that it has become perhaps the most important question in contemporary theology. It is the so-called "problem of hermeneutics" that divides the leading

* 3041 Broadway, New York, N.Y. 10027.

theologians today. This is not, however, a matter of being for or against a particular position, since such a position does not actually yet exist. Even Bultmann's own hermeneutical theory of pre-understanding and the revision of pre-understanding, of old and new self-understanding, does not constitute a final solution. He would undoubtedly agree that the theory of understanding has not yet become adequate to the phenomenon of understanding. Bultmann's great and lasting achievement lies rather in his having taught us to see the problem as such. The decisive issue that divides the theologians is whether or not one has grasped the hermeneutical problem *as such*, whether one has been sufficiently impressed by its inevitability.

The problem of hermeneutics is in a certain sense still up in the air in present-day theology. It is forcing itself upon us of its own initiative. In the twenties the appearance of dialectical theology signified a theological revolution without parallel. Today, in the continuation of that first revolution, we find ourselves in the midst of a second one signified by the problem of hermeneutics. But where the first revolution bore the imprint of a single prophetic figure, Karl Barth, today there are many thinkers caught up in the same stream. Although they do not yet have a particular goal clearly in mind, nevertheless they are all working, individually or together, on the same problem.

The problem of hermeneutics seems to unite the strands of several questions which theology has recently begun to consider: the question of "faith and history"; the missionary task of the church and the relation of the gospel to non-Christian religions; the relation of theological and psychological insights; and, lastly, even the ecumenical problem. All that Karl Barth envisioned in 1956, in what was for many a surprising shift in his terminology and his way of putting the problem, viz., in his phrase "the humanity of God"—or even earlier, under the heading of "the theology of the Holy Spirit"—seems now to be concentrated in the problem of hermeneutics.

It is under the influence of Martin Heidegger that the problem of *language* has most recently entered into theological discussions. There are today several theologians who have recognized the theological significance of the problem of language. But they sometimes appear too hasty in their conclusions, when one considers the slow and patient manner in which Heidegger for several decades now has been questioning and groping his way toward the mystery of language.

The problem of hermeneutics raises the question: what is understanding, and how does a given text become intelligible? The problem of language asks: what is the nature of language, and how, *quo modo*, does a given text speak (to us)? The two problems converge; in fact, they are both finally identical.

Now of course this complex problem of language and understanding has meaning outside of theology as well. But it is no accident that in our day it is precisely in theology that it has appeared with particular urgency. For properly speaking, theology in its very essence is hermeneutics. The problem of hermeneutics has accompanied theology from its outset. Theology itself is essentially directed toward the preaching of the church. Since its concern is with the intelligibility of its preaching, both in its concrete details and in its general nature, it cannot avoid the claims of the need for understanding. This understanding proceeds in a twofold direction: on the one hand, the correct understanding of the sources of the church's preaching, the biblical texts; on the other hand, the intelligibility of the sermon issuing out of these sources, both in itself and for its contemporary hearers. In both cases, however, what matters is the understanding of the kerygma. It is this which binds both aspects closely together, so that, when seen in terms of the subject-matter itself, they come in the final analysis to be one.

THE KERYGMA AND IDLE TALK

It is the kerygma, therefore, that provides the actual occasion for opening up the hermeneutical question. A brief illustration may clarify this point. Martin Heidegger says in *Being and Time* (§35) concerning *"idle talk"*:

In terms of the average intelligibility already present in the language used when one says something, the words communicated can for the most part be fairly well understood without the hearer's having to acquire a more primordial understanding of what is being talked about. One does not so much understand what is being talked about; one rather listens only to what is said as such. What is said is understood, but what is talked about is understood only approximately and superficially. . . . Hearing and understanding have beforehand fastened on to what is said. The act of communication, therefore, does not "impart" a primary relationship to the thing being talked about, but rather this kind of relationship to one another consists of talking with one another and being concerned with what is said. What matters is simply that talking is going on. . . . The unfounded character of idle talk does not prevent its becoming public; it rather promotes it. Idle talk is the possibility of understanding everything without any previous appropriation of it. Idle talk guards itself beforehand against the danger of foundering on any such appropriation. Idle talk, which anyone can come up with, not only releases one from the task of genuine understanding, but constitutes an undifferentiated sort of intelligibility which no longer excludes anything.

Heidegger here characterizes a possibility inherent in language as such, a danger inherent in the essence of that "most dangerous of possessions." Language presents us in this case with an understanding that is no understanding at all. Now experience teaches us that it is precisely in the church sermon that this possibility so suspiciously often realizes itself. And yet an understanding of the church's mission teaches us that the kerygma is essentially just the opposite of "idle talk." Kerygma is a kind of discourse grounded in a primordial understanding of the subject-matter being talked about, and which in turn is aimed at bringing its hearers into a primordial understanding of that same subject. God's Word does not return empty to Him!

Theology is thus the continual effort to ward off idle talk in preaching, the unceasing attempt to hold open or discover anew its original path to an understanding of its subject-matter. This effort takes place, however, precisely in the two-fold direction of the understanding of the biblical texts and the intelligibility of the gospel in the present. This could result, of course, in a strange hiatus, which would be unjustifiable in terms of the subject-matter and would lead instead to its being obscured or destroyed, were the continuity between these two aspects of understanding not protected! It is equally obvious that such an effort must belong to preaching itself. The preacher himself must, *as* a preacher, continually initiate the attempt to discover anew the original path to an understanding of the subject-matter, both for himself and for his hearers. To this extent the theological effort to assure the authenticity of understanding is a feature of preaching itself and is indissoluble from it. Theology is inherent in preaching.

The essence of theology, therefore, is hermeneutics. Heidegger makes this unmistakably clear in his book, *Unterwegs Zur Sprache* (*On The Way Toward Language*), when, in the course of describing the theological origins of his thinking, he confesses that without this background he would not have hit upon the problem of language and hermeneutics, and that in fact he would "never have reached the path of thought" (p. 96). Thus if Bultmann has shown his contemporaries the indispensability of the problem of hermeneutics, he has simply given fresh expression to the enduring nature of theology itself. In a time when the movement toward "idle talk" is assisted by the increasing technologization of language into mere information, advertisement and propaganda, the church is forced in its resolute response to reflect anew and in a thoroughgoing way upon that responsibility which is most properly hers, viz., a genuine understanding of that which is entrusted to her from God.

From this compressed account of the background of the problems of contemporary theological discussion, we turn next to the problems themselves. For this reason it is important to recognize the nature of the situation and to take it seriously. We are only at the beginning. We are placed under the unavoidable claim of the problem of hermeneutics. While the better listeners among the theologians have gradually become aware of this, all of us together still know very

little. Well-established as well as "introductory" theories of
the most varied sorts must not deceive us about this! In what
follows, therefore, we can only admit to this situation and
simply attempt to bring together, without any over-hasty
claim to having "the" solution, those points of view which
seem to us most important and fruitful for the further progress of the discussion.

To outline what follows: (I) we shall first attempt to characterize the problem of hermeneutics as such, to indicate both
the scope and the risk of understanding; (II) we shall then
consider more specifically the risk encountered in pursuing
the problem of hermeneutics and in consistently taking seriously the "principle" of understanding and its specific "scope";
(III) then we shall speak of the "universal intelligibility" to
which the "scope" of the principle of understanding leads us;
(IV) next we shall attempt to provide several points of reference for the problem of language, which, according to our
own thesis, is in the last analysis identical with the problem
of hermeneutics; and finally (V) we shall return to the concept of "understanding" and show its significance for the
various theological disciplines, in particular for dogmatic
theology.

I. The Fundamental Problem of Hermeneutics

We shall attempt to characterize the basic phenomenon
underlying the problem of all hermeneutics by starting with
the now famous assertion of Lessing: "Accidental truths of
history can never constitute the proof of necessary truths of
reason." "That, that is the ugly, broad ditch I can never cross
over, no matter how often or earnestly I have attempted the
leap. If anyone can help me over, let him do it!" (*The Proof
of the Spirit and of Power*, 1777.)

Lessing's words take us a bit too far. They are initially
illuminating, given no further explanation. But they no
longer correspond, in the way they were originally intended,
to the contemporary way of posing the problem. In any case,
as theologians we would no longer be able to repeat them

today in that particular way. For we understand the truth of "Christianity" as being existential and historical in nature, disclosing itself in historical encounters. No one today thinks any longer of talking about the Christian faith in terms of the "necessary truths of reason." Correspondingly, the opposition of "necessary truths of reason" and "accidental truths of history" has also become obsolete. Yet something of Lessing's way of putting the question remains valid. Indeed, I would like to go so far as to say that the question, rightly perceived, has lost none of its immediacy and indispensability! An appropriate transformation of Lessing's assertion allows us to see this: instead of "Accidental truths of history can never constitute the proof of necessary truths of reason," let us say "Judgments of historical probability can never provide the ground for the certainty of faith." In this reformulation both the actual intention as well as the stubborn *aporetic* character of Lessing's original assertion are preserved. The whole discussion of "faith and history" today must still pass through this *aporie*.

Lessing's assertion finally comes down to this: How do we get from then to now? It concerns that movement from out of the past into the present in which the present is actually established. To what extent do the historical phenomena of the past contain a truth or make a genuine claim that is binding for us today? How does the past "come toward" (or affect) the present?

Now we have a certain chance of overcoming Lessing's *aporie*, as translated into present terms, if we say that the problem we are concerned with is not one of "universal (necessary) truth of reason" at all, nor even of "accidental truths of history." We understand the truth that lays claim to us in the present not as something universally valid, but as something historical; accordingly, we understand the past also as something which in itself is already pregnant with meaning and not merely as some accidental "bare" fact. The past in itself is already constituted as that which in some way extends toward the present.

But how? How does this "coming toward" actually take

place? On the basis of this briefly sketched hypothesis, we apparently no longer have before us an insurmountable *aporie*, but in its place a genuine problem, no longer an "ugly ditch" which we cannot leap over, but rather a river, the bridging of which is difficult and not at all self-evident. Our attention falls next, therefore, upon *the process of translation as trans-lation. This is the basic involvement of hermeneutics.*

At this juncture the whole problem of hermeneutics can perhaps be divided into three questions: What is translated? How is it changed in the translation? And what is the nature of the river that has to be crossed, or of the two banks that determine its course? (It is obvious, of course, that none of these questions can be answered by itself in isolation from the others!)

These stipulations should hold for every sort of hermeneutics. Nevertheless, because we are confronted in the texts of the Old and New Testaments by an ultimate claim, because we in the church anticipate that what we will become aware of in the present on the basis of these texts is an absolute truth-claim on our existence, the hermeneutical question presents itself in this realm with particular urgency. Lessing, too, was really speaking with this theological situation in mind.

Hermeneutical reflection is always concerned with this phenomenon of translation. How complex the problems that arise in this connection really are can be seen in this simple but pregnant sentence. "Hermeneutics, understood as the 'art of interpretation,' is not so much the interpretation of a foreign language into one's own, or of a complex word into one that is transparent; it is rather the process of interpreting one thought into another, which is nevertheless intended to be the same. . . ."[1] Thus translation apparently involves something which is both the same and different; in fact, a similarity that maintains itself within the difference. This, however, opens up numerous problems: what kind of similarity? and what kind of difference? What does it mean to say: "Interpret

[1] From a small book, *Zur biblischen Hermeneutik*, by Kornelis Heiko Miskotte, a Hollander; Evang. Verlag Zollikon, Theol. Studien Heft 55, 1959.

one thought into another"? What after all is meant here by a thought? What is meant by thinking? Where does one thought end and another begin?

It ought also to be obvious that the phenomenon of *translation,* with which hermeneutics is concerned, is identical with that of *understanding.* Any particular instance of hermeneutical reflection has two aspects, or rather, asks the same thing in a twofold way: (1) Do we actually receive that which is to be translated, *i.e.,* do we understand it? and (2) Is what we understand or receive really that which is translated from the other bank of the river, *i.e.,* is it identical with what the text in question "says"?

II. The Risk of Understanding

We must now discuss the nature of understanding, in particular its essential "scope" along with its corresponding element of risk. To narrow the field of discussion, we shall proceed from three propositions:

1. UNDERSTANDING IS TO BE STRICTLY DISTINGUISHED FROM CONCEIVING

Conceiving is an intellectual type of explanation. "We explain nature, but we understand the life of the soul," says Dilthey. To explain something is to ground it in something already known. It is the result of an intellectual survey and comparison of several different elements. Understanding, on the other hand, is the unified act of grasping a psychological or historical situation in its unique individuality. But the distinction goes even further. Conception is an intellectual activity, a function of the intellect as a "part" of man. Understanding, however, is a function of man in the wholeness of his existence; it extends to the whole of the human situation. Bultmann is therefore correct in asserting that every act of understanding simultaneously implies a self-understanding, and thereby discloses the ontological structure of historical humanity itself. Understanding also makes possible that which is inconceivable or inexplicable, *e.g.*, the inconceivability of God, insofar as man understands himself in terms of God as the limit of his power to conceive. Man exists as man in that he understands himself. This brings us to our second proposition:

2. THE CONCEPT OF UNDERSTANDING HAS ONTOLOGICAL SIGNIFICANCE

Understanding is not simply a phenomenon of knowing; it is also a phenomenon of historical being itself, it has an ontic character. The concept of understanding has ontological significance in that it expresses the ontological structure of human existence. Man is in essence that being which understands. Man's biological existence provides the foundation for his actual, *i.e.*, his understanding being, and is at the same time taken up into it. We approach the phenomenon of understanding in hermeneutics primarily through concrete instances of understanding individual texts. But the horizon of hermeneutics is not confined to this specific situation. In hermeneutical reflection we are conscious rather that in the interpretation of texts the fundamental situation of human being itself makes itself known. For this reason, too, it would be inappropriate to force understanding, in contradistinction to other ways of knowing, into some *a priori* anthropological schema. Man does not stand over against his understanding; he is this very understanding itself. This leads us to our third proposition:

3. IT CAN NEVER BE DETERMINED IN ADVANCE WHAT WILL BE INTELLIGIBLE AND WHAT WILL NOT

To understand means to exist. And although man in his existing is ever planning, projecting himself ahead of himself, he can never fully anticipate his existence. In this sense, his existence is not at his disposal. What is intelligible only first proves to be such in the act of understanding itself. Understanding does not fit into any prearranged schema.

The seeming result of this last proposition is a twofold

situation that appears to be unavoidable when we turn to the phenomenon of understanding as it has been sketched above: it is the double fact of the scope and the risk of understanding. Because what can be understood is only disclosed in the act of understanding itself, we are able on the one hand to place unlimited confidence in understanding. Nothing that has meaning for us will be fundamentally unintelligible for another. On the other hand, however, we are given up or delivered over to future understanding. We never know beforehand what its outcome will be. The process of historical understanding is unending; it has no limits, at least none that we can see. Not even the much-praised laws of logic can define them. We dare not exclude in advance the possibility that someday someone will show us that, how, and in what sense the law of contradiction (for example) is no longer valid. Again, although the Roman Catholic Church cannot alter the dogmas which it has defined in virtue of its teaching office, yet it in no way knows what future formulations will appear as a result of the process of understanding and interpretation. That someday a future pope will authoritatively interpret or reformulate one or another of the doctrinal teachings that have divided the churches, *e.g.*, the doctrine of papal infallibility, in such a way that it could be acceptable to us Protestants, upon that rests a genuine ecumenical hope.

But if this is what understanding is like, then we are thrown into history as into a heaving sea, a sea of meanings, acts of understanding and interpretations—as in Nietzsche's saying: "Over against positivism, which remains standing by the phenomena, asserting that there are only facts, I would say: no, there are no facts, only interpretations."[2] Nowhere in this tossing sea do we find solid ground on which to stand; there remains nothing else to do but swim, that is, *we must entrust ourselves to understanding*. But because understanding has ontological significance, the above-depicted state of affairs discloses nothing less than the finitude or "thrownness" of human existence itself.

[2] *Der Wille zur Macht* 481. Mus. XIX, 13.

Then does not everything threaten to sink into a bottomless relativism? For understanding, which we are unable to leap over, is never fully protected from becoming misunderstanding. We shall discuss briefly the problem of understanding thereby indicated in terms of its particular theological context.

ORTHODOXY'S THREAT TO UNDERSTANDING

That understanding is not at our disposal, that we must rather surrender ourselves to it and can in no way escape it, is a theological insight that cannot itself be surrendered. It is found in the ancient dogmatic concept of the *testimonium Spiritus sancti*, the witness of the spirit, which is sent ever anew from God and which first makes possible the understanding of God's Word. To be sure, there is always the orthodox tendency to attempt to overcome the risk of understanding and to reach an established framework and solid ground, whether in the biblical canon understood as verbally inspired, or in dogmatic formulas put forward as definitive and unalterable, or in the authority of the doctrinal teaching office of the church. But even the canon, the dogmas, and the doctrines of the church's teaching office require continual interpretation. Orthodoxy attempts to provide a closed definition of the scope of understanding and to reduce the element of risk in understanding . . . but it never reaches its goal.

The argument of orthodoxy has always been that without a firm position of some sort, the church would be threatened by chaos and disintegration. Our reply is that the openness of understanding, to whose scope we in the church also entrust ourselves, in no way leads to chaos. For understanding itself always bears the mark of its content. In faith it is always something quite definite that is understood. And everywhere that faith occurs, the same thing is understood, whatever the various formulations may be that are tossed up against one another in the unending dialogue of the church. It is precisely non-orthodoxy which, by taking seriously the principle of the scope and the risk of understanding, does not lead to a fundamental relativism. Precisely in the certitude of faith (an integral part of which is consciousness of standing within the *communio sanctorum*) do we confidently dare to surrender ourselves in our theology to unlimited understanding.

We risk this with the confidence that the church cannot lose its proper knowledge of Jesus Christ and that the Spirit will lead its community into all truth (John 16:13). In this sense we too can speak of an "infallibility" of the church.

III. The Principle of Universal Intelligibility

This same feature of understanding shall next be considered in yet another of its aspects. Until now we have particularly emphasized the risk of understanding. Now we intend, more positively, to speak of the "scope" of understanding. Our guiding notion shall be that of "unlimited intelligibility," whereby the *intelligere* should be understood in the broader sense of "understanding in general," not in the narrower sense of "intellectual conception."

First, however, in order to view this unlimited intelligibility properly, we must consider two "limiting factors." On the one hand, the human dialogue, as the actual process of understanding, is an unending one; faced with this fact, we can do nothing but simply "let it happen." We must let this unending dialogue take place and allow the "phenomena" to speak to us through our own conversation, and then wait to see what emerges. On the other hand, we must naturally reckon with the fact that this particular mode of access, *i.e.*, that of language, is *ours* alone, and that *we*, as men, have no other. That we have no other can stand as an expression of our finitude. These assertions already point us toward the problem of language; for it is in language that both the finitude and the infinitude of human being are disclosed.

Let us return to a statement in the preceding section. We said that we can place limitless confidence in understanding, that nothing which is meaningful to us can be fundamentally unintelligible to another. But if this is so, then what we can call unlimited intelligibility or, with Jaspers, boundless communication has already become visible.

But Jaspers' position concerning this phenomenon is not fully correct, since he prematurely limits the scope of understanding. He breaks off communication when he recommends to us an intolerance of the "intolerance" of faith, with its "claim to exclusivism." He permits communication to take place only within a definite schema; so long, that is, as everyone presents his own faith-standpoint non-exclusively as simply *his* cipher for "transcendence." But what Jaspers calls the "claim to exclusivism" belongs to the very essence of a standpoint of faith. The Christian faith, for example, is no longer *understood* when its fundamental "claim to exclusivism" is taken away from it. It would be better understood were this claim genuinely disputed, or at least taken seriously. "Boundless communication" breaks down when confronted by this essential element of the meaning and structure of faith. Jaspers in fact places limits upon understanding.

We must counter this by taking seriously the idea of unlimited intelligibility! We are all familiar with the fact that often we are not understood, not simply in passing but with apparent finality. This is one of the real and tragic failures of being human, but not one of its necessary limitations.

The fact is that even in the encounter of representatives of different and mutually exclusive faiths, conversation and communication never really come to an end. The effort to make oneself understood (and that means also: of becoming intelligible anew to oneself) is an unending one. It is, theologically expressed, the effort of *fides quaerens intellectum*. It is unending reflection from out of actual existence and about actual existence. Faith drives theology forward as unending reflection—as it must, for the sake of the *communio sanctorum,* the world and itself—up to the Last Day. This reflection, as the process of becoming clear to oneself and to others, has no terminus, even when the partner in dialogue makes it clear that he does not wish to alter his own standpoint of faith. For we are not saying that something like an "understanding" can only take place when two standpoints have begun to approximate one another or when they have become indistinguishable from one another. This seems to be the case, however, with Jaspers' non-exclusivistic concept of faith-as-cipher.

Such concepts are premature. It ought first to be explained

what "understanding," understanding *in actu* as the occurrence of an event, could mean. The only thing that seems certain beforehand is this: that the struggle for intelligibility, the search for illumination, may not remain standing still.

CONCRETE, DAY-TO-DAY EXISTENCE

Behind this phenomenon of unlimited, universal intelligibility as a basic feature of understanding, there now appears a rather complex problem. It centers on the question: how is understanding, as an act of reflection, related to the existential "lived" reality with which it is concerned? How, in other words, are existential and reflective understanding, existence and thought, existence and language, related to one another? We must, generally speaking, take into account the *"levels of understanding."* On the one hand, historical life itself is already an understanding, while on the other hand, this existential understanding continually expresses itself in unending reflection—and in such a way that this reflective understanding in turn becomes a part of historical life. It is impossible, therefore, to draw any sharp line between existence and the thought which originates in it and accompanies and illuminates it. It is precisely in thought, as a thinking being, that man exists historically. In his existence as thinker man comes to understand the particular phenomena presented for his reflection. It is not enough simply to distinguish these two levels, however, for the levels of understanding are multiple.

Earlier we characterized understanding as a unified act of grasping an individual meaning-complex, in contradistinction to explanation as a grounding in something already known. This does not mean that understanding always definitively grasps the whole of that which is to be understood in a single leap. Understanding rather involves a process of articulation, a direction, a history, a progressive movement forward. A man can be led, existentially and reflectively, from insight to insight, ever closer to some phenomenon; but he can also be misled by the same process. Even with the fullest intention of understanding, he can be led along strange and errant ways. Understanding is subject to a certain destiny.

Although, like intuition, it can get a total grasp of some meaningful whole, it cannot do so in a punctual or unhistorical way. This must become obvious when one considers that understanding is actually nothing other than the ontological structure of man's historical being.

To give just a single example. As a believer, man understands the gospel of Christ existentially. He understands both this act of understanding and, in unity with it, that which is to be understood in the traditional dogmas of the church. These formulas permeate and to a large extent determine the language of his own faith, his prayer and preaching, and the understanding he reaches with himself, his fellow Christians, and those who stand outside. (This is the first level of reflection.) But he does not have the subject-matter firmly in his grasp simply on the basis of these previously given dogmatic formulas. The dogmas function rather as a stimulus to further reflection and to further illumination of the understanding he has reached with himself and with others. As a result of such ongoing reflection and fresh definition, he can subject the older dogmas to questioning; that is, he can attempt to understand them (and thereby his faith, and the gospel itself) in new, better, and deeper ways. Each basic definition is but a transitional step, calling from within the dialogue for fresh interpretations. Despite this tossing sea of interpretations, however, one remains in his understanding—and perhaps also misunderstanding—hard by the same object. This example allows us to be clearer about the process and the levels of understanding.

By now it ought also to be clear that the difficult question burdening our present-day theological conversations, namely, the relationship between theology and faith, or theology and preaching, can never be finally solved apart from the clarification of the complex relationship between thought and existence.

THE PRACTICAL OUTCOME

How then can this unending process of reflection, this unceasing effort to make oneself understood, this confidence in unlimited intelligibility, have any practical outcome? One way in particular commends itself. Whoever wishes to render his own standpoint intelligible will strive to show his partner in dialogue what this standpoint (for example, and above all, the standpoint of his faith, "that which he believes," his *fides quae creditur*) "means for him." He does this in the expectation that it could also mean the same for the other, and in Christian terms, he does this in the trust that the other is also called to be a child of God and to have eternal life. Thus we do not doubt, for example, that we, as Western Christians, can make the gospel in which we believe truly intelligible to other men, such as Asians or Africans, who come from totally different traditions and intellectual backgrounds. Showing what something "means for me," as an instrument for understanding, is in fact the method of every sermon. Each sermon gives expression to the gospel insofar as it reveals what the gospel means for the preacher himself and for his hearers. We call this necessary process *existential interpretation,* using this technical term, borrowed from Bultmann, in its widest possible sense. We may remind ourselves of a point already mentioned, that in all genuine understanding there is an inherent self-understanding, and that this understanding has ontological significance. For every understanding one has of something as meaningful, there is a corresponding "situational element" in his ontic, existential situation. In fact, understanding itself *is* this situational element. The intelligible meaning, or significance, is not something beyond ontic actuality; it is rather identical with it! Existential interpretation simply means: showing what existential (ontic!) element in this situation corresponds to a particular act of understanding, or again, making a particular act of understanding visible *as* an existential element in the situation. This may occur implicitly—as in preaching, or explicitly—as in theology. Theology, in comparison with preaching, is the next level of reflection. It is the reflective function of preaching itself. Theology is therefore just as involved in existential interpretation as preaching itself is. Now admittedly we do not have at our disposal (and we must firmly maintain this) any preestablished criteria for deciding what can or cannot be an "element of the situation." Otherwise we would be setting limits to understanding. Existential understanding, however, is precisely the vehicle of unlimited intelligibility.

We are coming to discover with increasing clarity that the problem of the historicity of existence, the problem of hermeneutics, and the problem of language are in the last analysis one and the same.

IV. The Phenomenon of Language

Bearing this identity in mind, we turn next to the problem of language. In order to get a preliminary idea of its theological significance, let us return to Lessing's assertion, which we reformulated in our contemporary idiom to read: "Judgments of historical probability can never provide the basis for the certainty of faith."

The problem is the *certainty of faith*. Christian faith refers to history that actually happened, above all to the history of Jesus Christ. It is the historian who is responsible for knowledge of the historical past. How then can faith achieve any certainty of its own in its reference to history, when the historian's knowledge of the past is never more than probable at best? How, conversely, can the contingent knowledge of history have any relevance at all for the certitude of faith? Martin Kähler, in reflecting upon the same problem, attempted to solve the *aporie* by bracketing off history (that is, the research of his day into the life of Jesus) and instead calling the Christ preached in the church the actual Christ. His distinction has remained with us.

Today the question runs: *is there perhaps yet another approach to history than the one resulting in judgments of historical probability?* Doesn't history speak to us in other sorts of ways as well? If we ask how history *speaks* to us, we must direct our thoughts to the nature of language. But even if a new way should be found, the question would still remain: how is this new way related to the traditional approach to history? Does each proceed along parallel tracks without any connection to the other? Or rather is a reorientation in the method of historiography itself forced upon us as a result of our reflections upon the nature of language?

A second avenue of thought might further establish the relevance of the problem of language for theology. It is sometimes said that faith is a reality transcending the *subject-object dichotomy* within which all thinking is carried on. Thinking and speaking are always objectifying. They are always "about" something. Faith, on the other hand, is a non-objectifying relationship to a non-objectified transcendence. It belongs to the realm of the "all-encompassing," which transcends the subject-object dichotomy. It never refers to an object, being rather a matter of continual historical decision. From this perspective, one specific aspect of the relation of faith to theology, and of faith to preaching, reveals itself to be particularly troublesome. We are compelled, namely, to come to terms with the inauthenticity and yet indispensability of all kerygmatic and theological discourse. We cannot authentically speak about God without making Him into an object, which is something He can never be. This being the case, every statement of the Bible and the theological tradition would at least initially appear to be made questionable.

It could be, however, that the axiom of the subject-object dichotomy is not at all binding. Were this so, a great deal would obviously follow. Modern science, of course, in all its branches, is an objectifying kind of thinking that presents and holds fast to some definite object or other. And language itself, at any given moment, involves an "about," an "object" about which it is speaking. But do we really know that the intentional structure of language is the same as, and not rather quite different than, that of scientific objectification? What makes us so certain that language, as well as science, is continually engaged in converting actuality into an object, standing it up in front of us and holding onto it as such, making "statements" and dispensing "information" about it? Let us be on guard against such premature conclusions! It could be that the facts of the matter are *toto caelo* different. It could be that a *genuine* analysis of the nature of language would render the subject-object dichotomy, and all the theological conclusions derived from it, permanently obsolete. As long as the nature of language remains insufficiently clarified, there is nothing really valid that can be said about the possibility of faith's speaking about God. But how can we get a clue to the nature of language?

We shall take our lead in what follows from Heidegger's reflections upon language, for we see no place where the nature of language has been more deeply pondered than in his thought. Although Heidegger is still underway in his own thinking about language, we can summarize his provisional conclusions very briefly in four points:

1. Language is not to be understood in terms of its sign-function, *i.e.*, as the denotation of intended objects by means of conventionally agreed upon phonetic symbols.

2. Language is not to be understood in terms of its expressive function, *i.e.*, as the expression of subjective inner life. Heidegger says that no matter how "correct" these two customary definitions may in their own way be, they do not sufficiently reflect the essential nature of language itself, *i.e.*, language as language.

3. Language is a "transcendental" (using this concept as carefully as possible!) event that overtakes man and in which man is allowed to participate: "language speaks," and mortal men, in response to its address, assist in its becoming publicly heard. This speaking of language is the transcendental "condition of the possibility" of the speech of mortal men.

4. Along with man's listening to language, the "dimension of the object" must also be considered. Our understanding of a text does not proceed simply between two points, ourselves and the text being apprehended. Rather it constitutes a triangle: by means of the text we perceive the object which addresses the text as well as ourselves, and only in so doing do we genuinely come to understand the text as such. It is not the "opinions" of the author that count, or that are relevant, or that must first of all be ascertained; we are not here concerned with opinions as finished products of some peculiar sort. If we wish to *understand* at all, then our con-

cern must rather be with the relation of the past thinker to
the object confronting him, an object which must be capable
of becoming ours as well. Historicism all too often forgot
these various interrelationships. It suppressed the element of
actuality present in the very nature of language as such.

We ought not to view this four-point summary of Heidegger's views as a finished theory of language, which we can
now simply appropriate for ourselves. It is more important to
remain with Heidegger "underway toward language" and to
keep our wonder before the mystery of language. Heidegger's
method of getting at the nature of language consists in "looking for the speaking of language in that which is spoken (cf.
the lecture on "Die Sprache"-"Language"-in the volume of
collected essays entitled *Unterwegs Zur Sprache-On The Way
Toward Language*). He restricts himself, in particular, to
that which is "purely spoken," that is, poetry.

V. Hermeneutics and Theology

If you wished to ask me as a theologian how, if we were
to pursue Heidegger's thought further, we could most fruitfully apply his insights to theology, I would say this: to begin
with, by looking with Heidegger ever anew for the speaking
of language in that which is spoken, in this case, however, in
that which is spoken in the biblical texts. Hermeneutical
reflection, and that also means reflection upon the nature of
language, can be appropriately understood in our contemporary discussion only as *"practical or applied hermeneutics."*
We have no acquaintance with understanding and language
in general. We can only apply ourselves to the "practical"
instance, the individual text, and must simply raise the question: how does that which is spoken in *it* speak? How do we
gain access to an understanding of it, *i.e.,* what is the specific
entrance into its particular way of speaking? We are continually inquiring into the *modus loquendi* of an individual
text—that is what characterizes the hermeneutical question.
It is entirely legitimate, indeed, even necessary to ask at the
same time: how does the text cross over *to us,* to our bank

of the river, in its speaking? Again, how (not *what*—that is a matter of concrete decision for the preacher in his own situation) are we to preach about it today? For this relationship, too, belongs to the speaking of language in a biblical text.

It is important that we enter into such questions without preconceived ideas. We ought not to presuppose any schema: we must, for example, neither interpret language from the outset in salvation-historical terms, nor attempt to press "salvation history" and the particularity of a biblical text into an imported theory of language. There is no way of knowing positively in advance whether a "theological" hermeneutics can be united with, or is different from, a "general" hermeneutics; nor is there any way of knowing whether and how the *modus loquendi* of the biblical text might differ from that of all others. That can only be settled on the basis of the texts themselves. The argument that it would be impossible to explain the biblical texts at all if we did not import hermeneutical principles and questions of some sort, is of no avail. For we here find ourselves already within the famous "hermeneutical circle": the "entrance" to the understanding of a particular text only becomes visible from within this circle, and vice versa. It is nevertheless useful, when inquiring into the speaking of a particular text, to cast an occasional sideways glance at the problem of the speaking of language in general and, with all due caution, to draw whatever tentative conclusions seem relevant.

We come now to the end. Our discussion has, as befits the present situation, been more a programmatic than a systematic one. It was not possible to provide more than a survey and a few points of reference. The chief work still remains to be done.

We theologians must stay conscious of the fact that the problem of hermeneutics and language also has significance outside theology: in philosophy, history, philology, literary criticism, psychology, and presumably in legal theory as well. We must listen attentively when something helpful or illuminating is offered to us from these areas. Whether, conversely, our work can come up with anything for these other fields of investigation is not our primary concern. However, we may expect with some confidence that if we simply do our own work properly and carefully, a more useful contribution to the dialogue among these various disciplines may very well be the result.

Theology and the Uses of History

Justus George Lawler

Justus George Lawler, who equivocates not in the least to affirm "the fundamental experience of being" and "the religious experience of God's presence to man," makes short shrift of the "cheap relevance" that seems to be the besetting temptation of many present-day theologians and eloquently pleads with them to stick to their last: "The theologian is a man in history; he finds himself there, he does not put himself there. And it is by being true to the demands of his own science, by making good theology, that he makes also his own contribution both to the spirit of the historical epoch and to man's understanding of it." Professor of Theology and Literature in the Graduate Theological Program of Saint Xavier College, Chicago, Dr. Lawler is the author of such books as *The Christian Imagination; Nuclear War: The Ethic, the Rhetoric, the Reality;* and *The Christian Image: Studies in Religious Art and Poetry*. His essay first appeared as an editorial in the Spring 1966 issue of *Continuum,** the distinguished Roman Catholic quarterly review that he edits.

ABOUT a year ago the present writer observed in connection with an article on the secular priesthood in *Commonweal:* "Pluck 'religionless religion' and what is left is a new apologetic, very good, very necessary, but in the end very much a matter of apologetic, a heightening of terminology *only*." This is a judgment which there is little reason for revising, even though it is evident that God's ardent theological undertakers are seeking to invest their earlier rhetoric with some substantive values. This latter stems in part from the demands of the intellectual community for payment in

* Saint Xavier College, 103rd and Central Park Avenue, Chicago, Ill. 60655.

hard cash on the inflationary vouchers which have been flooding the marketplace of religious speculation; it stems also, and more dangerously, from the mesmerizing effect the repetition of their own catch-phrases has had on the members of the death-of-God persuasion who are now driven either through psychological fixation or mere self-defense to reify their own jargon.

Yet nevertheless no one questions—though E. L. Mascall in *The Secularization of Christianity* comes perilously close to doing so—that the hydra-headed phenomenon known variously or collectively as religionless religion, secularization, God is dead, etc., constitutes a portentous sign of the times, the sources of which, as diverse as the manifestations, may be set forth serially as follows. There is, first of all, the response—strongly though not exclusively German—to the failure of the churches to withstand the corrosive force of fascism and nationalism: the churches having been too otherworldly in the past seek now to rectify the old failings, sometimes by a quasi-identification with the city of man. Parallel to this sociological reaction is the specifically religious rebound from the total negation of natural theology in Barth to the affirmation of the natural—meaning the secular—as the sole basis for theologizing: or not theologizing. There is, thirdly, the evident failure of traditional language and symbols meaningfully to express the presence of God among contemporary men; and on the one hand the consequent search for his presence outside of the realm ordinarily denominated "the sacred," and on the other hand, the conclusion that what cannot be adequately symbolized may not exist. Fourthly, there is the growing sense of the importance of the temporal and contingent in a religion, Christianity, which is so decisively history-centered and act-centered. Fifthly, there is the greater awareness of the selfness of man, of his unique spirithood—represented historically by the Romantic movement in all its facets—and the attendant disdain for the seemingly static categories enshrined in much of the theology of the West. Derivative from this on a more superficial plane is the assumption that the authentic utterance of any man, whether atheist or not, is a more deeply religious act, because more deeply human, that the feigned prayer or the sacramental confection of the professed believer. And lastly, there is modern man's experienced mastery of the universe—of which Teilhard is the Christian spokesman—and the recognition that this mastery is the fulfillment of man's destiny only when he envisions the "world" not as his enemy but as his co-conspirator.

All of these currents, radical, reactionary, liberal, evolutionary, have generated their own variants or composites of the central stream and their own enlargements of orthodoxy or extensions of heresy. The thrust of the larger drift is provided by the not very novel insight that all words used of God are inadequate and that whatever words man uses must come from his own self-appropriation of the absolute in his own temporal experience. The intellectual morass into which various of these channels have flowed arises from the failure to realize that precisely because man does shape his own destiny, does control his own evolution, not every manifestation of the age is by the fact of its mere appearance therefore ratified as good. Here the issue is to determine a standard relevant to the temporal order once the trans-temporal has been implicitly cancelled out. The world cannot be moved without a fulcrum, and traditionally it has seemed self-evident that that fulcrum cannot be the world itself.

It is this canonization of the exclusively temporal and this attendant exclusion of any prophetic surety in judging the world, which has been the butt of most orthodox Christian criticism of the religionless-religion current. This is a tenable line of criticism, but one which is patently more defensive than offensive, and one is therefore entitled to search out a much more fundamental criticism of those various new theologians whose implicit strategy seems to be the wholesale evacuation of the Christian position. A *radically* more fundamental criticism must necessarily concern itself not with theology and theologians but with humanism and man. And it is the contention here that such aberrations as the death-of-God theology can flourish only because of the exaggerated professionalism, the intense inbreeding, and the morbidly heightened *theological* consciousness of those many theologians who, having given themselves over to "the study of divine things," can glimpse human realities only in their most exaggerated and elephantine forms, and even then can glimpse them only "under the aspect of" themselves not as men but as theologians. The point of departure for the critique will not be the jets of paraphraseable or translatable thought that occasionally burst forth from the bogs of Emory University or Colgate Divinity School, but some observations of thoroughly orthodox religious scholars at the recent Notre Dame conference on the theological issues of Vatican II.

What is most striking about these various papers is their almost studied avoidance of any theological reflection as such; the great mass of the statements presented was concerned with assessments of the condition of modern man, with much shorthand sociology, history, artistic and literary opining—all embraced as indicators of the direction in which theology must go in the future. It is commendable that theologians should take into account the signs of the times; they simply must do so if they are to avoid exiling themselves to the deserts of irrelevance. But they must make such an accounting as theologians who are first of all men and who are therefore, and secondly, wary of the easy ascription of humane values to every human activity. One must therefore pause at Fr. Walter Burghardt's maintaining:

This man committed to Nothing is a frightening phenomenon of our time. It is an attitude towards reality that stems from at least four sources: (1) a creeping collectivism, where "the people" suppresses the individual; (2) a growing dehumanization, symbolized by Dachau, the mushroom cloud, and the shelter doorway; (3) an increasing automation, represented by the IBM card; (4) the apparent failure of organized religion to redeem the world. In this attitude, man's dignity and his hope lie in his ability to confront, with courage and indeed with joy, a life and a reality that is senseless, useless, absurd. Man is alone, isolated, a stranger to himself, to the world, to God. The hell of Sartre— hell is other people—has given place to the hell of Bergman—hell is being alone.

This affirmation of Nothing leaps out at you from the creative arts: from the painting of a Pollock, through the music of a Cage, to the poetry of Kazantzakis. It is splendidly summed up by Samuel Beckett: two times anything equals zero.

Fr. Burghardt is a careful and large-minded thinker, but nonetheless one can't help wondering what we really do know either about man of the past or of the present that would justify the claim that man as here defined is a "phenomenon of our time." Our awareness of creeping collectivism may be more intense than was that of thirteenth-century man's awareness of what might well have been—and historically, *contra* Christopher Dawson, looks very much like—an even more monstrous collectivism, simply because contemporary man can articulate what for men of past ages could only take the form of a suppressed grunt of outrage. Perhaps our awareness of such evils is greater only because man and his institutions in our time have reached so much higher a plane of humanism. And so too with each of the other "frightening phenomena of our time": why not parallel them with the dehumanization of the perennial pogroms of Christian Europe, with the Albigensian crusades, with the castles barred against the plague-stricken outside the walls, and so on? But the point is not to counter any of Fr. Burghardt's assertions with other perhaps equally questionable assertions, but simply to indicate that historical judgments such as his are not provenly well-founded and that therefore a theology based on them may be a chimera.

What Fr. Burghardt has given us—as the Quaker saying goes—tastes of the pipes. Christians of every denomination have been inundated by it before in innumerable articles and programs of study devoted to ferreting out Christ-figures and Adamic-types in all the English novels from Melville to Faulkner. It is the rare theologian—one thinks of William Lynch—who is so conversant with the contemporary arts that he can make religious sense out of them. More often than not he employs them as proof-texts for his own up-to-dateness (clerics in Harry Truman sport shirts: *that* up-to-date), as pegs to hang a thesis on (William Hamilton misquoting Stevens' "Sunday Morning") or as occasions for flying headers into *Kulturgeschichte* (Godot or Willy Loman envisioned as archetypes of contemporary man: *that* contemporary). In the latter instance, that sociologists or students of the behavioral sciences may view such heavily freighted symbolic fictions merely as the creations of cultural sports—in the strict biological sense—merely as expressions of the most involute subgroups, is usually ignored.

This is merely by way of noting (for the time being) that it is always desirable that one keep one's categories clean, that highly refined specialists like theologians ought to take measure only of what is actually known by those other highly refined specialists whose field of interest is man's present condition, his communities, his sense of the temporal, etc. This of course implies that all groups of specialists must rely primarily on their fundamental human experience (of which more shortly) and secondarily on their professional acquisitions. The fusion of religious commitment with amateur literary or sociological extrapolation does little to serve either theology or the citizen of the secular city. The latter, to the degree he can be shown to exist, will be better aided by theological speculation as such—undertaken in the light of the fundamental human experience—and less by spinning religio-cultural generalities out of Fellini and Camus.

The enormities which so much theology today easily assimilates can be explained only as the result of the atrophy of the human experience itself and the consequent attempt to compensate, necessarily at second hand, for this withering up of spirit by a junket through the arts in search of the lost innocence. Theology today—and this is true of most specialized disciplines save those that are directly rooted in the experience of being—is in a state with regard to the secular city comparable to the state of the whole literate culture vis à vis the mass of men in the thirteenth century. One shudders at the thought of what we might have if St. Thomas had devoted himself to being up on Guillaume de Lorris or—more up-to-date *and* secular—Guido Cavalcanti, rather than to experiencing the reality and elaborating the meaning embodied in the insight that "the intellect in the act of intellecting proceeds into infinity." And this, because the experience this insight represents is what defines man as man, whether he be the man of the dark ages or the man of the city of Nothing.

"It is the function of theology to be a servant," Fr. Burghardt notes. "In our time this demands service on three levels: the City of God, the City of Man, and what I can only call the No-City." One needn't question again: why "in our time"? Yet even after acknowledging the large truth in his formulation, one must inquire as to precisely how theology fulfills this ancillary function. The danger of enlisting theology in the service of "our time" is that theology may be made irrelevant to itself, that is, to its task of plumbing the infinite. This is all the more likely when one considers the plasticity, the vagueness and imprecision that attach to all serious efforts at precisioning with any kind of rigor the characteristic notes of our time. Given the fact that no theologian has any right to trust his private intuitings about the nature of *this* historical epoch, given the added fact that there is neither unanimity nor even a loose consensus among culture historians or social scientists about that nature, and given the final fact that there is no reason yet to assume contemporary man's radical dissociation from man of the past—the experience of the trans-finite is the single criterion and its application here would not confirm such dissociation—one can be optimistic about the future of theology only to the degree that theology is true to itself and its basic datum.

It could not unprofitably be borne in mind that the one massive theological achievement, though still in process, of a North American Catholic scholar stems not from any urgent, and however otherwise laudable, need for assuaging the anxieties of somebody's paradigm of the "man of our time," but from the exigencies of theological science as such. One will look in vain in the work of Bernard Lonergan for a theology inspired by the *ad hoc* dredgings of the present moment of history; and precisely because Lonergan's theology is to that degree "self-serving," precisely because it *is* theology, it continues to be of service and to speak to the needs of the contemporary world. The Christian community has been surfeited with skeletal theologies clumsily co-opted to this or that sociological conception, this or that literary school, this or that psychological or political theory: theologies which stand as objects of amusement or bewilderment to the practitioners or promoters of those various other disciplines and programs.

If it is rejoined that theology to be self-serving must both serve the world and draw upon the world's services in turn, the answer can only be, of course. Of course, all history is salvation history *in a sense,* but the determination of what in "salvation history *in a sense"* is truly salvific can only be made by the students of "salvation history *without qualification.*" And if it is further rejoined that whatever we know of God we know by his acts in history, the answer must again be, of course—with the proviso now, that while man in history can only know of God's acts, the knowledge of these acts does lead to, or *is,* a trans-historical experience. And it is primarily in reflection upon this experience that the theologian fulfills his mission.

Theologians ought to make no more of history than their inevitable immersion in its demands. That they do make so much more of it results mainly—among other things—from the separation of their understanding of God's acts from the trans-historical experience such understanding should have fostered but didn't. Without moorings in the transcendental experience, without the experience that the light one sees is the light by which one sees, their theology is irrelevant to itself and irrelevant to man who seeks such an experience as the natural end of his earthly being. In their search for this vanishing relevance, the theologians are more and more driven to directly relate their speculations to the immediate condition of man; they study his rootlessness, his anomie, and proffer their solutions—tricked out in whatever sociological categories may be current—from out of their compendia of religious data.

It is a truism that man comes to know himself only in the act of knowing another, and that he comes to know himself most fully in knowing, however inchoately, the being of God.

But many theologians rather than looking at this "other"—which implies a genuine alterity—look only at themselves; caught in endless mental ipsation, what they give to the living man is not the fruit of humane experience, but only the mirror image of their own insecurity, reinforced usually by the mirror images of other sciences, that is, only the fabrication known as "God is Dead." But this god, when stripped of his splendid verbal trappings, is only an abstraction of inhumane man, is what Wallace Stevens called "the total man of glubbal glub"—which is merely to say this god reveals himself in the language of Altizer and Hamilton.

Theologians no more than any others ought not to view themselves as divorced from the spirit of the times, from the flux of the present, and ought not therefore to feel they must compensate for their imagined divorce by an artificial and self-conscious immersion of their theology in what they take to be the dominant social, political, and cultural traits of the age. A little more confidence in themselves *as* men in history —that is, as beings defined as "vocations to the infinite"— would make them better theologians. Given their inescapable human disposition, they would do better to theologize out of the driving insights—born of the transcendental experience —into their own science and not out of their necessarily second-hand grasp of the materials of other equally specialized fields. They would above all be better off as men *and* as theologians if they ceased conning the arts for types or symbols of "the human condition" and "the existential situation," and let themselves be open to the esthetic experience itself. Our secularized theologians are like the caricature of Goethe making love with pad and pen in hand to immortalize his raptures. This is the "other" seen not as "other" but as a machine for poeticizing—or theologizing. The kind of hybrid vision to which this style of "doing" theology—as the new barbarism terms it—lends itself is apparent in some comments of Dr. Albert Outler who shared Fr. Burghardt's platform at Notre Dame: "Now the reality of God becomes the central issue once more—and new patterns of inquiry in religious epistemology, religious anthropology, religious metaphysics, ontology, and theology proper are the obvious tasks of the new generation who aim to convince men of the reality of God (of his presence and grace) in a world come of age and gone to pot." Bonhoeffer cum Spengler cum theodicy: the religious sentiments can be no more laudable than the historical judgments are incredible.

But not all the voices raised at Notre Dame harmonized with such a rendition of the song of earth. Fr. John Meyendorff, author of two important works on Gregory Palamas, in a few short paragraphs both broached the unchanging theological issue of our and all preceding times and also scored the current preoccupation with ministering to the needs of some contemporary image of man:

The Orthodox Church has committed itself, in the late Middle Ages, to affirming that God is absolutely and totally unknown in his essence, that no human faculty, not even the "beatific vision," is able to grasp the essence of God. Knowledge of God is possible only inasmuch as the living God manifests himself in the free acts of this love towards man. Between the honest agnostic and the Christian there is therefore this capital point of agreement: God is unknown to the human mind, and their dialogue consists in the responsibility of the Christian to show what is Divine Life, Divine Love, and where and how they are being met.

So, if we Orthodox join our Catholic brethren in facing the modern agnostic man, we are also led immediately in the discussion between the Palamite and the Thomist on the issue of the knowledge of God, on the making of the "spiritual senses," which are, according to the Fathers, our means of contact with the Living God; and whose existence we cannot prove to the atheist, nor even prove to ourselves, but whose reality we experience in the Church of God, as those things which, Paul said, "are prepared by God for those who love Him."

And if the knowledge of God is finally the very content of the Christian faith, and if this knowledge can be shown and accepted only *in the total freedom* of the human person answering with love to God's love, is the Roman Church always right in its traditional preoccupation—which is still certainly not totally absent in the Vatican II decisions—to administer human society, to find solutions to all human problems, to guide, to feed, to advise, to rule and to direct instead of *showing?*

There is much here to which one might take exception: it is too negative, and it assumes a gap between the Palamite and the Thomist which is largely non-existent. But it does raise the theological question, the question of plumbing the depths of the unknown God; the question of today as of yesterday as of the future. Unquestionably theology is made in history as God is known *somehow* in history; and the human ambiance affects the theologians no less than other men. But we know what little we do know of contemporary history only by indirection, and the theologian contributes in his own unique way to that knowledge not by gleaning the sociological data but by his necessarily historically conditioned and unselfconscious theologizing on the fundamental experience of being, and on the religious experience of God's presence to man in the Church. The theologian *is* a man in history; he finds himself there, he does not put himself there. And it is by being true to the demands of his own science, by making good theology, that he makes also his own contribution both to the spirit of the historical epoch and to man's understanding of it.

What the Palamite would call "the making of the spiritual senses," the Thomist would call the experiencing of the transcendent, an experience which though disfigured in much traditional Christian and even Thomistic thinking is utterly obscured by the theologies of the death of God. It is a stereotype of such modish trends that "the presence of God takes the form of a simultaneous and terrifying absence of God." The sentence is from an otherwise unexceptionable *Cross Currents* article (Winter, 1966) by Eugene Fontinell and parallels the following similar sentiment from an otherwise excellent book by Michael Novak: "If, occasionally, I raise my heart in prayer, it is to no God I can see, or hear, or feel." In both cases we have the utterance of a commonplace—though Novak's ambiguity is heavier by his use of "feel" which is both a transitive and intransitive verb—explicitly endorsed by a whole tradition from Dionysius on through the greatest medieval commentary on *The Divine Names* (Aquinas meeting Palamas); in fact, explicitly endorsed by virtually every Christian thinker, and implicitly, by the great God-haters such as Blake, Nietzsche, and Jeffers. But as understood by the radical theologians this commonplace is distorted to mean the total lack of any awareness of God's presence.

But traditionally even God as Absence is a knowledge, a way of knowing by not-knowing, a knowledge of the contours of what will go into a vessel from the vacuities, the emptinesses of the vessel which God has elected to fill. But this is a longing for the infinite, and as such still a negative knowledge. The positive aspect is an experience of God precisely *as* presence, as a presence which is a fulfillment rather than an emptiness seeking to be fulfilled. Obviously the two are aspects of the same reality for the nearer men draw to God, the farther He is from them and the greater is their longing *and* their fulfillment. Nor does it diminish the positive character of this sense of God as present that it can only be described in negative terms, as nada; or, more simply put, as the subjunctive to the indicative—which is the modal relationship of *any* expression of the experience of spirit, whether through a person, a poem, or a truth.

There are two aspects of this positive presence of God to man. The first, finely underlined by Bernard Lonergan, is an explication of the maxim central to Augustine, Aquinas, Pascal, and Newman that we would not seek God if we did not somehow possess him. The other is a "knowledge" which, though derivative of the preceding notion of "spirit as inquiry," "existential exigency," "vocation to the infinite," or, even "obediential potency," has a greater richness to it. This is the knowledge no less unformulatable, no less inenarrable, than any other knowledge of God, yet nonetheless and precisely because of its very ineffableness, a true and deep knowledge. This is the gradual shaping out—through a greater and greater frequency of recurrence of the experience of being—of one's sense of the infinite. It is not so much a question of an accumulation which results in an intensifying of the experience itself as it is of an accumulation which keeps adding new facets to the polygon of understanding as it seeks to embrace and be embraced by the infinite circle of mystery. And it is this shaping out—obviously never clearly, never definitively—this "habitus" of the transcendental experience, which alone when joined to theological competence can account for the insights of a Rahner, a de Lubac, a von Balthasar—though the latter would perhaps reject its present formulation. Not the most highly refined rational skills, however indispensable, can explain the fecundity of the elaboration of the Christian message evidenced in the writings of theologians such as these.

Parenthetically it should be noted that it is this understanding of the transcendental experience which is at the core of what is rightly regarded as the most significant attainment of truly contemporary and therefore truly traditional Catholic thought. It is the *point de départ* of Maréchal, the *Geist in Welt* of Rahner, the *surnaturel* of de Lubac, the *Metaphysik* of Coreth, the insight of Lonergan—and one could add, the basis of Novak's application of the latter in *Belief and Unbelief,* and of Boros' application of Blondel in *The Mystery of Death.*

Yet it is no mere cavil—rather it is the whole point of the earlier discussion above—to emphasize the fact that that this "new" understanding should be viewed as so significant an attainment can only strike the poet and the artist, that is to say, man at his best, as the astonishing proof of how detached from the experience of being is most philosophy of religion. Such are the pitfalls of the institutionalization and professionalization of intellectual enterprises, including above all theology as the subject of churchmen, that that experience which is most immediate to man in his authenticity should re-appear tardily as a novel discovery to academic thinkers. There is more to it than this, of course, for it is a question for the religious philosopher of not merely being aware of the undistilled experience but of validating as discursively as possible its reality and articulating as fully as possible its implications; and for the theologian as such, it is a question of distinguishing between what in the natural order is the element of *chance,* adventitiousness, in the encounter with being and what in the supernatural order is the absolute *gratuity* of God's addressing his Word to man in the Church. Nevertheless one cannot but be put in mind, when reading even the writings of the transcendental Thomists, of someone who came to realize the meaning of love only after researching, say, Fromm and Freud.

There is no evading "natural" theology and this transcendental experience which grounds it. If Barth in reaction to pietism feared the religious experience, so much the worse for Barth; theology is not politics and the fact that a theologian is a powerful intellectual force provides no guaranteed mandate for his views. It is this transcendental experience alone which preserves religious experience from anthropomorphism, whether the anthropomorphism of "Caliban upon Setebos," or the more refined though identical anthropomorphism of pop theologians who compose out of their own impenetrability and imperviousness the concept of god as the cosmic mortician who can only affect us after we are dead—if then. Yet such composition is in no way surprising: religious philosophers who never go beyond the conceptual, who traffic only in concepts, however sophisticated these may be, must conclude, when faced by their inevitable failure to conceptualize Being, that there is no Being at all.

And that is why the death-of-God theology is rightly denominated "pop." Pop art was the carefully tended nursling of neo-academic critics; it allowed them to appear as rebels against their own conventions and above all it allowed them to fulfill what they envision—indeed, what they get paid for and prove their raison d'être by—as the critic's highest function: *talk*. Since the pop painting was so negligible as to be almost non-existent as an artifact (Painting is dead!), all that really mattered to a truly contemporary critic was talk about, around, behind, and across the picture. Pop art made the critic more important than the artwork itself, even as pop theology makes the concepts of theologians more important than the being of God. (For tangential theological discourse going off aimlessly and telling us nothing about God but a great deal about himself and about his ideas and his feelings and his opinions one must heed the voice of Professor Altizer.)

Professor Altizer's colleague, William Hamilton, indulges

when theologizing his belletristic inclinations, and mythicizes the religious revolution through which modern man is believed to be passing with the assertion that Oedipal theology is giving way to Orestes theology, and that the epoch of Hamlet religion is being supplanted by the epoch of Prospero religion. This is an exemplary heuristic device. So let it be said instead that the revolt is *against* the religious, establishmentarian priggishness of a Prince Hal and is *for* the spontaneous, commoner's exuberance of a Falstaff. But the watchword is "demythologize." And no poetic imagery should blind us to the basic datum that monarch and fool are not distinguished rightly by their kingship or their buffoonery, but by their humanness, a humanness which remains, throughout whatever alleged revolutions, radically defined as "openness to the infinite." For this we must call upon the poet, not to put him to work for us, but simply "to hear the word of the bard":

> The voice I hear this passing night was heard
> In ancient days by emperor and clown:
> Perhaps the self-same song that found a path
> Through the sad heart of Ruth, when, sick for home,
> She stood in tears amid the alien corn.

The present epoch of the eclipse of light will pass; it is already a passing night, and Falstaff and Hal will be seen in the dawn for what they truly are: the everyman who is Ruth in exile gleaning what nurture she can for the journey home.

This is the tradition; this is man *with* a history. It may be expunged from the anthologies of the theologians; it may be driven out of academe. It cannot be annihilated in the human heart because it is what makes the heart human.

The Dilemma of Identity for the Emancipated Jew

Manfred H. Vogel

By "emancipation" Manfred H. Vogel means "the re-entry of the Jewish people into the concrete world and its profane history"—a world not of their own making, and one that they do not govern. Those whose world it is require that Jews enter as individuals, as "abstract" human beings, rather than as a nation with a particular history, and as a consequence a crisis has arisen for Jewry. For the price it is asked to pay for emancipation is the highest: abandonment of its distinctive religious vocation and its ethnic-national identity. Moreover, the old, diaspora-based rabbinic Judaism, with its stress on static law, is not equipped to cope with the contemporary situation. Dr. Vogel—a rabbi who is also assistant professor in the Department of History and Literature of Religions at Northwestern University—delineates the dilemma of modern Jewry from a theological perspective and finds hope in signs of a new, more biblically based mode of witness being manifested in the state of Israel. An authority on the thought of Ludwig Feuerbach, Dr. Vogel recently published a translation, with commentary, of Feuerbach's *Principles of the Philosophy of the Future*. His article is from the July 1966 issue of *The Journal of Bible and Religion* (now called the *Journal of the American Academy of Religion*).*

JUDAISM today is characterized by a question mark. For what finds expression most often and most authentically within contemporary Jewish consciousness is a question: "What is a Jew?" This question is manifest in all of

* 1010 Arch Street, Philadelphia, Pa. 19107. Copyright 1966, American Academy of Religion.

contemporary Jewish life—in detached philosophical-literary speculation, practical political-juristic formulation, and the ill-articulated but existentially immediate awareness of the ordinary individual. The existence of the Jew of today is marked by pervasive perplexity, which is thus authentically expressed by this recurring, nagging question. In the immediate lived reality of his existence he finds that he is unique. But what constitutes this uniqueness he does not know. He does not know what makes him a Jew.

Thus, Jewish life today can be most accurately characterized as a search for identity. Closely bound up with this search, however, is a search for the vocation that the adjective "Jewish" is supposed to connote. For the Jew's identity is intimately enmeshed in his distinctive calling and task in this world. Indeed, his identity can be determined and articulated only in terms of his vocation. Thus, underlying the question, "What is a Jew?" is the further question, "What is the vocation of the Jew?" In these two questions lie the crisis of present-day Jewry.

I

From a historical perspective we can see quite clearly that it was the phenomenon of Emancipation that posed these two questions for the Jew. Throughout Jewry's long history, from earliest times up to the recent era, the issue of vocation and consequently that of identity did not arise for Jewry. Generally speaking, Jewish consciousness had attained clearly formulated and acceptable answers to these questions. The Jew understood his vocation essentially in religious categories: his was the vocation of faith. He was called to be a witness to the presence, glory, justice, and providence of God. ("On this day you are my witnesses.") This vocation, however, was assigned not primarily to the individual but to the community, i.e., the nation, which was the primary carrier of the task and was, indeed, conceived to have come into being as a nation only by being assigned this vocation. Such vocation as the individual had was derived from that of the nation, and only by belonging to the nation could he participate in the religious vocation. His religious vocation implied and, indeed, required his ethnic identity as part of the peoplehood of Israel. Accordingly, the Jew understood his vocation and identity in terms of an inextricable union of religious and ethnic categories. This self-understanding characterized the Jew throughout his entire history until recent times, and served as the constant, unshakable foundation of his self-image. Clearly, in these circumstances the question of what constituted his Jewishness could never arise.

However, while this call to witness through ethnic identity remained constant, the concrete form of its expression, i.e., the *mode* of witnessing, could and did change. For the mode of witnessing is, after all, contingent upon the conditions of life, which provide it with material for its expression. Thus, if and when the conditions should change radically, the mode of witnessing, if it is to continue to be viable and concretely to articulate the witnessing, must likewise change and adapt itself to the new conditions.

Indeed, viewed from this vantage point, the radical turn which separated and distinguished rabbinic Judaism from biblical Israel was due to a change, not in the nation's vocation or in its content (these remained constant), but in its expression. Jewry's mode of witnessing changed because of the radical change in conditions: from an existence in its own sovereign state to an existence in diaspora. When it possessed an independent state, biblical Israel had at its disposal the machinery and the reality of exercising power. (How limited this power might have been in comparison with the power of other states matters little in this context.) The state could make and enforce decisions, and thus actively and concretely fashion the course of its history in all its dimensions: political, economic, and social. Biblical Israel lived in the concrete political world and had the task of charting its destiny within profane, secular history. Consequently, its life was in turn fashioned by that history into an on-going process that was ever-changing and ever-new. Correspondingly, its mode of witnessing was made into an ever-open, situational kind of witnessing. This mode expressed itself in and through profane, secular history by the very exercise of Israel's power. The witness of Israel could not be pre-determined, but had to enter the flux of profane, secular history, there to risk and expose itself ever anew in specific decisions. A succession of such open decisions, the warp and woof of the fabric of history, made its witness by directing and transforming profane, secular history in response to the divine challenge. Thus, the biblical mode of witnessing can be characterized essentially in two aspects: 1) the material of the mode was the power afforded by the concrete world and its profane, secular history; 2) the form of the mode was the open, situational decision-making.

The loss of the state and the exile into diaspora-existence signified a radical change in the conditions of life of the Jewish people. Essentially, it meant that having lost their state, they no longer had at their disposal the possibility of exercising power, for the exercise of power is afforded a nation only through the machinery of the state. Without power the Jewish people as a people could no longer exist in the concrete political world nor influence and impinge upon its profane, secular history.[1] To exist outside that world meant, however, that the essential pattern and structure of Jewish existence was no longer submerged in the on-going, ever-changing process which characterizes the concrete world and its profane history. Hence, Jewish existence became a closed, unchanging and complete pattern, which let the concrete world and profane history flow by it.[2]

[1] Of course, as isolated individual human beings the Jews continued in a sense to exist in the profane world, as there is no place else for individual human beings to exist. But as the Jewish nation they were excluded, and it is in terms of the Jewish nation that this analysis is conducted. Our very understanding of the concepts "concrete world" and "profane history" in terms of power and the machinery of the state applies quite evidently only to an analysis of nations rather than to that of individuals. Furthermore, even as individual human beings the Jews, precisely because of their Jewishness, led a passive existence. They were, by and large, objects receiving the action of the world and its history, not subjects who directed and fashioned the world.

[2] Naturally, in the course of almost two thousand years of diaspora existence there were also changes. But many of them were accommodations necessitated by the strategy of survival, while others were very often imposed from the outside. In neither case did these changes really affect the essential structure of Jewish diaspora-existence. They were incidental changes—necessary and minimal compromises and accommodations.

Franz Rosenzweig's description of Judaism as "outside the world and

The rabbinic statement that prophecy had ceased in Israel since the days of Ezra and Nehemiah is not to be read as a mere descriptive one. It is categorical—it had to be so. While holding fast to the substance of biblical Israel's vocation of faith, diaspora Judaism had to reshape its mode of witnessing to correspond to the new conditions of its existence.

The new mode of witnessing through which diaspora-based rabbinic Judaism expressed the vocation of faith was the Law.[3] We do not imply that this mode of witnessing did not exist prior to rabbinic Judaism; rather, the newness lay in rabbinic Judaism's understanding of the nature and status of the Law.[4] The Law was now conceived as an eternal, un-

---

history" is thus a perceptive and profound description of diaspora Judaism, though not of the community of faith of Israel as a whole. It does not apply to other modes of witnessing which the community of Israel could and, indeed, did assume. Only if we equate diaspora Judaism with the community of faith of Israel can Rosenzweig's analysis stand. Such an equation is impossible. Along the same line, Arnold Toynbee's description of Judaism as a "fossil" can be understood only as a judgment upon diaspora Judaism given from the viewpoint of profane history. From that viewpoint, with its essential criterion of power, diaspora-existence is essentially a "fossil" since it cannot participate as an active, living organism in the fashioning and directing of profane history. Thus, Toynbee's description must be taken seriously. But this is not to say that there is no other dimension of living beyond that of profane history. Here lies the basic justification for accusing Toynbee of "intellectual anti-Semitism," since he himself, when he ceases to be a descriptive historian and turns into a religious "apostle," preaches a mode of existence which is akin to that of diaspora Judaism.

[3] The word "Law" stands here for both the *Halacha*, "the way," and the *Torah*, "the Teaching." Although strictly speaking the two terms refer to two distinct entities, the *Torah* referring to the source from which the *Halacha* is formulated, they are related in a very intimate way. The point we are trying to make here applies to the Law as both "the way" and "the Teaching."

[4] Witnessing through the Law was always characteristic of the Jewish community and certainly manifested itself in the biblical period. But in that period (1) the Law was only one among other modes of witnessing and by no means the most basic and characteristic; (2) the Law did not presume to encompass the totality of life in all details; (3) there were a number of codes of law reflecting the legislation of certain parts of the country and certain segments of the population. Hence, the Law of the biblical community was anything but monolithic, unchanging, and all-encompassing. Rabbinic Judaism, on the other hand, while continuing the mode of witnessing found in the biblical period, radically transformed its nature and status by (1) making the Law the only normative mode of witnessing; (2) extending it to all possible contingencies of life in all their details; (3) hypostatizing the Law, giving it independent existence as a permanent, unchanging, unitary, and all-encompassing code. Thus, it was through these changes in the conception of the nature and status of the Law rather than through the introduction of a totally new mode of witnessing that rabbinic Judaism signaled a radical turn in the history of the Jewish people and their faith.

changing, and all-inclusive teaching. Consequently, the way that followed from its teaching was a completed, closed one—a way that had already arrived at the end, that was already "there." He who travelled this way was following a pre-charted, pre-determined way, with the navigation of each new turn already known. Indeed, the way was more like a static system that covered and decided in advance every conceivable situation. There was no room for the genuinely new, undetermined, and open situation. All-inclusiveness and permanence rather than flux and on-goingness were this way's characteristics. He who witnessed, therefore, through the Law was not called upon to take his ground in open response, risking his decision in the face of ever-new situations. His response was already determined and formulated, at least theoretically, for every conceivable situation. His task was merely to discover the right answer.[5]

Quite clearly, the mode of witnessing through the Law

[5] Thus, the office of the rabbi, the office *par excellence* of rabbinic Judaism, was simply that of interpreter and explicator. The *Torah* revealed once and for all at Sinai was taken to be eternally and absolutely valid, or at least (as taken by some, e.g., Rabbi Yosi, a third century Babylonian Amora) absolutely valid until the coming of the messianic age, which was, by the way to coincide with the end of diaspora-existence. (This latter view is certainly most suggestive and intriguing when seen from the vantage point of our interpretation, though it was certainly not the reasoning behind this rabbinic view.) Furthermore, and this is the crux of our point, the *Torah* was taken in principle to cover every conceivable situation. When confronted with a supposedly "new" situation (from the viewpoint of *Torah* there was of course no genuine newness), the rabbi's task was merely to discover, interpret, and apply the appropriate response. Of course, some responses did not fall into this pre-determined category but were authentically new and open—evolving from man's decision in face of a concrete situation. These were the *g'zerot*, the rabbinic edicts. They resulted from the fact that in however limited a way, diaspora Jewry was still inevitably involved in profane history. But even here the rabbis were extremely reluctant to resort to a "new" mode of response. They sought with all their ingenuity to find the appropriate, pre-formulated response in the *Torah*. When the genuine newness of profane history made this impossible, recourse to the edict was inevitable. However, even then, the rabbis considered such recourse a forced temporary exception (*g'zerat Hashaa*, an edict of the hour) placed in a separate category from responses formulated in the *Torah*. Furthermore, the view that in many instances the rabbis were really formulating their own response, which they then read into the *Torah* as the alleged source, does not present a problem to our interpretation. What is important here is not what we maintain or even the reality of the situation, but the claim made by the rabbis. That claim is very clear: The *Torah* given to Moses at Sinai is all-comprehending, unchangeable, and eternally valid. The rabbis did not see themselves as initiators or bearers of new responses but as technicians discovering the old ones. How different, then, was the office of rabbi, the symbol of rabbinic Judaism, from that of the prophet, the symbol of biblical Israel.

corresponded to the conditions of diaspora-existence. Diaspora-existence and the witnessing through the Law were alike outside the flux and on-goingness of profane history. They were already "there," "waiting" at the end of profane history, complete, finished, and static. Indeed, the Law could guide and encompass the life of the diaspora community so thoroughly, precisely because it corresponded so intimately to the conditions of diaspora-existence.

II

On the basis of our analysis above regarding the change in the conditions of existence that characterized the transition from biblical Israel to rabbinic Judaism, we should expect that the Emancipation would involve yet another radical change in the mode of witnessing of the Jewish people. This indeed is essentially the case, except that the change in conditions signaled by the Emancipation presents serious difficulties, which make highly problematic the emergence of an appropriate mode of witnessing. Thus is precipitated the crisis of vocation and identity for the present-day emancipated Jew.

The essential feature of the Emancipation is the exact reverse of the conditions under which rabbinic Judaism lived. It means the re-entry of the Jewish people into the concrete world and its profane history.[6] This, quite clearly, has to precipitate first of all a crisis in the mode of witnessing of rabbinic Judaism. For the Law as permanent, unchanging, and all-inclusive simply does not fit the conditions of the concrete profane world. We should not be surprised, therefore, that

[6] We must emphasize again that the object of our analysis is—and indeed, as pointed out above, can only be—the Jewish people as a whole and not Jewish individuals. Of course, there were prior to the Emancipation individual Jews who were emancipated. As such they provide a fascinating study of how on an individual basis witnessing in the framework of rabbinic Judaism was combined with participation in the concrete world. The price exacted, however, from such persons was a double life, which an individual person may get away with but which a people as a whole cannot endure. Thus, the distinctive mark of the Emancipation is precisely that the people as a whole, and not just a certain number of individuals, enter the profane world.

the neglect and even abandonment of the Law follow closely upon Emancipation.[7]

That the Emancipation collides with the mode of witnessing of rabbinic Judaism can be seen not only through the mass exodus of emancipated Jews from under the wings of the Law but indeed in the very religious movements that are representative products of the Emancipation. All of them—Reform, Conservative, and Reconstructionist—center around the question of the Law. For all, the Law is the basic issue of division and all (though in different degrees of radicalness) compromise the *in toto* conception of the Law insisted upon in rabbinic Judaism.[8] Clearly, emancipated Jewry is searching for a new mode of witnessing, struggling to find a more open and flexible expression of that witnessing.

It might seem, therefore, that our analysis ought to come to rest at this point to await the emergence of a new way.

[7] Emancipation has set in at different times in the various geographic segments of the Jewish people. Thus, the correlation between the onset of Emancipation and the precipitation of the "crisis of the Law" can be observed in a great number of instances. No sooner does the former occur than the latter follows.

[8] The "*in toto*" is all important for our interpretation, since the crisis is precipitated precisely because of the incompatibility between the changing character of the concrete world and the mode of witnessing through an unchanging Law. To do away with the "*in toto*" (no matter how infinitesimally small the compromise) means the surrender of the essence of the Law as conceived in rabbinic Judaism.

Emancipated religious Jewry's need for a new mode of witnessing is seen not only in its institutionalized religious movements but also in its theological thought, which has attempted somehow to preserve the Law. Resort is made to the principle of "selectivity," either as (a) existential selectivity, whereby the Law is turned into a "reservoir" from which the individual person is to select as binding only what he can truthfully appropriate as his own authentic expression (e.g., F. Rosenzweig), or (b) ethical selectivity, whereby the Law is divided into (1) a small kernel of supposedly unchanging and eternally binding ethical injunctions and (2) the large remaining body of the Law, which is seen as the strategy devised to protect the ethical injunctions and which therefore is time-bound and changeable (e.g., L. Baeck). Although a principle of selectivity of sorts is found in rabbinic thought (e.g., the distinction between Scriptural Law and rabbinic Law, or even that between the Law and the "fence around the Law," a distinction that would seem particularly close to the modern way of ethical selectivity), it is quite different from the two formulations just mentioned. It is only a principle of methodological selectivity. For one thing, it locates the selectivity objectively as a means of classification within the Law itself rather than making it subjectively dependent either upon the individual's authenticity or upon extra-revelatory ethical criteria. Second, and more important, in the rabbinic view the principle of selectivity is not allowed to compromise or mitigate the binding force and obligatory nature of the Law as a whole.

Yet in truth the situation of emancipated Jewry is much more problematic and precarious than we have shown thus far. It is not merely that emancipated Jewry is going through a period of transition, though that is a difficult enough problem. The issue goes far deeper than the search for an adequate, specific mode of witnessing. *It questions the possibility of there being any mode at all that can authentically express the witness of emancipated Jewry*. In other words, it questions whether an emancipated Jewry is at all possible.

The issue lies in the fact that the re-entry into the world takes place in diaspora. This means that it is a re-entry into someone else's world, a world fashioned and governed by, and expressing and manifesting the ethos of, other nations, cultures and religions. It is a world that Judaism and the Jewish people did not create and therefore do not possess or control.[9]

These circumstances imply two important considerations, which radically question the possibility of a full Jewish Emancipation in diaspora and introduce a certain element of estrangement and ambivalence into the Emancipation. First, it is difficult to see how Judaism in its vocation as a religion can truly enter into this world and its history. For how, then, will it be able to fulfill its task of guiding and directing the destiny of this world and its history, and, moreover, of sitting in judgment upon the world and the nations? How can a Jewish mode of witnessing authentically express itself in terms of this world and its history when the *sine qua non* for this is the use of power, power that Judaism cannot have because the world and the history which it enters are not its own? Thus, even if we were to suppose that Jewry, as a people, could be emancipated, the truth is that Judaism, as a religion, cannot

---

[9] This description applies to diaspora Emancipation in all parts of the world, e.g., the Arabic-Islamic as much as the European-Christian world. Of course, the Emancipation has been manifested most clearly and importantly in the latter world, which therefore primarily guides our analysis. The situation in the United States is somewhat different from that in Europe due to the fact that the ethnic-national character of the American people is relatively new and is, indeed, still in the process of formation, thus lacking a clear and definite structure. Also the presence of the Negro minority complicates the picture. Nevertheless, it is our provisional contention that the position of Jewry in the United States will finally prove to be basically the same as in the rest of the Western world.

follow suit and thereby be in a position to formulate and express the vocation of the emancipated Jew. Emancipation, therefore, must be partial—applying to Jewry but not to Judaism, and implying a necessary estrangement between the two. To the extent that Jewry is emancipated, Judaism simply cannot be meaningful to it, for Judaism ceases to be in a position to formulate and express its vocation. But by the same token, Jewry, to the extent that it is emancipated and yet remains Jewish (in the sense at least of not becoming something else), is left without vocation. For from where else can it receive its vocation than from Judaism? We should not be surprised, therefore, that secularism should quickly engulf the majority of emancipated Jews and that simultaneously the crisis of vocation and identity should be precipitated for them.

This predicament is further shown and, indeed, made even more radical by a second consideration: the Emancipation of the Jewish people *as a people* is simply not possible. This truth follows from the fact that the re-entry of emancipated diaspora Jewry into the world is not by right (since the world is not its own) or through its own power, but through the grace and permission of the nations who possess and control the world. In the last analysis, it is the nations of the world that determine the nature and extent of Jewish Emancipation, and the permission that they extend to Jewish re-entry is far from open and unconditional. The most essential and important thing for us to realize is that the nations exclude, as indeed they must, the entry of Jewry *qua* nation. For how can they permit another nation to share the power and control of their world?[10] We should not be surprised, therefore, to find that to the extent the door is opened at all, it is opened

[10] This, of course, means that the kind of Judaism which as a religion is inextricably bound to the nation is excluded as well, since its carrier, the Jewish nation, is excluded. But even if the kind of Judaism that witnesses "horizontally" through profane history could somehow enter the world without the Jewish nation as its carrier (which in reality is not possible), it would still not be allowed to enter. For how can the nations of the world as custodians of their religions accept another religion to share with their own the guidance and judgment of their actions and policies? (And insofar as they are secularized, Judaism *qua* religion certainly does not have a place in their world.)

not to the Jewish people as a nation, but only to the Jew as an individual.[11]

But what does the term "Jew" signify now, since it can no longer signify either the vocation of faith of Judaism or ethnic membership in the Jewish nation? It has become an empty term, which at best may signify the past but not the present, not the belongingness or vocation of the emancipated individual. Indeed, we must realize that in the last resort, permission to enter upon Emancipation is withheld not only from Jewry as a nation but also from the Jew as an individual. True, there seems to be a distinction with respect to the *offer* of Emancipation; i.e., while the offer cannot even be made to the Jewish nation, it can and is made to the Jewish individual. Yet in the latter's very acceptance of the offer, his Jewishness (to the extent that Jewishness can have any specific distinguishing meaning for the emancipated individual) must be left behind. The individual may enter the world, but not as a Jew, only as a human being.[12]

[11] We are thus witnessing a unique phenomenon in Jewish history: it is the individual Jew, not the nation as such, that is emancipated. The term "emancipated Jewry" signifies, therefore, only a collection of individual Jews. This situation is entirely different from the phenomena of the exile into diaspora and of the birth of biblical Israel (i.e., Sinai), phenomena appertaining essentially to the nation and not to the individual. This does not contradict what is said above in note 6. There attention is called to the fact that the Emancipation in our day engulfs the vast majority of Jews in contrast to the emancipating of isolated, individual Jews in the past. In this sense, Emancipation today affects the Jewish nation as a whole. Nevertheless, attention must be called to the primary subject of Emancipation in our day: the individual Jew. In other words, the Jewish nation is "emancipated" only because the vast majority of its members are emancipated.

[12] That this condition could have asserted itself in the first place arises from the fact that the offer of Emancipation did not extend to membership in the peoplehood of the nation but only to membership in the state. Under the influence of the Enlightenment, the state was conceived as a separate, independent, neutral entity, which could accept any human being as a member, i.e., as a citizen, as long as he swore allegiance to it and abided by its rules. The fault lay in assigning to the citizenry of the state an independent reality that could furnish full identity for its members. This meant a betrayal of the intimate relationship between individual identity and an ethnic-national entity. In truth, the state and its citizenry are but conventional political-legal expressions of an ethnic-national entity. Consequently, while outsiders may participate as citizens in the conventional political-legal structure called the state, they do so only through the toleration of the ethnic-national entity. Unfortunately, as has been demonstrated only too clearly in our day, the tolerance is not too abundant. The ethnic-national entity seems to possess an innate drive to try to appropriate the state exclusively, tolerating outsiders only when they are few and then only on an individual, temporary basis. Thus, the entry into the citizenry of the state that the Emancipation offered was in the last analysis a sham. Authentic

Thus, we are forced to conclude that the re-entry of diaspora Jewry into the world, as signaled by the Emancipation, is anything but simple and straightforward. Jewry must pay the highest possible price, a price so high that its very vocation and identity are shattered. Judaism, which formulates and articulates the Jewish vocation of faith, cannot accompany Jewry in its re-entry and must remain outside. In the same way, the Jewish nation, which defines and determines Jewish ethnic identity and belongingness, must also stay outside. Yet these are the two pillars that from the very inception of Jewry, always defined its vocation and identity. Once these are taken away, the term "Jewish" is robbed of all significance. The only "identity" left to the emancipated Jew is to be a member of the human species. But this puts him in an impossible position. To be a human being in general is to be nothing in particular, a mere abstraction.

Theoretically, there are two ways out of this plight of the emancipated Jew. One is to carry the process of Emancipation to its logical conclusion, and enter not only the world and history of the nations but also their ethnic reality and, if need be, their religious vocation.[13] (True, the individual cannot

---

and full entry could only take place in terms of the ethnic-national entity, and it is here that our dilemma arises.

[13] It would seem that the major stumbling block erected by the Emancipation is the question of ethnic-national identity rather than religious vocation, since the latter is a changeable factor while the former is not. Thus, it is quite possible that the ethnic-national entity into which the emancipated individual seeks full entry should be essentially secularized, in which case "conversion" would not be necessary. (If "conversion" were required or, more likely, desired, there would be no problem in embracing it since "conversion" to the religions of the world, unlike "conversion" to Judaism, does not require simultaneous entry into an ethnic-national entity.) The fact remains that ethnic-national identity is always required and yet is never available to the emancipated individual. Here is the insurmountable stumbling block to the full emancipation of any individual.

This perennial factor of ethnic-national belongingness operates just as effectively from the Jewish side. In holding fast to the view, "once a Jew, always a Jew," Judaism refuses to surrender its claim on anyone who ever was a Jew. But this is a result not of capriciousness but of the fact that being Jewish implies necessarily belonging to the Jewish ethnic-national entity. One simply cannot give this up. Even conversion out of the faith cannot dissolve the ethnic bond. (Since the vocation of faith is the other inextricable element in being Jewish but one that can be renounced, the act of conversion leads to a clash and an impasse in the Jewish status of the convert. The only solution possible, and it is indeed the one which Jewish Law follows, is to relegate him to a state of limbo. It is as though he has ceased to exist.) Thus, both from the side of the world and from the side of Judaism it is the ethnic bond that obstructs the exit of the Jew from Judaism and his entry into the nations of the world.

enter himself, no matter how much he may want to do so, but he can ensure entrance for his descendants fairly easily through intermarriage and conversion). The other way is to withdraw from Emancipation and thus make possible a complete and authentic return to Judaism, to both its religious vocation and its ethnic-national identity. On either course, the popular understanding of Emancipation as a means by which the Jew can belong simultaneously to two worlds, the Western and the Jewish worlds, is seen to be untenable, an illusion. The only resolution of the dilemma is to go in one or the other direction. Evidence of both these alternatives is apparent today. On the one hand, intermarriage is very widespread and the prospects are that it will engulf more and more emancipated Jews in the days to come. On the other hand, within some quarters of emancipated Jewry faint but nonetheless real signs are appearing of withdrawal from the world of Western culture. And hand in hand with this withdrawal has come a return to the mode of witnessing of rabbinic Judaism.[14] From the Jewish viewpoint it is this latter trend that will provide the surviving remnant (no matter how small its numbers), a remnant that can alone and without self-contradiction or ambiguity live an authentic Jewish life in the world of diaspora.[15]

III

Thus far the present analysis has concentrated upon the predicament of emancipated Jewry in diaspora. It is against this background that we may appreciate more fully the tre-

[14] In this connection it is interesting to note the recent rise of the Jewish day-school movement and the "return to Orthodoxy" manifested in some quarters of emancipated Jewry.

[15] Only if we understand Jewish identity and vocation in religious categories can Jewish existence in diaspora make sense and in a way be justified. For the essence of Jewry is then formulated in terms that transcend the world of diaspora. If we understand Jewish identity in secular categories, its identity is exclusively ethnic. But what justification does an ethnic-national group have for living outside its own land in the midst of other ethnic-national groups? There was no escape from this abnormal state of affairs when Jewry did not possess its own state. With the restoration of the State of Israel how can one whose understanding of Jewry is exclusively secular, i.e., ethnic-national, in character, justify the continuous existence of Jewry in diaspora?

mendous theological significance of the reestablishment of the state of Israel in our time. Indeed, that event can be understood as the answer to the dilemma of emancipated Jewry—not only from a secular-nationalist viewpoint but from a religious viewpoint. In direct contrast to the situation in diaspora, the emancipated Jew can now enter a concrete world and a profane history that are of his own making. It is a Jewish world that he enters. Consequently, he enters by right and not by sufferance. Every aspect of the world is open to him—political, social, economic, ethical, and cultural. He is given full power and unrestricted opportunity to determine the course and destiny of the concrete world. Most important, no longer does he have to enter as that dubious and ambiguous entity, "man"; he enters as the concrete being he is: a Jew. No one stands in the way to place conditions and qualifications on how he is to enter. Nor is Judaism excluded from entering this concrete world and its profane history. Judaism is there to define and articulate the vocation and identity of the Jew, to give guidance but also to pass judgment.

And yet, while the dilemma of Jewish re-entry is positively resolved by means of the re-established state of Israel, it does not follow that the other question posed by the Emancipation, the question of the viability of the rabbinic mode of witnessing, is similarly resolved. On the contrary, the crisis of the rabbinic mode of witnessing through the Law is precipitated all the more radically. For while the rabbinic formulation of the Law as all-inclusive, and hence static and unchanging, could serve so admirably as the mode of witnessing of diaspora and unemancipated Jewry, since it corresponded so well to Jewry's trans-historical and trans-worldly mode of existence, the rabbinic formulation fails miserably to serve as the mode of witnessing of emancipated Israeli Jewry. This is because that formulation no longer corresponds to, but is indeed at an opposite end from, its new mode of existence, which is immersed in the open and ongoing character of the concrete world and its profane history. The crisis of the Law as the mode of witnessing, as analyzed above regarding diaspora emancipated Jewry, applies just as much here. If anything, the crisis can be seen more clearly and poignantly, precisely because the entry of the emancipated Israeli Jew into the concrete world is so complete and unambiguous, without any qualifications or half-way accommodations. Consequently, there are no theological "backdoors" through which the Law can partially re-enter, if only in a mitigated and qualified way, to serve as a vague, half-hearted mode of witnessing. We should not be surprised, therefore, that there should be such a radical crisis of the Law and hence of rabbinic Judaism in the State of Israel today.

However, the contemporary rejection of the Law and of rabbinic Judaism in the State of Israel should not be taken as necessarily a radical secularization of the community, in the sense of an abandonment of the vocation of religious witnessing. This latter is indeed possible, but the collapse of the Law is not necessarily indicative of it.[16] What is clearly indicated is that the mode of witnessing of rabbinic Judaism has been rejected. But we must not identify rabbinic Judaism with the Jewish community of faith. Rabbinic Judaism is but one expression of this community, an expression resulting in large part from particular historical conditions. We are not permitted to forget the peculiar mode of witnessing of biblical Israel during a time when Jewry lived in the concrete world and possessed its own state. It is therefore very interesting that with the simultaneous rejection of rabbinic Judaism in modern Israel, we should be witnessing a conscious, enthusiastic turning toward the Bible. Modern Israel feels a strong kinship with the Bible while rabbinic Judaism has become an estranged, alien phenomenon, and this in spite of the fact that the latter is so much closer in time. The mode of existence is evidently the determining factor in the mode of witnessing.

---

[16] Our assumption here, as above with respect to emancipated diaspora Jewry, is that while it is possible to interpret what is happening in Jewish life today in terms of a thorough and fundamental secularization of the Jewish community—secularization in the sense of a renunciation of the religious vocation—this is not the only interpretation possible. We contend that the facts may suggest a less radical secularization, in the sense of a collapse of one mode of witnessing and the not-yet emerging reality of a new mode. Such secularization is partial since, in principle, it does not reject the religious vocation and is itself transitory.

Consequently, we may perhaps expect a new mode of witnessing to emerge in modern Israel, with some resemblance to that of biblical Israel.

Today's Jewish community of faith is living in the midst of a period of radical crisis. In the thousands of years of its history, there has been only one comparable instance: the change from the biblical to the rabbinic period. We can see only the negative, destructive side of this crisis—the collapse of a structure and pattern of life, or, as formulated in the present article, the collapse of a mode of witnessing that defined, guided, and regulated the vocation of the community. Accordingly, this exposition had to deal primarily with the negative side. The positive side has not yet emerged. One can only hope for the coming of another mode of witnessing that will implement the vocation of the community. We are not able to project the course of the development. The future remains always open and does not admit of prophecies.

The Issue of Transcendence in the New Theology, the New Morality, and the New Forms

Gabriel Fackre

In the view of Gabriel Fackre, secular theology's thirst for freedom and its attack on the autocratic theologies of the past are to be applauded. At the same time, Fackre suggests, the new radicalism in its repudiation of transcendence is in danger of exchanging an old imperialism for a new one— one dominated by monolithic, monological man, a tyrannical megalomania. Fackre doubts that one must write God's obituary in order to affirm humanity, or espouse codeless love as the only answer to a loveless code, or deny the being of the church because of its failure in doing. As an alternative to the accommodationist theology of the anti-transcendents, Fackre outlines what he terms a "Eucharistic theology for the new age"—a theology "which has learned to love God for God's sake alone, and therefore, has also learned to love man for his." From *Theology and Life* (Spring 1966),* Dr. Fackre's essay originated as his inauguration address delivered February 4, 1966, at Lancaster Theological Seminary, where he is associate professor of Historical Theology and Christian Ethics. *The Pastor and the World* and *The Purpose and Work of the Ministry* are among his published writings.

"THE ONE I like the best is really very satisfying, very good . . . It eases my mind, makes it more clear. It makes me forget some of the other things . . . Seems more enjoyable to be on the streets. The world seems like a much better place to be in." So reports Richard Dobbins who for

* Lancaster Theological Seminary, Lancaster, Pennsylvania.

a long time had been subject to violent fits of depression and rage. Now with electrodes embedded in his brain, attached by wire to a little box he carries on his hip, Mr. Dobbins can with the press of button one alter his own personality. He can create peace of mind, joy, a feeling of harmony with the world.[1]

Let's change the scene. We are at a Singspiration Sunday night at the little church around the corner. The congregation is lustily sounding forth on No. 52.

Are you sad and lonely? Lift your heart and pray;
Though the clouds may hide the sunshine—God is not far away.
Clouds will turn to sunshine, night will turn to day;
If you'll just remember, God is not far away.[2]

What possible connection could there be between an electrode implantation and a gospel song? The startling thing is that they share a basic mark of these modern times: They are both through and through secular.

"Secularization," says Harvey Cox, "is man turning his attention away from the worlds beyond and toward this world and this time."[3] Thus, Mr. Dobbins and his medical and psychiatric helpers do not spend their time reflecting on the three persons of the Trinity, nor do they write monographs on the furniture of heaven or the temperature of hell. Their pulses beat faster and their forehead veins distend at the promise of shaping the human being as a whole and happy self, here and now.

But then again, so does song No. 52 and its numerous companions from "God will take care of you" to "Anywhere with Jesus." The heart and mind of the singer are not drawn to the great God who is who he is, and who is to be loved for his own sake because he is who he is. Nor is there much talk

[1] See interview filmed for "Frontiers of the Mind," a documentary produced for television by Wolper Associates, Los Angeles, Calif.
[2] Favorites, Number four: Gospel songs for solos, duets, trios, quartets, and group singing. One of the Singspiration series, compiled by Alfred B. Smith. Grand Rapids, Michigan: Zondervan Publishing House, 1956, No. 52, "God Is Not Far Away," words by Sidney E. Cox and music by Alfred B. Smith and Sidney E. Cox, copyright by Alfred B. Smith.
[3] The Secular City, New York: Macmillan, 1965, p. 2.

even about the world to come. No, these things are too religious—they have to do with another world, and the next world. The gospel song turns men's eyes to *this* world and *this* time, its heartaches, its loneliness, its cares, its burdens and its promise of relief from them for the Mr. Dobbinses. Yes, religious words are used, but the goal is this-worldly—hence as secular as the electrode technicians adjusting the wires on Mr. Dobbins' skull. One is scientific secularization; the other is pious secularization. Both are a long way off from the genuine otherworldliness of an Eastern Orthodox prayer.

If "the new age" means a fundamental "mutation in human consciousness" for scientist and pietist alike, a turning of men toward absorption in the business of living in this world and this time, then the church needs to examine its ways of speaking to the new man. It needs a *theology of secularization*.

An increasingly active candidate for the role of interpreter of faith in the age of secularization is a point of view which we shall call here "secular theology." This perspective begins with the assumption that "the transcendent," that otherness from which the new men of the new age have turned their interest is a suspect notion. The solidity, objectivity, and overagainstness of what the church has called God, and/or the network of relations he sustains with his world, are put in question. The secular theologian, therefore, seeks to state the meaning of Christian faith without reference to the transcendent, a dimension which he feels is a barrier to communication with modern man and which he himself finds to be unbelievable.

But there is an even deeper impulse at the heart of secular theology—a passionate humanism which believes with Feuerbach that the transcendent is a threat to the human enterprise itself. The imperious God "out there" is seen to sap the creativity and energy of men "right here." Hence, the announcement of the divine demise is the proclamation of human freedom.

Secular theology has something to say to us. It is shaking the church awake to the fact of secularization. It is driving us to launch the task of communicating faith in an idiom that is real to the man of the new age. And most of all, its ethical sensitivity has exposed abortive notions of transcendence that have too long held the field.

In its missionary zeal to talk the language of the new day, however, it has crossed a dangerous line not unknown to evangelists of other days. In its eagerness to "go native," it has excised a fundamental motif of Christian faith itself, the motif of otherness suggested by the word "transcendence." It has passed from communication to accommodation.

How is it possible to speak intelligibly to man in our age of secularization as Christians of other generations have talked the language of their day in the going intellectual styles of Logos, or homoousios, or the symbols of feudalism or the law court, without letting these words and concepts "call the shots" for faith itself? What is the genuine wisdom of secular theology that must be incorporated in any new statement of the meaning of transcendence for our time? We examine these questions by looking at three expressions of secular theology, different in many respects (proponents of the latter two often do not wish to be linked with the first), yet bound by common misgivings about the transcendent as it is understood in their area of concern: the new theology, the new morality, and the new forms. In our sketch of the service and disservice of this trinity, the contours of an alternative to secular theology will begin to emerge, what we shall call here, "Eucharistic theology."

The phrase, "the new theology," is, of course, a slippery one used in different ways in our time and other times. By it, we mean the contemporary point of view in the church which seeks to interpret Christian faith without reference to a divine Other. Identifiable proponents—those both vocal and unambiguous about their intentions—include the British lay theologian Wren-Lewis, the European Herbert Braun, and the so-called "death of God" theologians in the United States, William Hamilton, Thomas Altizer, and Paul van Buren. They speak of the elimination of talk of "behind-the-scenes," "occult" reality about which we can know nothing empirically.

They point to healing personal and social events, the validity of which can be established without One who is alleged to be their source, an encounter without an Encounterer.

To appreciate this revolt against classical theism—and its corollary "for man" theme—it must be placed in the setting of the revolutions of our time.

Our world is seeing at an increasing pace the emergence of many sectors of mankind from the period of social, economic, political, and cultural captivity. Currently new nations are fighting their way out of a time of western tutelage. The Negro is breaking out of the prisons in which we have locked him. The poor, overseas and at home, cry to be recognized as human and for the right to have a say in their destiny (note the current poverty programs). The laity in Roman and Protestant communions are coming into their own as free responsible subjects rather than objects manipulated by hierarchies and clericalism. Our own revolutionary era was foreshadowed by the struggle against monarchy, the overthrow of slavery, the fight of women for their citizenship and social rights, and the surge of working men to have some control over their destiny. Already there are hints of tomorrow's struggles: the pressing forward of the growing numbers of aged people whose power is already manifest in the passage of Medicare; the increasing interest in the rights of the prisoner before a police establishment that is under attack in many places; the surge of parent and citizen to be partners in the educational destiny of their children as is seen in the contest with de facto segregation; the struggle of youth to be accorded some voice in their own destiny, be it educational or military; the restlessness of persons before the growth of an omnicompetent state. In short, there is everywhere to be seen the struggle of man to come of age, to be accorded the dignity of speaking his piece, to be recognized as a person. We are seeing the revolt of the V.L.P. (Very Little Persons) against the V.I.P. (Very Important Persons).

The radical theology is an almost predictable ideational phase of this coming of age process. In fact, it may be the "ideology" of revolution, the epiphenomenon of a society which is moving toward maturity. It looks at the transcendent and sees in it the religious expression of tyranny. The word itself has these overtones. Secular theology hears of a Ruler, King, independent, and omnipotent who calls for man's abasement, dependence, and submission. It sees a religious institution which has, in fact, resisted the Galileos, fought the development of human ingenuity, imagination, and science. It looks at the God of faith and sees the Autocrat of the Communion Table, and it concludes that this Deity must go. To preserve the integrity and creativity of man, the secular theology seeks to turn God-lovers into man-lovers, theology into ethics. It must slay its own Dragon who, it believes, has sapped human energies, as the Negro, the woman, the worker, the poor, the laity, and the new nation have downed their tyrants. Hence the battle cry, "God is dead!"

For those who believe in the release of men from old captivities, it is impossible to take issue with this thirst for freedom found in secular theology. The question is, does one have to write God's obituary in order to affirm humanity? To that question we shall turn after canvassing the protests of two other anti-transcendent positions.

The New Morality

The new morality—again a label which is subject to no little confusion, applicable to points of view that run from Hugh Hefner's *Playboy* to J. A. T. Robinson's off-again-on-again contextualism. We shall confine our remarks here to the new morality understood as that perspective on moral life which seeks to eliminate the transcendent referent in the definition of a Christian style of conduct. Joseph Fletcher is a clear representative of this position, a position characterized often as "situationalism."[4]

While not questioning the existence of God, Fletcher takes issue with any conception of Christian ethics which would

[4] For a more detailed analysis and appraisal of current types of the new morality see Gabriel Fackre "The New Morality," *Theology and Life*, Winter, 1965.

"reify" value. This position he terms "intrinsicalist." The intrinsicalist doctrine, he maintains, holds that there is an ethical absolute which stands above, which "transcends" every critical decision-making moment. Thus the intrinsicalist position would assert that it is always wrong to lie, to commit suicide, to violate the ten commandments. While the intrinsicalist might allow that there are occasions when one cannot follow rigorously this absolute (Christians in a World War II underground movement who believed that it was right to lie to the Gestapo to save the life of a refugee), such an act would be considered evil, though the lesser of two evils.

Fletcher denies the existence of any transcendent norm that stands in judgment upon decision making. Nothing is intrinsically evil, since there are no absolute principles, codes, norms, mandates except one—good will or love. Love operates ad hoc, seeking afresh in each new unpredictable situation to discern what action may be the natural expression of the benevolent will. It is bound by no "prefabricated" norms coming from revelation, natural law, etc. Such norms prejudge what love must do in a situation and hence impair the true work of a sensitive benevolence. Fletcher has gained some notoriety recently for applying his thesis to sex morality, asserting, "We cannot dogmatize . . . any sexual act (hetero - homo - auto) engaged in, in or out of marriage will sometimes be good and sometimes be bad depending on the situation . . . Sex for procreation or sex in marriage only is to me warmed over natural law."[5]

What lies in back of the protest of the new morality? The universal plea sounded by its interpreters is for a person-centered compassion. The note is regularly sounded that the old morality is a fiat morality whose heavy-handed legalism destroys the inquiring, seeking spirit of the new age—one who wants to be a partner in the conversation on "why" such a mandate is set forth, one which pleads for the recognition of persons, one which wants explanations and not uninterpreted commands. The new morality points also to the fact that law in itself is no guarantee of love—that in the case of marriage,

[5] Quoted in The Christian Century, Vol. LXXXII, No. 13, March 31, 1965, p. 409.

a person may be defiled within the bonds of marriage by an unloving spouse as seriously as by a breach of that bond. Through it all, the transcendent moral principle, the code handed down from on high, looms for the new moralist as a threat to the fulfillment of person-ennobling love.

Who can deny the power of this criticism against those whom Hefner rightly calls "the hat-pin brigade"? Yet is a codeless love the alternative to a loveless code? To this question we shall return.

New Forms

Under the impetus of the ecumenical movement, renewed biblical studies, contact with Roman Catholic and Eastern Orthodox traditions, the Lundensian theology, patristics, the renaissance of Mercersburg theology, there has been in recent years a fresh appreciation of the singularity of the people of God. We learned to capitalize Church, the Body of Christ, the Bride of Christ, One, Holy, Catholic, and Apostolic. The pedestrian congregation on the corner of Fifth and Main was seen in a new light—it glowed with mystic incandescence.

Then came the blistering criticism of the sixties, criticism of the introverted, self-centered, pietistic, over-institutionalized religious establishment. Allied with it was the birth of a new fighting word, "the world."

Upon closer scrutiny of the church in the light of the new ferment and critique, the light of transcendence dimmed. Further, man looked at the world and saw the dedicated people in the civil rights movement, the peace corps, and the poverty programs. A new formula surfaced: God→world→church which nudged the older one, God→church→world. One group of new formers concluded that this meant Christians must gather in new ways outside the obsolete religious establishment—particularly outside the local congregation—around the places where God was at work making and keeping life human in the world. Other and more radical new formers asserted that the people who lived at these strong and humanizing poles of divine grace in the world themselves constituted the church, regardless of whether they identified themselves as such or not. The old battle cry was "join the church!"—the new one became "join the world!"

In the restatement of the meaning and mission of the church, the word "church" loses its transcendent referent. It is not the community in which God is. It is the community in which man does.

Those who have been caught up in the "for man" movements of our time understand the scathing indictment made by new formers who watched the priests and Levites in a religious establishment pass by on the other side of the wounded of our time—the Negro, the poor, the disinherited. Comprehensible as well are the bitter denials that an unconcerned Christianity is in any sense "the church," for it is entirely possible that modern priests and Levites are going to hell. But is there any biblical warrant for denying the being of the church because of its failure in doing, to deny the freedom of God to be even among the stiff-necked and the wayward?

New theology, new morality, new forms—protests in one vein or another against a transcendent which shackles, dehumanizes, and justifies inauthenticity. Can we too not join with the protesters in reading the burial service over such an enemy?

But is trans-humanity itself a tyrant? That is the question. The answer to it is "no," not the "yonder" that comes to us in Jesus, Emmanuel. To the quest for a meaningful and compelling conceptualization of biblical transcendence we now turn.

Freedom

The conviction that God is a genuine Other with whom one has business to do is born for the Christian in his life within the faith community. The transcendent is not a general abstraction, but a term forced on the believer by his encounter with the Christ he meets in the covenant life together.

The very *otherness of God* rejected by the graveyard theologies is implicit in the freedom which is at the heart of the

Christian message and encounter: the freedom over the judgment which the self knows to be rightly his own, the freedom which is the divine forgiveness, a freedom not bound by the structures and demands of justice. In the Christian's confrontation with the biblical events, he is made aware of the Inexhaustible, the More Than, the Second Mile that goes "beyond" the normal expectancies of one who looks for and deserves the just punishment of the universe on his breach of good faith. In finding this More, he learns the meaning of freedom, and thus the meaning of God. In short, divine transcendence is the free spilling over in-spite-of Care that Christians call God. It is the not-boundedness, the non-captivity, the pressed down, shaken together running-overness of Love.

When we speak of transcendence as Freedom, we are far from the Autocrat so rightly excoriated by the new theology. To affirm that God is free is to say that his will and his presence are freedom. Therefore, where men break out of their prisons, throw off their yokes and down tyrants, there God is, for he is Freedom! The transcendence of God is not a robber of human integrity, but a celebration and encouragement of it! To throw off shackles is to do what God is. Therefore, the emergence of man, the coming of age of the world, the revolutions of citizen, slave, worker, Negro, woman, laity, poor are the work of God himself.

How can one affirm both the free integrity of man and the reality of God? Does not one threaten the other? So an autocratic theology of another day taught with doctrines of predestination which obscured human responsibility. So Feuerbach and latter-day death of God theologians contend as they opt for human responsibility at the price of the reality of the transcendent. Still others speak in terms of a sequential or yoked partnership in which God and man have a go at it together (Cox). We know something about these options from reading the minutes of the last meeting. In the history of Christian thought the church has experienced in other contexts sundry reductionisms—Ebionite or Docetic—and various synergisms and semi-Pelagianisms which in their effort to give half the credit to God and half to man end by giving neither man nor God their due. To honor both the human and the divine, the church learned to speak of Very God and Very Man present in the one Person of Christ, the divine initiative and the human responsibility imbedded in the Pauline exclamation, "It is I, yet not I," and the sacrament that is fully bread and wine yet at one and the same time the vehicle of divine grace. It has chosen the way of *paradox* which in its non-logic makes more sense than the neat logics of all or none, or half and half. Thus, we speak here of the freedom of God which expresses its solidity and vitality in, with and under the freedom of man—the activity of Very God which in no way impairs the creativity of Very man.

For modern man, freedom is no esoteric thing. It is part of the political idiom of our time and found in the mouths of Birchite and SNCC worker, Marxist and democrat. Whatever the meaning the partisan pours into it, the common note is the resistance to slavery. The free man is nobody's captive. Modern man understands and wants that.

In the deep recesses of the private landscape, as well as on public political terrain, modern man also reaches for freedom, to understand and to protect it. He may call it "subjectivity" and analyze it as first awareness, critical reflection, and the drive to understand as Michael Novak has done in his fertile new work, *Belief and Unbelief.* He may worry about its demise as the decision-making center of the self with the emergence of prenatal genetic control and the electrode personality. He knows that the capacity to "stand over," to rise above the creaturely structures and responsibly choose is the heart of his humanity.

The transcendence of God is freedom, no enemy of the human enterprise, no absolute stranger to contemporary idiom.

In passing, it is interesting to note the parallel between the death of God theology and several strands of thought in contemporary human revolutions. The legitimate drive for the emergence of the Negro into participatory democracy may become transformed into black nationalism. The struggle of the worker for his rights may lead some toward the goal of a dictatorship of the proletariat. Thus the effort to emerge develops into a new tyranny with the oppressed seeking to liquidate his oppressor. Proclamation of the "death of God" is simply a theological version of the same megalomania which seeks to turn an old imperialism into a new one. Here there is no talk of God-man partnership or covenant dialogue, but the appearance of monolithic, monological man.

Continuity and Finality

As the commitment to a theological transcendent is born from the life of the faith in the Christian community, so too is the conviction concerning a moral transcendent. What in fact are the biblical mandates concerning human behavior? Are they verbalizations of the Deity himself etched with a jack-hammer into some Cecil B. DeMille-like tablets? Or perhaps they are "eternal forms" in a Platonic heaven? This is the caricature of biblical morality which appears with regularity (fueled by inept fundamentalist interpretations). Biblical morality from the ten commandments to the New Testament conception of marriage is something quite other than this. It is covenant action rooted in God's own covenanting care. Covenant codes are disciplined decision-making continuities, in which one moment is bound to the next by "steadfast love." As God's own love is not erratic, not a passing fancy, so men's love for one another is always firmed by continuing bonds. A code such as that against bearing false witness, and a covenant such as that of marriage, are person-affirming mandates which reflect the kind of faithful love that is in the divine heart itself. They are transcendents in the sense that they are trans-occasional—persisting through a sequence of situations—commitments born from the covenant community's research on what makes and keeps life human. This research has learned something about the finitude and sin that do their work in each situation when not disciplined by continuities. The community knows that there is no such thing as a pure or omniscient reason which reads each fresh situation with a perspective uninfluenced by partial perspective and personal interest. Moral principles are transcendent therefore in that they are not captive to the capricious atomism of situationalism (Paul Ramsey identifies atomistic conceptions of morality as a hangover from the bourgeois individualism of another age), but trans-situational commitments based on the covenant style of the Judeo-Christian tradition.

There is another dimension of moral transcendence that is honored in the Christian community: the eschatological. Christian behavior has as its final norm a horizontal transcendence—a vision of what is yet to be, what lies "out there" ahead at the End. When we say that the beating of swords into ploughshares and the lying down together of the wolf and the lamb is an "absolute" under which every lesser act is judged wanting, we are speaking of a trans-historical affirmation that is part of the story of the mighty acts.

Are not these notions of transcendence foreign to the modern mind? No. Increasingly, for example, in the political community there is a movement from ad hoc to continuity, a realization that over-all *planning* and reflection on the meaning of the good society are crucial factors in metropolitan renewal that ought to replace current piecemeal efforts of reform. This mood is paralleled in student circles these days by the growing feeling that the pragmatism of the Movement must mature in the direction of developing a coherent overview. Continuity, what we have called here covenant, is part of the coin of today's realm.

And eschatology? Eschatological morality is "hope in action," as Hans Margull puts it. Hope is the currency of a new age whether it be found in Martin Luther King's "I have a dream" or the rising expectations of the new nations. To speak to men of the things which are to be is not to speak in a foreign tongue.

Steadfastness and vision, continuity and hope—a trans-situational morality for the new age.

For-His-Own Sakeness

It is no accident that a high doctrine of the church and an honoring of worship tend to go together. So it has been in catholic Christianity whether eastern Christendom, Rome, or

Mercersburg. The reason is the same as the one behind the great opening words of the wedding service, "Compared by St. Paul to the mystical union between Christ and his church." It is interesting to note that in all three—the church understood as the bride of Christ, the liturgy, and the conjugal union—there is a reality men point to with particular awe, describing it in common terms—holy church, holy communion, holy matrimony. In each there is a recognition and celebration of a mystery, an elusive plus which exhausts human conceptualization. The Orthodox have learned to live with this mystery and have developed their own language for it—apophatic or negative theology.

Perhaps the best we can do also is to say what it is not. It is not functionalism. It does not collapse the being of a reality into its doing. It is not the technician mentality. It is not only interested in how something works, and particularly not how something works for me. It is awe before the awesome, adoration before the adorable. It is a belief that there is something that counts for something above and beyond, "transcending" what is available, manageable, productive, useful. Ian Ramsey, the linguistic analyst, comes close to describing it when he compares religion to the relation of two lovers who say to each other, "I love you for a hundred-thousand reasons, but most of all I love you 'cause you're you." Now that will not make much sense to the hard-nosed pragmatist who will take nothing seriously unless it has results. But it will to a man in love. And it will to a worshiper who lifts his heart to God, not because it will make him feel better, or even be better, but simply because God is there to be worshiped, loved and delighted in for his own sake.

New formers who demand that the faith community show its moral credit card before they serve it up with the name "church" do not do justice to this dimension, this being of the church which rests on God's own promised presence, not on man's productivity. The transcendent in the church is God's simple readiness to be with us in spite of our lovelessness. (How he is there, to burn or heal, is another matter, of course—here we are simply speaking of the presence which persists even in the midst of our unfaithfulness.) Here is the church, morally diseased, a company of the uncommitted, no bodies for the battle to make and keep life human, nothing to offer. Nothing to offer, nothing but the One who gives himself in worship so that men may love and praise and enjoy him. One is reminded of Bethlehem and of a God who had nothing to give to the world but himself.

Can modern man make any sense out of this strange talk? Is his answer to our belief in "for-his-own-sakeness" simply "so what," as van Buren puts it? No, for modern man understands something of the reality of for-his-own-sakeness. Consider the love between a husband and a wife. Is the meaning of that relationship exhausted by the functional inter-dependence of these two people? Is the relationship justified so long as it is mutually useful, so long as the wife is a satisfactory child producer, housekeeper, lover, companion, and the husband a good father, provider, romantic, and friend? Let us suppose that the wife is stricken and becomes an invalid, or the husband is incapacitated as a wage earner. Is this cause for separation? A strict functionalism would have to say that it is. But for those who know of a mystical bond into which two people are drawn, such a separation is unthinkable. The service of marriage celebrates and seeks to firm that bond when it speaks about a tie that persists in sickness as well as health, in sorrow as well as joy, in want as well as plenty, "for worse" as well as "for better." Can we say that this has nothing to do with the transcendent bond that is spoken about by men of faith? As the marriage service itself indicates, conjugal love is reflection of the relation of heavenly Bridegroom to Bride. The marital union goes back to the heart of God himself, to the unconditional love that faithfully covenants, that remains steadfast in the midst of the unlovely and unlovable.

The belief in this kind of transcendence not only is understandable to the man of the new age, but crucial for his survival. Again, it is, ironically, precisely the "for man" concern of the new formers that gives the belief in transcendence its peculiar power in the new age. The man of faith trained to believe that reality is not exhausted by its functionality—whether that reality be the universe, the church, or another person—will look with different eyes on all he sees. Nature will not be merely lumber for buildings, minerals for tool making, water for power, but trees and rocks and sea which are transparent to what Gerard Manley Hopkins calls "the dearest freshness deep down things." And human beings cease to be functions that fit into our designs and ambitions, be they that of totalitarian, racist, or manipulator, and become "Thous" affirmed in their essential humanity.

The anti-transcendents have said an important word. They remind us that the eyes of men are now turned to the human plane. Further, they have underscored the serious misunderstandings possible in our present conceptions of transcendence. What is properly a corrective, however, must be just that—a corrective and not a new gospel which merely accommodates to going notions and sensitivities.

There is another way to greet the new age with joy and yet not be captive to it—to learn from its exhilaration and insights, and yet have something to teach us well as learn, to engage in dialogue rather than revert to our old ecclesiastical monologue or succumb to a new secular monologue. This other way is the way of "Eucharistic theology."

As the Christian Eucharist—the Lord's Supper—is a turning to God in and through the actions and elements of time and space and history, so too Eucharistic theology believes that Deity is met not in some private flight of the alone to the Alone, but through the grubbiness and glory of the time-space world, through the struggle to make and keep life human. As the Eucharist affirms the co-presence of the divine and human—the grace that is in, with, and under the action— so Eucharistic theology welcomes the emergence of man and sees in, with, and under this human struggle the favor and power of God himself. As the Eucharist is a sacrifice of praise and thanksgiving, so too in this time of scientific secularization when man will be able to do many of the things that were formerly thought to be the special province of "religion," Eucharistic theology seeks to move from the lower rungs of petitionary worship directed toward a God who "fills the gaps," to the higher rungs of adoration and thanksgiving to a God who is present in the human and secular work of scientist, doctor, psychiatrist, revolutionary, and statesman. As the Eucharist is a family meal, so too Eucharistic theology affirms the primacy of covenant continuities in moral style rather than the discontinuities of a bourgeois individualism. As the Eucharist is the foretaste of the heavenly banquet, so too Eucharistic theology never rests uncritically with the status quo for it is lured by the divine discontent of faith's final vision. As the Eucharist climaxes with the communion of the human I and the divine Thou, so too Eucharistic theology affirms the reality of a transcendent God who does not have to be justified by his usefulness to us, by Gospel song or reformer, but is simply to be adored for who he is, a Eucharistic theology which has learned to love God for God's sake alone, and therefore, has also learned to love man for his.

Veni, Creator Spiritus:
The Doctrine of the Holy Spirit

Albert C. Outler

All too rarely does one encounter a theologian who can convey serious ideas with verve and wit. Albert C. Outler is such a theologian—even when he is tackling the difficult, often-avoided subject of pneumatology, or the doctrine of the Holy Spirit. Relating divine mystery to human mystery, Dr. Outler advances the view that it is spirit which accounts for man's uniqueness, and while rejecting mystical and magical interpretations of spirit, he is also critical—indeed, scornful— of contemporary theologians who advocate the desacralization of culture. "Life in the Spirit is as worldly as being human is being worldly. But life in the Spirit is the only valid mode of being truly human, since other forms of 'worldliness' are self-defeating deviations." A noted ecumenist, Dr. Outler was a delegated Methodist observer at all four sessions of the Second Vatican Council. He teaches at Southern Methodist University's Perkins School of Theology, and his article —initially a Peyton Lecture at Perkins—was published in the *Perkins School of Theology Journal* (Spring 1966).*

MY ASSIGNMENT in these lectures is to speak of God the Holy Spirit—"the Lord and Giver of Life, who proceedeth from the Father . . . , who with the Father and the Son together is worshipped and glorified, who spoke by the prophets," who formed the church at Pentecost, and who has been her resident governor ever since. The likeliest place to begin, I think, is by noticing the strange reticence and ambiguity of the traditional teaching about the Spirit, both in the Scriptures and in the church tradition. Despite heroic

* Southern Methodist University, Dallas, Texas. 75222.

hermeneutical efforts by recent exegetes, the biblical notions of pneumatology are far from simple and clear. The creeds of the early church are almost cryptic. The earliest form of the Apostles' Creed has merely the bare phrase "and in Holy Spirit" for its lame conclusion—and there is nothing more ample in the Eastern Creeds until the pneumatomachian controversies of the last half of the fourth century. The bibliography of important literature in pneumatology is downright skimpy; we have no "classics" here to compare with those in theology proper, in Christology or Christian ethics. Orthodoxy has tended to subordinate pneumatology to the doctrine of the church—since the notion of the radical freedom of the Spirit tends to dissolve fixed patterns of church order and ecclesiastical discipline. At the other extreme, the pentecostalists and the pietists—in their typical stress on the personal and emotional effects of life in the Spirit—tend toward what Wesley called "enthusiasm properly so-called . . .: a religious madness arising from some falsely imagined influence or inspiration of God"[1]—or as Luther said scornfully of the Saxon *Schwärmer:* "They pretend to have swallowed the Holy Ghost [symbolized by the *dove*], feathers and all!"

What this adds up to is that the doctrine has been and remains unstable—and this has been more often complained of than remedied. Methodists are particularly apt to descant on the importance of a doctrine of the Spirit or to call for improvements on the general view. There has not been much to show for all our agitation, however, and so we continue confused, but cozily convinced that *if* we and others had an adequate pneumatology, all other things theological would be added to us as well.

At least two reasons might be suggested for this unsatisfactory state of affairs. The first, of course, is the inherent ambiguity of all talk about God as Spirit—which is to say, any human language about the living God as present and efferent in human existence and history. For weal or woe, human language is designed to deal literally with finite entities and

[1] *Works*, V, "The Nature of Enthusiasm," Sec. 12, p. 470.

their relations—only these and nothing more. God, if he is real at all, is infinite and ineffable. In liturgy, readily and naturally, we speak to God and to each other of God. This is what we mean by liturgy. But it also means that liturgical language is not literal and is not meant to be. The language of theology is not meant to be literal, either, but it does pretend to be *clear*. And there is where we regularly have our troubles, finding the way between a *false* clarity, on the one extreme, and a *genuine* obscurantism, on the other. In pneumatology we are concerned with God's personal presence in our midst; hence, nonliturgical language is bound to be as awkward as it is necessary—if we are to avoid mere pious muddle. But this makes for inhibitions on easy talk about pneumatology.

A second reason why pneumatology is a low priority topic in classical theology is that it is the most easily abused of all the great Christian doctrines—by one or another of our human passions to domesticate the divine or to become divine ourselves. Mysticism and wonder-working are antithetical expressions of the very same basic idolatry; and yet they are very hard to avoid, in one degree or another, in the discussion of the Spirit "in the heart" or "in the world."

One assumes that, in this audience, it is a commonplace that the root soil of all religion, high and low, is *animism:* the primitive and generalized awareness of some sort of an all-encompassing, all-suffusing mystery as the matrix of existence. The world of the primitives is peopled by ghosts (good, bad and wayward); pervaded by all sorts of "spiritual" forces which are, by definition, "supernatural." In such a world, a man's proper life-purpose is to make his peace with the spooks and to exploit their well-known susceptibilities to blandishment. This way lies superstition and magic; and from this common magma of wishful thinking both religion and science have developed: religion as what man can do with the "supernatural," science with what he can do with "nature." Conceived in these terms, however, the relation between science and religion falls into a desperate disjunction—with religion presiding over a shrinking domain of the ghostly and the ghastly, while science goes on from strength to strength, subduing nature and enlarging its boundaries to coincide with the cosmos. There is at least one clue, however, that suggests that any such disjunction is false. For all its success, science has not dispelled our sensitivity to the encompassing mystery of existence: life and thought still begin and end in wonder. Modern man is still haunted, even after he has renamed and reclassified his ghosts. We are still driven in our search for a ground that can bear the weight of being. In this process, though, there has been an all too easy disavowal of the supernatural as an omnipresent dimension in all that is truly human —partly because we've infinitized nature and partly because we've settled for a disjunction between nature and the supernatural—leaving the latter to "the ghost riders in the sky."

It was one of the chief virtues of biblical religion that it turned man's primitive animism upside down—by the recognition that the sovereign creator is ethically involved in his creation but not bound by it; that the Creator Spirit is omnipresent and immanent but on no account amenable to human management, that spooks and people are all and equally creatures—and all created *de nihilo*. It is precisely this denial of the final autonomy of both matter *and* spirit that is the special genius of ethical monotheism.

For all their variety, the notions of God's Spirit in the Old Testament, the Rabbinic writings and the New Testament have a common central theme: the Spirit is God himself at work in *human* affairs—present, active, and yet immune to human manipulations. This understanding is the death knell of superstition. The deepest chasm in biblical *pneumatology* lies between the unfaithful man's idolatrous efforts to harness and exploit the power of the Spirit and the faithful man's grateful reception and use of the gifts and fruits of the Spirit in the faith that works by love. The deepest chasm in biblical *anthropology* lies between all spirit-flesh dualisms, on the one hand, and the concept of *imago Dei,* on the other: man as a special project in creation, an integer of inspirited flesh and enfleshed spirit, neither by itself nor on its own.

Generally speaking, the Holy Spirit in the New Testament

is God at work in human hearts, in the midst of the church and in the crises of history, making real in human experience the self-manifestations of the divine mystery—in the Torah, in the Christ and in the Church. William Temple used to speak of "the immanence of the transcendent," but the Holy Spirit is never a whit less transcendent when most foully immanent, no more easily exploited because he is "closer to us than breathing, nearer than hands and feet." Always his domain is the *human* and the *communal*—which is to say, *history*. His unique office and ministry is the realization of the effects of the grace of our Lord Jesus Christ in the hearts and lives of men. Specifically, for Paul, the Spirit is the agent of the new creation in Christ; for John, he is the Spirit of Truth, our divine safeguard against our natural propensity to self-deception.

The doctrine of the Trinity, as it evolved through the centuries, followed the typical course of a theory expanding to meet the confusing pressures of Christian experience and heretical deviation, within the Church and without—but never by more than enough to defend, conceptually, the gist of what was intended by the language of the liturgy. The heart of the matter, for the patristic Christians, was their conviction that since Pentecost, the Holy Spirit has been the resident governor of the Church, inspiring her in her mission, validating her ministries and sacraments, leading her into a fuller awareness of the significance of her origin in the Incarnation and her destiny in the Parousia. Such a ministry was surely the work of the living God, and so, eventually, the Holy Spirit had to be affirmed as sharing equally with the Son in the divine mystery—the third so-called "person" of (not *in*) the Blessed Trinity. Even so, there has always been an ambiguity in Christian teaching between the Holy Spirit as a separate hypostasis and the Holy Spirit as a modality of the Father and/or the Son. This is reflected in the tortuous differentiations, in classical theology, between the generation of the Son from the Father and the procession of the Spirit—and the clumsy, and mildly heterodox, addition of the *filioque* to the Latin Creed. In every case, the basic patristic theme

is the same as the biblical one: the Spirit is God creating
and fulfilling the human possibility, investing men with their
true identities and assisting them in the knowledge of faith.
The Spirit does not reveal himself as such (John 16:13);
rather, he leads us into the truth that is in Christ Jesus and
ingrafts us into the mystical body. Thus the Church lives by
the power of the Holy Spirit, since faith has no knowledge
of God in Christ save in the Spirit. This is the point to that
hymn of the Wesleys that we sang a moment ago:

> Spirit of faith, come down,
> Reveal the things of God;
> And make to us the Godhead known,
> And witness with the blood.

> No man can truly say
> That Jesus is the Lord,
> Unless Thou take the veil away,
> And breathe the living word.

The doctrine of the Trinity means that the living God is
utterly transcendent and, as such, unknown and unknowable
—absconded, *ab-sent*—utterly beyond the reach of any of our
defining notions or any of our confining desires. And yet, it
is this utterly transcendent God who became utterly immanent
in a man of His own choosing in our time and space—Jesus
of Nazareth: Lord, Savior, Son of God. But this event is not
fully open to historical inquiry as such (as demonstrated in
the spectacular confusions of the old and the new quests for
the historical Jesus). Neither is it patient of metaphysical
constructions as such (witness the contortions of Christological speculation, old and new). But both before and after the
Incarnation the Wholly Other was also actually present in
history and amongst his people—the constant dynamic ground
of all reality and process, apart from whom no thing nor even
any possibility exists: the eternal Spirit in whom we literally
live and move and have our personal identities. God is beyond
conceptual definition, beyond our finite knowledge, having
no assignable locus in time, space or causality. Nothing in our
experience is more positive than our certainty of his encompassing reality; nothing more negative than our competence

to specify his existence as a logical object. The knowledge of faith is not some special or privileged access to some arcane order, vouchsafed to some, withheld from others. It is, rather, our apophatic awareness of the dynamic presence of the divine mystery within our existence—in *all* of our existence—and *the sacral character of the world because of God's presence in it.* On principle at least, we can explain all the causal processes that we know without any reference to God's efference. But since we are ourselves captives of the causal process, we try to locate God—in it or at its beginning and end—and we find it easy to construe God's absence from it as proof of his unreality. If God exists, so the syllogism runs, he exists as thus and such. But he does not exist as thus and such (and this includes any logically specifiable "thus and such" you can name). Therefore, he does not exist. It seems so simple, so final—and so devastating to *conventional* religious belief (as indeed it is!). But it is also simple-minded and desperately irreligious.

The current hullabaloo about the death of God is, of course, largely an affair of religious journalism (with some of the journalists writing for the newspapers and *The New Yorker,* others teaching in seminaries and such). Its protagonists are men bored to the point of recklessness with the patent pretensions of popular religious faith and practice; they are half-educated in the history of the *via negativa* and apophatic theology; and they all seem to have the journalist's typical taste for violence and excitement. Just two weeks ago, I was visiting with an old friend of mine—a distinguished professor of English who has often chided me about the way theologians play games with words. He had just read Ved Mehta's articles in *The New Yorker* about the new theologians. "Now," said he, "we must be approaching the acme of privileged communication. Bonhoeffer rejects religion in favor of Christianity and is reputed to have been a saint, Cox extols the secular city in the interest of the Kingdom of God and Altizer celebrates the death of God by professing faith in Christ. It's all a rather bad imitation of *Alice in Wonderland,* what?"

Then there was also the story that Father Frank Murphy

told me about himself. He is, incidentally, the man who is all, or part, of Xavier Rynne but, more importantly, perhaps, he is an eminent patrologist, a professor at the Gregoriana, a *peritus* of the Vatican Council, and a vigorous "new breed" theologian. The previous day he had met his old and beloved theology professor, Father Francis J. Connell—also a Council *peritus*, an emerited professor of Catholic University, and a very staunch conservative. In their conversation they had agreed to disagree about something or other, but Father Connell had had the parting shot: "Frank," said he, "the reason you've latched onto this new theology is that you would never take the pains to learn the old one!"

On the other hand, it is startlingly clear that these self-appointed morticians to the Almighty have squeezed an aching boil of over-belief and misbelief in many a churchman's mind that was worse than it looked. They have thereby brought us smack up against the climax of the drama of modern atheism. For if the reality of God depends upon his demonstrable existence in space, time, and causality as a definable object of experience and thought, then the atheists have got us (and have had us all along). But if *this* is what the brouhaha amounts to, then it is—and always has been—quite fatuous to speak of God at all, dead or alive. Not even in the secular city is there much of a future for the First Church of Christ, Atheist!

It is as if these men had finally lost their fears and hopes of the spooks, had finally gotten free of their ghostly father-figures (which they had mistaken for God), and had finally come to realize that man is really on his own in this world—the maker and the victim of his own history and culture. And since animism, in one of its versions or another, has always been more popular in our churches than the biblical faith, the rumor that the Head Spook has "bought it" was nicely calculated to shake up the weaker brethren.

By the same token, however, it is useless to counter the report of God's death with a simple denial, buttressed by the claim that we've just been talking to Him on the cosmic intercom. Such sentences as "God is dead," "God is alive,"

"God wears a beard and contact lenses" all allege more by way of logical specification than any classical theist ever supposed he was entitled to. It is not merely that such statements are incurably ambiguous—that would go for even valid religious statements. The peculiar fault of this particular sort of language is that it's *useless:* it cannot be verified or disverified, it doesn't make good poetry or liturgy, and it lacks the lilt of really imaginative nonsense:

> 'Twas brillig and the slithy toves
> Did gyre and gimbel in the wabe.

But if it is unfruitful to refute these "Christian atheists" on their own terms, it is also unedifying to yell at them in panic (like that man in the headache ad)—unless, perchance, you, too, still are an animist, after all.

It is more helpful to notice that in all the different types of religious skepticism in our time—from real titans like Heidegger and Bultmann to our current crop of pygmies— there is not the slightest tremor of suspicion about the reality of the human self nor about the self-evidence of valid *self-*understanding. Indeed, human self-awareness is their obvious substitute for a fading certainty about God. "Man is all we know on earth and all we need to know." As the spooks slink back, their enchantments broken, secular man shakes off his awe of heaven and celebrates his own divinity. The *civitas Dei* descends to earth and is ensconced in our megalopolitan jungles where man is left to suppose that he can live by what he is and what he knows and what he can make of himself.

This is actually quite remarkable. For if the divine mystery is thus to be relegated, it is at least as certain that the human mystery will have to go, too. Elsewhere, I have summarized the evidence from contemporary psychedelics to the effect that, if you apply the same epistemological canons to the human self that our religious skeptics have to God, it turns out to be a fiction, quite literally—a non-identifiable function of the biological processes and of alterations in the organism's blood chemistry. The point to any such *reductio ad absurdum* is to suggest that the perspective of the whole analysis is cock-eyed and needs rather fundamental recasting. By any account of contemporary psychotherapy the human self is an inexplicable *proprium*, in nature but not wholly of it, with the problem of its source and sustenance unsolved by psychological analysis. And, if existence applies only to entities that have location and causal explanations, then the human self exists no more, nor less, than God.

Men may, mistakenly, apply this nihilistic mode of reasoning to God, but they cannot go and do likewise with themselves even if they are so minded. Human self-transcendence is a marvel, but one feat it cannot bring off is the self-conscious awareness of the unreality of self-consciousness. Augustine, Descartes, Heidegger, all had a heave at that and gave it up. It may be a jest of God, this lunatic eventuality: that the conclusion of rigorous skepticism is the unreality of the skeptic—who is, however, unable to draw any such conclusion. And yet the man who can pretend to such a conclusion cannot affirm it nor can he affirm its consequent, not even by self-rejection or suicide. The alternatives: chaos (which is in fact what modern man has opted for) or else a radically different concept of the self and its ground—one that recognizes in the human self a fit analog of that radical mystery that environs and pervades our existence in all its dimensions and occasions.

Our true identity comes from our self-participation in the processes of nature pervaded by that truly encompassing mystery which sustains us in all our ventures, in order and disorder. All the various ways in which the human self transcends the energy systems of which it is composed point to an ultimate reference quite beyond the sum of these energy systems. This would suggest that each human spirit is a project of God, a chosen and unique creation with an invested identity which is part of the intent and purpose of the *Creator Spiritus*. It is God's personal love of each person which defines his specifically human possibility, it is God's grace in Jesus Christ that creates the context of each man's self-realization, it is life in the spirit that guides and guards our growth in grace.

And so our reflections on the Spirit and the human self have turned out as an anthropological mode of the cosmo-teleological way of being aware of God. God the Holy Spirit is that without which no self-conceiving self can be conceived or be realized. Our consciousness of God is no more credulous than our consciousness of self. It is, indeed, its ground. The obvious difference—that one's self seems to be inside one's skin whereas the divine mystery seems to be outside—is merely an illusion, for the mystery within is surely a function of the mystery without. It would, therefore, appear that the self and its ground are in real and quite specific communion. Insofar as he is *human,* man is a finite spirit (a perduring identity that orders and disorders "body" and "soul" and "history")—not a spook nor a blob of animated matter, but "living soul," "son of God," *imago Dei.*

It is in this direction that we should look for an adequate account of what it means to be truly *human*—kin to both the beasts and angels but neither beast nor angel really. It is, I think, significant that psychologists and anthropologists have never solved the question of man's uniqueness—and this because it is not a problem but a mystery. Thumb-forefinger opposition, cranial expansion, cortical elaboration, linguistic capacities, psychological mastery of some of the biological processes, complexity of reflex-conditioning, the making of cultures: these and similar notions illuminate the human condition, but none of them really differentiates us from the rest of animate nature, save in degree along the biological continuum. What really is uniquely human, however, is *spirit.* This does not mean that man is a spook or that ecstasy is the apex of experience. Rather it means that selves are more—both in themselves and in their interpersonal relations—than "objects" or "subjects."

The man who has helped me here more than any other (once I got past my prejudice in favor of myself as a local-ized entity) is the greatest of contemporary Roman Catholic theologians—Bernard F. J. Lonergan, whose essay in epis-temology, *Insight: A Study of Human Understanding,* is a landmark in religious philosophy. This is neither the time nor the place to expound 748 pages, in small print, of tight-packed argument that is cast in a quite different mood and mindset from those we are accustomed to. All I can do here and now is to point to the notion—developed by Lonergan into a metaphysics—that *insight* is a unique function of the *human* spirit, that it is ontically prior to understanding and judgment, that it is spontaneous and stochastic and yet also the very stuff of rationality, that its effects may be known but not its ground. Insight is a *human* activity—but this is also to say that it is an affair of the Spirit, of our own finite spirits in interaction with their Creator Spirit.

But to be human is also to be "spiritual" in many divers ways and I cannot tarry now to count them. One will have to do for a sample. Man is uniquely human in his patterns of community and in his experiences of *worship*. We are, of course, political animals, gregarious mammals—and our societies have ample analogs in the herds and hives of our 4-legged and 6-winged cousins. But there is such a thing as human community that is unique in nature, that is crucial for the emergence and maturation of persons, that is uniquely *spiritual*. We participate in it, but it is beyond our powers of origination *and* consummation. To be human is to be social and to be social is to be *spiritual*. Men live by the company they keep, but the quality of their communities is never the sum of their gregariousness and mutual self-interest. This is why we congregate and covenant in religious communities, as a recognition of the basically spiritual character of our lives alone and of our lives together. For this, the church is the archetype—and it is no accident that, in the Christian tradition, the Holy Spirit is always uniquely related to the church. But then neither is it an accident that there is an elemental cleavage—often in the same community—between the notion that the Spirit belongs to the Church and that the Church belongs to the Spirit. In any case, it is the proper ministry of the Spirit to edify the Church—to build it into "a royal priesthood, a dedicated nation, a people claimed by God for his own." And the Church lives and is renewed in its life and mission by the Spirit.

My suggestion all along has been that the fatal flaw in animism is not that there are no spirits—we all are spirits—but that the animist misconceives the spiritual as something spooky and un-natural and so misconstrues the "supernatural" as the antithesis to nature. This is why I think that our secular city boys, with their demands for the desacralization of culture (which means purging it of all spiritual concerns), are actually lapsed animists who want to save *us* from the *false* spirituality from which they have just been rescued. But the whole point to Christian living is that we become fully spiritual as we become fully human, fully human as we become truly spiritual. Holiness, therefore, is humanity raised to its highest power *by the Holy Spirit,* since man-centered efforts at self-improvement are notoriously fatuous. Obviously, the locus for all this is this *saeculum,* for this is the locus where we have been set and in which God is working his purpose out.

To be spiritual is, then, to be human in this world and in our human condition. This is far from commonplace, however, nor is it purged of the mystery that we thought the spooks would take with them when we sent them packing. The most fully secularized people I know are men still capable of awe and ecstasy, of exaltation and of shuddering at the edge of the abyss, of glimpses of the sublime and of moments of disinterested love—which is to say, *worship.* This is natural enough, and yet also "supernatural"—for worship is the apex of the experience of being human, even for my desacralized neighbor. In worship, we get both the feel and the notion of what it means to be in the world but not fully of it, in worship we realize the sacramental character of all of life—viz., that the whole of it is suffused by the outward and visible signs of the inward and invisible Spirit. In worship we renew our true identities by a fresh recognition of their grounding in grace.

But man-centered, man-directed worship is naturally idolatrous, as Calvin told us long ago on the authority of St. Paul. Valid worship is an enduement of the Spirit, just as faith is and just as selfhood itself—*all* are gifts of the Spirit. "We do not even know how we ought to pray but through our inarticulate groans the Spirit himself is pleading for us and

God who searches our inmost being knows what the Spirit means, because he pleads for God's own people in God's own way; and in everything, as we know, he cooperates for good with those who love God" (Rom. 8:26–28, NEB).

Thus, the power to be human is the power to be spiritual and vice versa, and the energy for either is from the Holy Spirit who is God at work in us actualizing the possibilities he has already created for us. The way to holiness—to the wholeness of God's design for us—is life in the Spirit, which is neither mystical nor magical but the life of love in and for the human creation which is the Holy Spirit's special domain. Life in the Spirit is as worldly as being human is being worldly. But life in the Spirit is the only valid mode of being truly human, since other forms of "worldliness" are self-defeating deviations. Life in the Spirit is life defined by Christ, redeemed by Christ, in the body of Christ, for the only safeguard against the human corruptions of the spiritual is the revelation of God in Christ, whereby we come to know and trust God's free unbounded love, and to accept ourselves as nothing apart from that love.

Life in the Spirit is the life of prayer, of worship, of devotion, of withdrawal and recollection—"the life of God in the soul of man," to quote a favorite slogan of John Wesley's. But the life of prayer is not to be identified by ethereal feelings and pious exercises. It is, rather, the venture of sustained attention to the Spirit within, above, beyond. It is one's withdrawal from the distractions and distortions of life in order to test the inner witness of the Spirit "that we are God's children and, if children, then heirs—God's heirs and Christ's fellow-heirs" (Rom. 8–17).

But life in the Spirit is, above all, the habitude of God-consciousness—the settled disposition to rest the weight of our being in the upholding buoyancy of God's grace—not without the anxieties, pains, and travail of an agonized existence in a tragic world, but with a steadying sense that it is all of grace, that both life and death are gifts of God, that He means to redeem them for us, that none of our labors is ever in vain in the Lord and that they all *are* in the Lord, one way and another. Thus, holiness and humanity are nearer being twins than the animists had thought. The communion of saints is both here and hereafter. The gifts of the Spirit are for us to receive in gratitude just as the fruits of the Spirit are for us to cultivate in faith and hope and love.

> Go not, my soul, in search of Him,
>   Thou wilt not find Him there,
> Neither in depths of shadow dim,
>   Nor heights of upper air.
>
> For not in far-off realms of space
>   The Spirit hath His throne;
> In every heart He findeth place,
>   And waiteth to be known.
>
> Thou answereth alone to thought,
>   And soul with soul hath kin;
> The outward God he findeth not,
>   Who finds not God within.
>
> And if the vision come to thee
>   Revealed by inward sign,
> Earth will be full of Deity,
>   And with His glory shine.
>
> Thou shalt not want for company,
>   Nor pitch thy tent alone;
> The indwelling God will go with thee,
>   And show thee of His own.
>
> O gift of gifts! O grace of grace,
>   That God should condescend
> To make thy heart His dwelling-place
>   And be thy daily Friend!
>   *The Methodist Hymn Book,* No. 281

Problems of a Protestant Spirituality

John Kent

Contending that "post-metaphysical piety has relaxed too much in its aspiration towards both God and holiness," British Methodist John Kent, lecturer in Ecclesiastical History and Doctrine at the University of Bristol, finds the present time woefully lacking in suitable models for the Christian life— a time when the relationship between social activism and spiritual discipline is seldom alluded to, much less attended to. While monastic asceticism clearly is no answer, perhaps, suggests Kent, we have been too quick to equate striving for righteousness with self-righteousness, to relinquish the God-relation in our eagerness to relate to our fellow men. Kent's may be a rather isolated voice among the myriad touters of "holy worldliness"—who, as he points out, generally leave the "holy" part undefined—but all the more reason that he be permitted to address a wider audience. His essay originally appeared in the *London Quarterly and Holborn Review* (January 1966).*

SOREN KIERKEGAARD said that Christianity meant forsaking the world and that Protestantism had lost touch with this aspect of Christianity. With some such statement any serious discussion of spirituality must begin, because it is not spiritual techniques that are all-important—how often one should pray, what one should pray for, what is the value of confession, and so forth—but the end for which the technique is accepted. What is the proper model of the Christian life—this is the question the answer to which determines in advance the choice of spiritual techniques, and it is the unsatisfactory nature of the model—so often accepted very much on trust—which stultifies so much Christian endeavour.

* 25-35 City Road, London, E.C. 1, England.

Kierkegaard defined the Christian category as the absolute relation to the absolute; he even granted a limited approval to the theoretically absolute renunciation of the world practised in the middle ages and in his closing years was inclined to defend the idea of celibacy. He explicitly rejected, however, a revival of monasticism as a solution to the spiritual problems of Protestantism, and here it seems to me that he was right. There is something more than slightly comic in the spectacle of young married ministers who have no intention of putting away their wives haunting the courts of Taizé as a way, one supposes, of sublimating their sense of guilt at not being more completely devoted to God. The sense of guilt is proper—it should be common to all of us—but the solution offered is a dead-end cult. It involved the very assumption that monasticism is spiritually superior to common Christian living, against which Martin Luther protested, saying, "however numerous, sacred and arduous these works may be, in God's sight they are in no way superior to a farmer labouring in his field or a woman working in her house" (cf. *Babylonian Captivity of the Church*).

Monasticism took too literally the idea of absolute mental concentration upon God. Experience showed that enclosure did not make it easier to concentrate absolutely upon God, and the most famous of all monastic reforms was that of Saint Benedict, who in effect partially converted his brethren into farmers and housewives in the hope of saving them from the devils who wait for the victims of accidia. Now if our major problem is how to work out a discipline for groups, a spirituality which will enable Christians more easily to live together and remain Christian—a spirituality of the housing estate rather than of the isolated country house of the member of the professional class who has fled to the country to avoid his social responsibilities—then monasticism once again is less help than the psychiatric workers and sociologists and others who are analysing the nature of small groups, the meaning of group therapy, and so on. The monastic community is too artificial, contains only one sex, has no children, does not relate to the industrial and social patterns of our time. If one wants a significant model in the same basic tradition one should turn to the worker-priests, who have just received a very guarded Papal permission to resume some of their activities in France. I am well aware that the Bishop of Middleton has openly doubted the relevancy of this experiment to English conditions, though before accepting this judgement one should certainly have read both *The Church and Industrial Society*, by Gregor Siefer, and an Anglican manifesto by a group of Englishmen who are trying to apply the worker-priest approach to English industrial life, *Priests and Workers*, by John Rowe. The Anglican group, incidentally, is not vowed to celibacy and has thus avoided one of the pitfalls of the original French movement. The worker-priest is facing the problem—what difference does it make to be a Christian?—in the nakedly secular context of a factory, whereas the monk has constructed an artificial context which permits superficially attractive solutions. The worker-priest approach does attempt to combine the idea of forsaking the world with the deliberate embracing of it in its most typical form of industrial work.

The natural development of Protestantism, however, has transformed Luther's emphasis on the housewife and the farmer into a Christian activism from which the spirituality has often evaporated and to which the idea of forsaking the world seems alien. Spiritual discipline degenerates into little more than ethics, which may mean private good behaviour, such as not stealing, not lying overmuch, and so on. Or it may mean support for more communal, if rather more vaguely defined, good works, such as Christian Stewardship—of which one might hazard the guess that Luther might have called it the Indulgence system of our century. In any event, the links between this activism and spiritual discipline are not thought out; instead, it is usually taken for granted that personal holiness—the aim of the classical discipline—will emerge as a kind of spiritual by-product. A whole case for trusting to one's spiritual luck seems to have grown up around the alleged truism that conscious holiness is impossible. Here is one of the great dead-ends of modern Protestantism, faithfully illustrated every year by many honest Scottish Calvinists and their churches in their attitude to the Edinburgh Festival. It is not what one does that makes one holy; the degree of holiness to which one has already attained largely determines instead how one acts. Christ could afford to trust to his spiritual impulses but his followers cannot. Trusting to luck means that both ministers and laity often live spiritual lives which are dominated by models which they have neither designed nor examined, and which may be completely self-defeating.

One's judgement here depends very much upon how far one feels that Kierkegaard was right in his contention that Christianity means forsaking the world. He was saying in effect that some form of the way of negation is necessary for a personal approach to God, even if poverty and the surrender of one's own will into the keeping of another are no longer very fruitful outworkings of the principle. I imagine that Kierkegaard derived his own interpretation of the way of negation from the Lutheran doctrine of justification, according to which there is at the root of any non-egocentric sort of piety a sense of having died. The dead man posseses nothing except memory, certainly does not possess himself, and so is sharply aware that apparently an existence must derive immediately from the will of God. He should have known this when he was alive, but the fact of his spiritual death brings this knowledge to life and liberates him from the pains of possession, ambition, and time. As long as he lives this borrowed, divinely-sustained existence he pays back what he owes in his love for his family (from which he is at the same time utterly detached, he has obeyed the dominical injunction to love Christ more than father and mother, wife and children), in the faultless discharge of his secular duties (from whose purposes he is again spiritually detached, seeing the irony of their human finiteness), and even having time for a walk in the Deer Park with the children (a human echo of the moment in the Old Testament when in the cool of the evening a God who is almost off duty and who loves his children comes to talk to them in the pleasure-garden). He needs no other set of spiritual techniques because his death and resurrection leave him no option but to fulfil, ghost-like but almost angelically, the will of God which is the underlying substance of his being. Monasticism and secularization have both become meaningless words as far as he is concerned, because they apply to stages which he has survived.

Kierkegaard, of course, was a reactionary, and I doubt whether he knew enough church history—a subject which theologians often rashly despise—to grasp in its entirety the historical context of his impulse to rehabilitate the classical asceticism in some new, nineteenth-century form. He was also a contemporary of the English Oxford Movement; both were expressing a rather similar horror at the apparent second-rateness and complacency of the so-called Christian living which surrounded them. They differed in that the English reformers went much further than did the Dane in reinstituting medieval piety. The Anglo-Catholics achieved much by personality, and more because they knew by instinct how to capitalize the discontent with classical Protestantism which was stirring among the Anglican clergy. But they were not original intellectually, they were content to borrow their spiritual techniques from French Catholic sources, a vice which seems to have become almost inherent in the Church of England. They restored the prestige of the old ideals of poverty, chastity, and obedience, they tried hard to persuade the laity to accept aural confession and spiritual direction, and they set up new Anglican monastic orders which have survived into the present. Nevertheless, the Victorian world suspected that all this was a refusal to think out the nature of the spiritual life in the world which was being produced by the industrial and scientific revolutions, so that in the end the Catholic revival stopped far short of being a national religious movement.

Protestant spirituality lacked an authoritative note in its answer. If the revival of Catholic techniques was a dead end, little more could be said for the Protestant alternatives, in so far as they were alternatives and not half-hearted copies of what was suggested elsewhere. Protestant spirituality had been in difficulties, however, ever since the moment somewhere in the late sixteenth century when it became evident that the new Gospel (and Karl Barth still sometimes calls Romanism "another Gospel") was not producing an increase in Christian efficiency—that old monk was as good (or bad) as the new presbyter. Methodism, about which Kierkegaard probably knew next to nothing, had been the last major Protestant attempt to solve this problem, by bringing holiness (almost as absolutely defined as Kierkegaard would have liked) down to earth, but the London holiness crisis of 1760 convinced some, and the Methodist schisms of 1827–57 convinced those who still doubted, that no lasting solution had been found. The point about Methodism, as has become clearer with the passage of time, was that so far from being raised up to spread scriptural holiness throughout the land, it might be said with more truth to have been raised up in order to show that scriptural holiness could not be spread throughout the land. Wesleyanism was by no means a reaction towards Rome, as Maximin Piette argued in his well-known book, but a tremendous effort to make a case for Protestant spirituality, and it was the comparative failure of the experiment which led to the middle-class repudiation of Evangelicalism which in its turn caused the real reaction towards Rome which would have to be named after Newman, if any individual could be said to have been responsible for what was really the culmination of a process which had lasted at least two hundred years. After Newman's very logical withdrawal into the Church of Rome many Protestants either joined in the Anglo-Catholic redevelopment of sacramental piety, or seemed to lose confidence altogether in spiritual techniques and in the doctrine of justification by faith alone for which Kierkegaard was pleading so powerfully. From this disaster flowed the complacency of the days of the Nonconformist Conscience when sanctity consisted in making others toe a moral line (often a very wavy one), and now, in the aftermath of two global wars, we seem to be re-approaching the kind of spiritual crisis at the height of which Newman attacked the Church of England and Kierkegaard the Church of Denmark.

By this I mean that we are once against dissatisfied with the results of having become Christian, and with the religious experience which is available through the Christian Churches. We are also torn, not very fruitfully, between a knowledge that the scriptures talk about forsaking the world, and also talk about housewives and farmers. We do not know what model of the Christian life to choose. We flit from one to another. We are seduced easily by spiritual headlines. The dead ends emerge very clearly one by one.

There is Taizé, of which enough has already been said. There is sacramental devotion; but the adoration of the Reserved Sacrament and Benediction require an elaborate theological underpinning which most of us as Protestants cannot provide. And sacramental devotion without theological backing becomes self-indulgence, a sophisticated way of believing what one knows is not true. The same will be true of the cult of the Virgin Mary, renewed efforts to popularize which in Protestant circles are inevitable on ecumenical grounds. A dying man still draws a certain relief from swallowing medicine which he knows cannot cure him: for us as Methodists the dead end looms close at hand because we have never depersonalized the Gospel as completely as those who talk so much of the time about "the Church," or who magnify Christ to the point at which he becomes invisible: if our piety has been almost too Christocentric, at least this means that other sources of spiritual support always seem thinner, less necessary to us, than they may to other people.

Perhaps the most pervasive new approach to spirituality is what might be called the belated Bloomsbury element— the tendency to believe that in the post-metaphysical age so cruelly devised by the philosophers, God (if the expression may be momentarily permitted) is to be found, if not very easily identified, in personal relationships, recognized suddenly in personal situations. This might, if it had been taken with the original Edwardian seriousness of high Bloomsbury itself, have caused orgies of self-examination, finely drawn moral analysis, fierce spiritual quarrelling. This would have brought us, oddly enough, close to the classical piety, with its instinct for perpetual self-examination, and to justification by faith, which turns always to God the face of a pardoned sinner. It didn't, however, because the man busy in Church and State, anxious about the recovery of membership and the reconstruction of morality, at work reuniting Methodism and Anglicanism and fighting simultaneously for peace in Viet-Nam becomes too sure that he himself is all right because he is sure that his targets are all right (his targets, of course, are often completely wrong). Or this Bloomsburyish piety ends in the feeling that everything is all right as long as one has personal relationships, and these are sincere, and as long as somewhere in the background lurks the fact that one still wears a clerical collar, still attends a Sunday service, still goes to the Bright Hour, so that in the moment of truth the fact will pop decisively out, that one is a Christian.

One imagines then a man, still haunted by some pietist negations, unhappy about gambling even if reconciled to the occasional glass of wine; a man who is simultaneously determined to make everything religious and to secularize the Gospel, to achieve holy worldliness without ever defining what is meant by "holy" in the famous phrase. This depends partly upon the misleading exegesis of the New Testament idea of holiness which implies that it always means something which is "set apart" for divine use, rather than something which is moving towards perfection. Paul's denunciations of the immoralities of his converts suggest that tradition was not far wrong in suggesting that "saints" ought to be striving for a perfected relationship with God, not just with the problem of communicating the Gospel to industrial man. Christ himself said not only that our righteousness must exceed that of the scribes and pharisees but also that we must be perfect, as our Heavenly Father is perfect. The dead end implicit in the Bloomsbury ideal of spirituality is that it becomes content with an ignorance of God for the sake of a knowledge of people, that it easily substitutes worldly wisdom for Christian insight, that it assumes that converting other people is more important than converting oneself.

This brings us back to the classical ideal, the striking thing about which is that it makes the relationship with God the all-important one, and insists that it must be perfected. In an allegedly post-metaphysical period such a relationship cannot even be described, becomes impossible by definition, or would at least be impossible to define. Hence suspicion falls on all the traditional methods—asceticism, justification-based piety, self-sacrifice, even holy-worldliness itself—because their God-relation has got lost or become obscured, and what remains visible is their human aspect, their slice of the human will to power, their human cruelty and temptation to exploit others, the human rejection even of humanity itself, in celibacy. And so the emphasis falls inevitably on to the relationship with men, and one has the substitution—love your brother, whom you can see, and perhaps you will be loving your invisible Father in Heaven. But this will be concealed from you as long as you remain in the body.

This post-metaphysical piety has relaxed too much in its aspiration towards both God and Holiness. And the real pressure, one suspects, is not so much scientific and philosophical, although this is the kind of expression which its rationalization takes, as social, the colossal pressure of western capitalist society, the strength of which is seen as soon as the build-up of West Indians in Smethwick has passed a certain point, or whenever Mr. Smith's hold on Southern Rhodesia is seriously challenged. One cannot accept the social aspirations and assumptions of western society at the present time and simultaneously accept the classical goal of personal holiness. Forsaking the world does mean something in the twentieth century, but too much of our perfectly genuine piety is aimed at integrating people in a society in which they ought not, spiritually, to become integrated. If what you are praying for is fundamentally wrong it does not matter much whether you pray as a holy worldling, as a monk, as a Central Missioner or as a missionary in that East End of Africa which is the slums of Johannesburg. The problem is not just the choice of a method, a choice between Catholic asceticism and some Protestant variety of the same approach, but a choice between models of the "saint," and the truth seems to be that for the moment we have rejected the classical image but have only Holy Worldliness to put in its place.

Toward a Theology for the New Social Gospel

Max L. Stackhouse

A half-century ago Walter Rauschenbusch called for a systematic theology to sustain and extend the social gospel of which he himself was a principal proponent. Today, when Christians are once again involved in efforts to achieve a more humane society, are responding to a newer social gospel, there is need for an adequate conceptional framework for that gospel. So argues Max L. Stackhouse in an article from the *Andover Newton Quarterly* (March 1966),* a journal published by the seminary at which Dr. Stackhouse is assistant professor of Christian Ethics. The basic question for the needed theology, says Dr. Stackhouse, is, How is Christ historically mediated to the present? "Indeed, a new theology for the social gospel . . . must be primarily a theology of history calling for a new reformation." Then, with a view to how they might help or hinder the development of a social-gospel theology, the author assesses current discussions in theology (e.g., the death-of-God movement), theological ethics, and ecclesiology and polity.

IN 1916 WALTER RAUSCHENBUSCH penned the initial words of what was to become his most famous writing: "We have a social gospel. We need a systematic theology large enough to match it and vital enough to back it."[1] One half century later, we who see Christian involvement in civil rights, poverty programs, housing projects, community organizations, and international affairs as legitimate and central, we

---

* Andover Newton Theological School, 210 Herrick Road, Newton Centre, Massachusetts. 02159.
[1] Walter Rauschenbusch, *A Theology for the Social Gospel* (New York and Nashville: Abingdon Press, 1917), p. 1.

who see the definition, criticism, vindication, and transformation of the *ethos* as a crucial task of Christian theological ethics, and we who have a hope for a more humane society have also a social gospel. We too need a theology capable of sustaining and broadening it. Our social gospel is not a recapitulation of the old one, although it could not have developed without its parent, and although we claim that the earlier movement has too frequently been slandered and, just as frequently, suffered the more ignominious death by dismissal. Yet, it is true, the old social gospel did fail, for it claimed more than it possessed; it spoke of God without sufficiently saying what it meant; it developed a theology of history laden with idealistic conceptions; and it was never able to deal with the charge of "culture Christianity," although it was a protest against other "culture Christianities." The newer social gospel has been duly chastised by subsequent theological movements; it does not make the claims of its predecessor. We do not claim to *have* a message of redemption and sanctification that needs only to be implemented in the social order to be fulfilled. Instead, we have the "good news" that we think we know where the gospel is located in a day when many think it irretrievably lost. And we think we know what some concrete implications of the gospel are, even if we don't *have* it. It is by involvement in, reflection upon, and transformation of the social, political, and economic dilemmas of contemporary history that one comes closest to the whence and whither of human existence, for the Lord of history has been incarnated into that history's possibilities, the values that govern life have been plowed into the furrows of time, and the fundamental convictions of men about the ultimate with which man has to do, positive or negative, have been built into the institutions they have constructed.

We who are proponents of a new social gospel, like Rauschenbusch, need a theology capable of sustaining our inklings, at least until we find out what is valid and invalid in them. We need a conceptual framework upon which to work out our emergent sensitivities and by which we can defend these sensitivities against the premature attacks of the perennial spiritualizers, reductionists, privatizers, and ideological dogmatists of Christianity. We assume, let it be noted, in part what Rauschenbusch assumed: that theologies are constructed as critical, polemical, and expressive tools to build a frame around some segment of experience which is thereby designated as central and becomes the organizing principle for other dimensions of life. A social gospel theology, for example, points toward a reality that is actually at another level of experience than the theology itself—the historical level. We also assume that theologies may be judged valid or invalid in part because of their ethical power in history; that theology is of instrumental, not consummatory, value. Theology, thus, is a necessary but not a self-validating enterprise—one that involves the construction of fundamental conceptual models to allow the identification, interpretation, and actualization of that most significant reality with which all men have to do. In the present situation, however, we have no ready-made models for that toward which the new social gospel wants to point. We can neither transplant the old social gospel (although a renewed and thorough reading may be helpful), nor can we adapt any present theology ready-made. Rather, we, like every theological generation perhaps, need a more subtle combination of recovery, reconstruction, exorcism, and elaboration. And to do this we must engage in an assessment of the theological resources at hand and make some suggestions as to the potential shape of a new theology for our new social gospel.

"Three Debates"

The contemporary debates in theology and theological ethics that have gained the most widespread attention are only partly helpful in providing tools for the construction of a new theology for the social gospel.

The "Death of God" movement is an unavoidable case in point. It may be, as Harvey Cox has suggested, that the Death of God proponents and the defenders of God need each other "like Punch and Judy." It is certainly true that the slapstick scrimmaging between those who shout "God is dead, for I don't experience him" and those who shout "He lives, for I experience him" are of that order, but they offer nothing of substance to the debate, since their arguments are equally vapid.

But the "Death of God" movement is not to be dismissed so easily, in spite of the ways it is sometimes represented or refuted. The spokesmen for the position are raising fundamental issues, in a semi-popular way, that concern more serious theological efforts as well. One of the most crucial issues is the question of the continuity of faith. What kind of continuity do we have with previous believers? Do we believe the same things? Hardly, else theology would have frozen into the recapitulation of implicit faith. The "Protestant Principle" allows no such possibility. Theology must, and indeed frequently does, continue to reformulate explicit faith with candid integrity. But that is part of the problem, for each generation and each geographical area has its distinctive, explicit theological style. How then can there be continuity of faith? Two related possibilities have been widely suggested.

The first sees theology as an outworking of the interior logic of the language of theology. Ironically, the position that is usually engaged polemically in a refutation of developmental theories of history assumes development in theology. Thus, Christianity is seen as a special variety of intellectual history, and it is at the level of the outworking of doctrine or dogma that essential Christianity is grasped. Further, theologizing, the constructive task of the church in each generation, is seen as the projection and filling out of the logic of past ideas through the present toward the future. In this case, Christian intellectual symbol manipulation is seen as the activity that primarily bears the "essentially" Christian continuity of faith. This mode of thinking has not only been part of theology in the twentieth century, but also of much philosophy. In both cases, there has been a frequent and noticeable tendency to shift from engagement with historical problems to a concentration on the ideational level of culture whether that is discussed as dogma, myth, or language games. Significant segments of both Continental theology and British philosophy have tended to engage in the outworking of the internal logic of a given symbol system rather than to struggle with concrete historical and ethical issues, in spite of a few noble stands *against* history that had important historical consequences.

Now, we can explain why they made this shift: we can speak of a loss of moral nerve (in spite of a courageous theological or philosophical audacity) in the face of morally incalculable events, the need to assume an absolute position not relative to historical contingencies of the time for which adequate analytical tools were not available, or we can speak of the need to find a security for the two disciplines at a time when they were threatened by ideological inundation and a revolution in physics that upset the philosophical interpretation of "the nature of things." But such explanations do not show that the efforts are right or wrong. Some contemporary secular theologians, interestingly and deeply influenced by these previous movements, are, it seems, illustrating the frustrations to which their immediate forebears led and are calling for a recovered openness to culture and history as well as asking, indeed praying in an excruciating way, for a new sense of continuity with the Christ and "meaningful language systems" they want to continue to confess.

The second possibility sees not the process of theologizing, but the object of theology as that which alone bears the continuity of Christianity. The eternal is placed over against the temporal in a way that makes any temporal continuity, even theologizing, religion, and ethics, a pretension. This option describes only a succeeding series of discrete moments in human experience, each of which is empty except for the *a priori* character of "the Word," understood as either divine judgment-affirmation, or the divine inducing of existential decision. Our only continuity with Paul, Augustine, Thomas, and all the others is that of analogy. As they were existentially related to the Word, so may we be. As they pointed authentically to the eternal in their day, so we can point to the eternal in ours. Or as they spoke "the Word," a contentless, eternal, decision-inducing, super-historical, function, so must we. We are among the faithful when we speak such a word now. History is not finally informative about either "the Word" or about the ultimate decisions evoked.

The "Death of God" movement in its various forms seems to me to be the result of the above tendencies and a powerful indictment of both options. While it may be that the former option is the easiest to teach and hence will continue to have considerable reputation in the academic centers, and while it may be that the latter is the easiest to preach and hence will ever have its chief defenders among the priesthood who need to invoke sanctity and evoke commitment, the Death of God theologians are forcing us to ask again as to our continuity with our fathers. It is, I think, no accident that one of the initial and primary discussions of the whole problem is William Hamilton's *The New Essence of Christianity,* for there is indeed a quest for a new statement of that core that is continuous with today's past. William Hamilton speaks to the question as posed by the first of the two options by rehearsing the intellectual history of previous "essences of Christianity." From Feuerbach's effort to transform theology into anthropology, to Harnack's attempt to separate the husk from the simple and powerful kernel of the teachings of Jesus, to Schweitzer and Troeltsch and Nygren, Hamilton shows that "neither philosophy nor historical method . . . can give us any theological residuum that we can adopt from the past, without change."[2] Hence, "all our theology, even our essence of Christianity must be done afresh in every generation."[3]

It is ironic that, in showing the relativity of those whom he interprets as having tried to establish an intellectual-historical interpretation of Christianity, he adopts their dilemma. For, as they were seeking for an essential *idea* that needed to be worked out intellectually or conceptually, Hamilton also

---

[2] William Hamilton, *The New Essence of Christianity* (New York: Association Press, 1961), p. 19.
[3] *Ibid.*

wants to preserve a theological or ideational "residuum." He does not ask whether Christianity and the essence of Christianity is "idea" at all, but only whether it is a particular God-idea. He wants to see it as Christ-idea, or rather, a set of christological fragments that suggest an idea-style.

Hamilton is not worried so much about faith understood as trust. Indeed, he says, "faith is, for many of us . . . purely eschatological. It is a kind of trust that one day he will no longer be absent from us. . . . Faith is hope."[4] The problem is faith as the outworking of essential ideas in theologized belief and conceptualization. As the theological revolution of the early twentieth century is usually seen as a response to the poverty of its parents, so might we see the Hamilton branch of "Death of God theology" as the response to the poverty of the first theological alternative.

And Altizer prevents the adoption of the second option. He points out that, in the face of crumbling Christendom, Christianity has tried to establish an unassailable position. "Faith is then declared to be either *a priori* or autonomous. Transcending a historical ground it is open to no human experience whatsoever. . . . Wholly isolated from our history, the word of faith is now silent."[5] And later, he makes the point in an even stronger fashion:

A proclamation of the Incarnate Word can never be simply a negation of history, even if the history which it confronts is a radically profane moment of time. A final no-saying to history is a renunciation of the incarnation, a refusal of the word which has actually become incarnate. . . .[6]

There are, of course, a good number of other themes that continually crop up in the essays and books of the "Death of God" theologians, but again and again they return to the question of historical continuity posed by the late nineteenth century and shouted down, not answered, by the twentieth.

4 *Ibid*, p. 64.
5 Thomas J. J. Altizer, "Creative Negation in Theology," *Christian Century*, Vol. LXXXII, No. 27 (July 27, 1965), p. 864. His formulations here, however, seem directly to contradict the major themes of "Nirvana and the Kingdom of God," *New Theology No. 1* (New York, Macmillan, 1964), ed. M. E. Marty and D. G. Peerman, pp. 150 ff.
6 *Ibid*., pp. 865–66.

Indeed, much of the dilemma is that they are attempting to ask a question in a post-Barthian and post-Bultmannian era when whatever tools theology once had to answer it have been swept aside.

The "Death of God" theologians, thus, represent a dead end of those branches of Christianity that see "essential Christianity" as borne exclusively either by the process of theologizing or by a super-historical object of faith wholly other than anything experienced or known in human history. Yet, they sense, evidently, part of the way out of their dilemma, for they ask as to the historical character of Christ and attempt to suggest styles of Christian obedience. Further, they suggest that we begin a de-eschatologizing of history and propose a historicizing of faith and eschatology. That is, rather than seeing each historical moment as a discrete absolute of finality, as Barth does in making eschatology the eternal that stands over time and breaks it at each juncture, or as Bultmann does in making each decision-moment the eternal now, historical moments become part of a pattern of expectation toward future possibility in which we have some, if cautious, trust.

A second debate that is only partly helpful is the running exchange between the "contextualists" and the "principialists" in theological ethics. Although James Gustafson[7] has shown that the terms "contextualist" and "principialist" each apply to sets of figures whose theological-ethical stances are so different as to make the terms quite imprecise, one can say in general (and only in general) that the disagreement lies between those who, on the one side, see the task of ethics as one which tries to spell out the fundamental guiding rules for moral life in a way that makes them pertinent to new situations and those who, on the other, see rules as a cumbersome legalism to restrict the freedom and honesty of the loving self as it tries to work out a mature and appropriate response to the inevitable uniqueness of every moral situation. The principialists tend to rely upon the "new law of Christ,"

[7] James Gustafson, "Context versus Principles," *New Theology No. 3* (New York, Macmillan, 1966), ed. M. E. Marty and D. G. Peerman, pp. 69 ff.

"the command of Love," the moral function of reason, and/or the rich traditions of natural law theory. The contextualists tend to rely on the perennial Protestant critique of legalism, the radical historical tradition that recognizes the individuality of each event, the inner resources of a dispositional ethical theory, and much of the pragmatic tradition.

The debate between these two perspectives has sometimes been tedious, and even cantankerous. Yet, in spite of efforts to get beyond the dispute, it lives on. James Gustafson, in the article referred to above, not only shows that there are four levels of moral discourse to which a mature ethic must refer (following H. D. Aiken's "Levels of Moral Discourse") and that the principialists speak more flexibly to the context than their detractors admit, while contextualists use hidden principles, but also claims that any systematic ethic must deal with all the four levels of the moral situation. He is, I think, right, and many ethicists on the basis of the article have laid the debate aside.

And the debate might well be over for the radical principialists and the radical contextualists, for the moral experience of man entails more than either historically unaffected norm or totally unguided situation. The absolutists of the authoritarian, though thoroughly "principled," variety are indeed not much help; but no responsible moralist would claim that a principialist must needs be one who applies a principle in exactly the same way in all cases, irrespective of circumstances. Nor are the existentialist contextualists much help, for surely some kinds of factors besides the authenticity of the self in each momentary context come into the play of moral decision-making. Indeed, those few moralists who are on the extremes are only recapitulating, in even less edifying terms, the problems of continuity and discontinuity that the secular theologians point to. Yet, the debate persists.[8]

Is it possible that something is at stake that has not been seen? To say that ethics must, and for the most part does, touch all bases does not seem to mitigate the dispute; for

[8] Cf., for example, Paul Ramsey, "Deeds and Rules," *Scottish Journal of Theology Occasional Papers*, No. 11, and Joseph Fletcher and Herbert Mc-Cabe, "The New Morality," *Commonweal*, Vol. LXXXIII, No. 14 (January 14, 1966), pp. 427–440.

much, much, rests on accents. Perhaps the question is at what level of human historical experience we are to find that which is most real, most capable of providing Christian moral power. To answer that it is at all levels does not seem helpful. Indeed, one may suggest that this dispute takes the question that the "Death of God" theologians are raising one step further. For the principial-contextual protagonists, as ethicists, are all convinced that one of the principal features of "essential" Christianity is its historical character and its ability to suggest "styles" of Christian obedience. Their dispute, then, is not whether historical reality in contrast to ideation or a non-historical object is that which sustains continuity of Christianity. The best theological ethicists of both stripes are interested in man in history for the sake of Christ and the glory of God. But they ask whether creative continuity is to be found by successive definition and re-definition of ethical-legal formulations (for the principialist), or by "responsive" personal engagement in the moral situation and pragmatic calculation of consequences (for the contextualist).

At stake in this dispute, we might suggest, are complex issues. One is a primal perception as to whether the "problem" with history is that it continually threatens to break into chaos and must be ever and again ordered constructively toward righteousness, or whether the "problem" of history is that it has been over-institutionalized and ordered so that new freedoms and creativities cannot break forth. In short, is the creative continuity of history to be found in breaking free from false bondage, or providing frames for organized purpose? A second dimension of the dispute is whether induction or deduction is the proper ethical logic. But we are here accenting a third issue, although a fundamental one that may well call for the development of an analytical ethical method. While the "Death of God" theologians point to (and often illustrate) the emptiness of non-historical interpretations of Christianity, the principialists and contextualists are asking, among other things, as to the level of human historical experience that bears the preconditions and consequences of viable historical Christianity.

Paul Ramsey places this question squarely when he points

out that most "contextualists" seem to find that Love sees "only decisions to be made and acts to be done, never any order or at least no moral order in the world surrounding personal claims."[9]

Yet, he continues, the contextualists, when pressed also admit that the construction and maintenance of a series of moral nets are necessary in society. "Christians are bound to construct a net, to repair the net, but also to criticize and transform it in the direction that love requires. . . . This is one form of rule-agapism."[10]

The question, then, that we wish to extract from the contextualist-principialist debate is: can one establish a particular level within history as the central bearer of the Christian "essence" in history?

The third set of discussions that seems to occupy much of the semi-popular, semi-scholarly discussions of contemporary Christianity is the masochistic self-lashing of the church by those who have learned some sociology. In this movement, perhaps a little past its peak of influence in the seminaries, but not yet in the churches, the historical manifestations of Christianity are assumed to be "essential," and the structural factors are more important in the analysis than the "contextual" response. At least, so it would seem in terms of the methodological assumptions of the sociology of religion. However, after adopting modes of analysis that show the church to be a part of the structural and historical setting in which it occurs, the church and the moral nets it represents are scolded for being "culture Christianity." And, usually quoting H. R. Niebuhr,[11] it is assumed that everybody knows that Christ should only transform culture.

The problems, however, remain. How is Christ present to transform? Is he mediated from a super-historical locus? Is that the realm of religious *a priori*? If he is not mediated but direct, where is he? Are we speaking of a metaphysical spirit? Is Christ a universal *logos*? Then how do historical phe-

9 Paul Ramsey, *op. cit.*, p. 26.
10 *Ibid.*, p. 27 (quoted from Bishop Robinson's *Christian Morals Today*).
11 H. R. Niebuhr, *Christ and Culture* (New York: Harper & Bros., 1951).

nomena that are manifestations of that *logos* become separated from their roots? But these are strange and awkward ways to speak and to think today. Is, then, Christ only Jesus, the man? In what way is that first-century historical person related to contemporary life?

The quasi-sociological critics want, it seems, to see Christ as being borne from the first century to the present by sociologically traceable structural effects, but they draw back for fear of the "Christ of culture" charge. They chastise the church, on the one hand, for its lack of cultural relevance and for not being on the vanguard of every cultural change (as if God only works in history through the conscious intentions of the Board of Deacons), while, on the other hand, they "prophetically" indict the church for not withdrawing sufficiently from the world to establish its peculiar (and hence more real?) faith and identity.

Yet these critics raise a third question that follows on the two previous ones: Can a historical view of Christian continuity ever become more than a sanctification of what is going on in the culture at large?

"Why Important: An Aside"

The three sets of discussions that we have just reviewed may call ultimately for a throwing up of the hands in despair. Indeed, the frequent reaction of many academic theologians is precisely a contemptuous rebuff. But I do not believe that we can do so, so easily. One of the distinguishing marks of most theology, in contrast to, say, some movements in philosophy, is that theology is called upon to speak from academic heights to an institution that is not primarily academic. This can often lead to a drive for a Sunday supplement interpretation of "modern man" and a cheap "relevance" without long-range substance, but it also preserves theology from systematic irrelevance. Christian theologians have a constituency, the church, which demands a recognition of the fact that meaning, goodness, significance, and truth may be best stated by, but they are neither limited to, nor identical with conceptual facility. The questions raised by these discussions are, in a sense, widespread in the church today and could be dealt with if for no other reason than that.

But we might further point out that much of the debate on these three fronts takes on its importance precisely because it is being carried out in a semi-academic and semi-popular way. Whereas theologians of previous generations had two poles to their work, the pulpit and the theological tradition, each informing the other, the level of contemporary preaching has fallen into a state of relative deprivation (for it is, after all, a rather obsolete form of communication), and the level of academic research has become more specialized. Hence, an intervening level of discourse, always present but not always as important, has come to the fore in a new way. This semi-scholarly tractarianism, related both to academic and to the kerygmatic, apologetic and critical tasks of the vital preacher, has captured sizable sections of the paperback book market, church related journals, and, more recently, even the slick commercial magazines. Now, this is not altogether new, for one can see strong precursors in the social gospel movement, the Christian Socialist movement on the Continent, and the historic production of tracts by the sects; but its importance shows every sign of pending and dramatic crescendo. Further, the consensus shaped by this new, slick tractarianism is widely reforming the social and theological sensitivities of Christian pastors. We might therefore suggest that professional theologians no longer have their point of contact with the churches *directly* but only *mediately* through a growing body of middle-level literature (and through middle-level organizations such as conferences, seminars, institutes, and denominational or ecumenical associations where this literature is discussed).

Further, the problems that concern these men are, in fact, crucial for professional theologians as men, whether it is their primary vocational concern or not. It is no small thing that all these movements are dealing in one way or another with the problem of history and that all the persons involved in these various debates, it would appear from their writing, have an intense commitment to efforts for justice, freedom, and renewal that has shaped their theological efforts. They are, I would suggest, pointing toward the new social gospel in significant ways, partly because of their social engagement. The fact that the theological frameworks they employ leave us woefully dissatisfied should not obscure their contributions nor the importance of their level of discourse.

"What Is Required?"

But what, precisely, are the questions, and how can they be phrased in manageable ways? And, most important, how can we begin to deal with them? I say "begin," for it is beyond the scope of this paper and the competence of this writer to finish the task. But due to an irritable impatience with those who tell us what needs to be done without trying to do it, a constructive, if provisional and skeletal, series of options and choices will be made.

The question about a new essence of Christianity, with hints about its Christological and hence its historical character, is almost the right question. There is a dramatic need for Christian thinkers to attain some clarity about that which is peculiar to Christianity, to specify where in the world Christ is. But posing the question in terms of a "new essence" and a "Death of God" vocabulary is not helpful, for the connotations of "essence" are laden with idealistic metaphysics and a tradition that continually draws a distinction between interior and exterior, with anything exterior and formal being unauthentic. The "Death of God" language, further, misdirects the writers and the readers, for it leads them to speak of a kind of emptiness at the level of nonhistorically conditioned experience rather than toward the partial fullness that they want to speak of at the historical level. Their readers, whether enthusiastic anti-religionists, confirmed theists, enterprising journalists or whatever, therefore continually press the questions concerning that about which they cannot speak rather than that about which they can speak. What they want to do (or, at least, their strongest theological move) is to construct a theology that delineates history as the primary locus of revelation and signification.

Yet the "new essence" language is better than the "Death of God" language. A new theology for the new social gospel may well be deeply informed by the "quest for the essence of Christianity," old and new, for it is precisely a quest for some kind of historically borne continuity with Christ.

The essence of Christianity has been placed, displaced, and replaced at several levels of historical experience, as has been shown by Hans Frei's brilliant essay on the theological background of H. R. Niebuhr.[12] The "essence" has been variously conceived as a unifying consciousness that stands behind all particular acts and teaching; a unique and uncaused event, the continuing interpretation and re-interpretation of which forms a chain of continuity; a novel set of interrelated symbols or images that have an interior logic that can be inexhaustibly developed in each historical epoch; a kernel of historically taught truths separable from their cultural husks; or the ideal rules governing the process of historical development itself, cut off from any metaphysical ground. In nearly all cases, the definition of "essence" was deeply influenced by residual idealism.

An effort partially to recapture and partially to reconstruct, for the new social gospel, the centrality of the historical sensitivities that obtain in both the old and the new quests for the essence of Christianity, requires first of all a departure from the notion of essence. But it does not thereby abandon the effort to find an answer to the question of how Christ is historically mediated to the present. Indeed, a new theology for the social gospel, viewing theology as a heuristic framework or model that delineates that which bears the continuity in a way that focuses on creative change, must be primarily a theology of history calling for a new reformation.

Nor must we allow our efforts to be confused by the traditionalist interpretation of the relationship of theology and history. It is not sufficient to make a distinction between "reform" and "reformation," between reform of the moral and institutional life and reformation of doctrine and theology, seeing one as a secular and the other as a sacred task. The new theology must not allow its center to be reduced to moral energy *or* new symbol manipulation. We cannot allow Luther's formulation to stand on this point: "Doctrine and life are to be distinguished. Life is as bad among us as among the papists." "But if doctrine is not reformed, the reform of morals will be in vain, for superstition and fictitious holiness cannot be recognized except by the Word and by faith."[13] While it may well be that we are no better than our Catholic brethren, as we now call them, he has missed the point. The aggressive sectarian tradition that is the root of the social gospel movement, old and new, is frequently confused with populist, humanist, often apocalyptic reform movements in which the reform comes first and for its own sake. But the aggressive sectarian tradition, which the sentiment quoted above helped suppress on the Continent, but which cropped up again in the British semi-Calvinist traditions and which is now recurring in the second generation sectarian churches of the developing countries and in the "conciliar denomination-alism" of the World Council of Churches,[14] moves by quite a different logic. For it says, as do its American counterparts concerned with history and life and the new social gospel, that a right, if partial, theology directs one to the proper locus of meaning and demands an empirical and consequential reform precisely at the historical level so that the promise of seeing in full may become a more immediate reality. Further, reform is not constructed out of man's own resources, but is an integral part of the response to and of grace that is historically mediated. Thus reformation is not mere reform and certainly not mere reformulation, but a thorough reformation

[13] Quoted by G. H. Williams, "Friends of God and Prophets," *Harvard Divinity Bulletin* (October 1965), p. 14, in a discussion of H. Oberman's "Das tridentinische Rechtfertigungsdekret im Licht spätmittelalterlicher Theologie," *Zeitschrift für Theologie und Kirche,* LXI (Tübingen, 1964).
[14] See the four volumes of papers prepared for the 1966 Conference on Church and Society: J. Bennett, ed., *Christian Social Ethics in a Changing World;* Z. K. Matthews, ed., *Responsible Government in a Revolutionary Age;* D. Munby, ed., *Economic Growth in World Perspective;* and E. de Vries, ed., *Man in Community* (Association Press, 1966).

of theology and history. And that integral relation of the two demands a theology of history, a historical theology of history.

The phrase, historical theology of history, demands explanation. It implies a theology, a set of related, formal categories, that points to history and that is itself subject to historical correction. Let us look at each of these terms in more detail.

Theology, as here understood, is a discipline that attempts to set a frame around the center of meaning and righteousness. It requires, thus, some conception of "reality," "Being," or "God." But in view of modern man's inability to know or experience anything much of a super-historical person, it may be that we shall have to utilize one or another of the "natural theologies" or, as I prefer, "apologetic theologies," that attempt to state the formal conceptual and/or functional requirements for speaking of historical experience. There are, it seems, formal categories that are *a priori* required for the interpretation of life and meaning. Not only do mathematical and logical relations seem to have this character, but every people in every culture has a concept of "ought" or "requiredness," and a sense of what is "real" or "final." Even if these formal categories are, as some claim, very deeply rooted *conventions,* and not *a priori* forms at all, the fact that every people requires these conventions points toward a formal boundary that does not seem to be affected by historical events.

A theology for a new social gospel, however, would have to claim that these boundaries are discovered by historical experience and that, further, they serve not as the shape and plot of life, but as a stage whereon the real drama takes place. The same stage is sometimes a ship, sometimes a drawing-room, and sometimes a forest; the historical outworking of conflict and resolution, interacting plots and characterization impute the meaning. Theology must provide proper lighting for the stage (to press the metaphor), not to illumine the stage itself, but to allow the drama to be seen.

History consists of the remembered and interpreted patterns of events that define the present and give rise to expectation.

Various dimensions of the patterns are organized into systems. Thus our focus is upon a dynamic and creative set of interacting "systems," each of which undergoes interior structural change and is involved in a continual series of constellational changes. Among the major "systems" are some that we can delineate: language systems, legal-political systems, educational systems, mores and folk-ways (that amorphous context of pragmatic expectations that pervades every *ethos*), economic-technical systems, and psycho-biological systems.

We come, then, to the question posed in part by the Principialist-Contextualist debate, namely, which level of historical experience is to be accented?

A truly "historical" theology of history for the new social gospel would not be caught designating one "system," or level of experience, as crucial and calling that "the essential one." But, as we have pointed out previously, neither is it sufficient to say they are all important all of the time, for the question of accents is crucial. Rather, we must suggest a shifting point of reference. At some periods of history, it is historically shaped language that bears the burden of recovering, preserving, re-defining, and transforming that which was brought to life in history by Jesus Christ. At other moments, the economic-technical systems bear the crucial values, or the legal-political ones, and sometimes a combination of several, and so forth. It is possible, for example, to say that the shifting of levels by Barth, vis-à-vis the nineteenth century, from an understanding of history that had become highly subjective and interior to a recovery and renovation of an objective language system, was a way of keeping alive the historical influence from Jesus Christ at a time when other levels of experience or "systems" were faltering or actively consumed by an orgy of self-destruction.[15] But that is not to claim that

---

[15] But even the success of this singular language system was partially assured by the military aspects of the political-legal systems of Switzerland and the allies. Hence one must postulate a relationship between particular language and political-legal systems in this period of crisis that is not sufficiently accounted for by the proponents of the Barthian language system. Cf. Reinhold Niebuhr's scatching indictment of Barth and the Barthians on this point. "Karl Barth and Democracy," *Essays in Applied Christianity* (New York, Meridian Books, 1959), pp. 163 ff.

we should stay there, or that one kind of language is the only authentic bearer of Christianity. To say that leads to a linguistic Amishness. Rather, the kind of analysis that leads us to such a suggestion about Barth leads us also to the conclusion that we can never claim that we should always stay in one language system. Not only does the aggressive sectarian position, out of which an historical theology of history grows, force us to other levels, but it drives us to suggest that an exclusive claim by any one "system" or level leads to idolatry. Indeed, the proponents of the new social gospel are now suggesting that it is another level of experience besides a historically conditioned system of "God talk" that now bears the crucial set of influences and to which we must attend if the gospel that we know in part is to be known more fully.

Now, of course, one might ask how are we to know where, among the "systems," one is to find that shifting cipher that gives life to the empty stage? Or how, within a theology of history that points to the dynamic interaction of creative "systems," are we to discern which "system" or set of "systems" is crucial at the moment?

The question calls in part for an empirical answer. By technical analysis of historical data some indications can be found.[16] But the answer can also only be understood through a concept historically related to some sectarian interpretations of "Spirit."

A theology for a new social gospel can only deal with spirit as a historical phenomenon. It does not know what would be referred to if by "spirit" is meant a metaphysical substance. Metaphysical substances do not provide discerning power. They are, if anything, what is supposedly discerned. Nor is it necessary to retreat to subjective interiority. A careful theology for the new social gospel does not want to choose between misplaced objectivity and unreliable subjectivity. It turns instead to the structured *esprit de corps* of those cove-

---

[16] Robert Boguslaw, *The New Utopians* (Englewood: Prentice Hall, 1964), makes some very suggestive remarks to this point in a quite different context, Cf. also my article, "Technical Data and Ethical Norms," *Journal for the Scientific Study of Religion*, Vol. V, No. 2 (Spring 1966), pp. 191–203.

nanting together to discern the signs of the times. It sees participation in the organized body of the committed as crucial. The primary, although by no means exclusive, institutional form of interacting systems that attempts to be that body is the church.

We are led thereby to the question posed by the quasi-sociologists of religion. What is, and what is to be, the role of the church in modern society as it attempts to find and define that which it knows to be enlivening and transforming in history? An absolutely fundamental ingredient of the new theology for our new social gospel, thus, is ecclesiology. The church that is alive is one that re-enacts the unity, linguistic, legal-political, educational, moral, economic and psychological, of the implications of Jesus Christ. It attempts continually to sustain appropriateness of the several systems for each other and for the prospective shape of history as we look to future possibility. Indeed, the church is a meta-historical model of history living in history that attempts to preserve the integrity and transform the sustaining power of all the systems, within itself and for society at large. Marx was right when he said that the criticism and transformation of society begins with the critique of religion. And, we might add, organized religion at that. Thus, the theology for the new social gospel must concentrate on ecclesiological polity and action, the ways in which the systems can be and should be arranged and the things the church can do, so that the effects flowing from Jesus Christ are not stultified and the holy *esprit de corps* is not suppressed. It is the conviction of this writer that the best models for this reconstruction of a historical theology of history, focusing on ecclesiology, may be found in four places: in the "polity" sectarian churches, i.e., those defined by their principle of organization—Presbyterian, Congregational, Baptist, etc., in the church of the emerging countries and the "conciliar denominationalism" referred to above (p. 235), and in the debates about conciliarism, collegiality, and "people of God" of Vatican II.

But more, the church can be, and sometimes prophetically is, the anticipation of the potential transfigured integrity of the interacting "systems" of the future. The conception, borne by the church, of the eschatological Kingdom and the vision, borne also by institutions indirectly influenced by the effects of Christ, of a universal society constitutionally bearing the conditions in its economic, social, and political life that would allow "seeing in full" have ever been important ingredients of theology, but require particular attention in view of much contemporary obscuring of the issues.

Two issues are raised by the preceding suggestions. First, there must be a fresh reading of church history itself, for much church history sees the activity and polity of the church as only secondary. Gabriel Fackre struck precisely the right notes in an address given at the first annual meeting of the United Church of Christ ministers who teach in theological seminaries:

Much present reading views the period of the world's tutelage as a time of priestly imprisonment. The church smothered human creativity, and now when the world comes of age its tyranny is thrown off. While this interpretation does, in fact, describe the priestcraft that resisted the Galileos, it does not do justice to the better sallies of the church onto secular terrain—scouting parties that did not go out to imprison but to release captives, not to wound but to heal and humanize. The hospital, welfare, educational, crusading, justice-seeking and peace-making ministries were in large part efforts of the church to stumble onto the Jericho roads following the secular Christ. Why? In order to "fill in the gaps"—to be the Dutch boy at the dike—yes, let us use the awful words to be a kind of "Deus ex machina," filling a human need for which the secular community had neither the will nor the way. From the care of the prisoner, hungry and aged and the attack on the exposure of female children in the ancient world up to monitoring the Jackson, Mississippi, TV station's segregated programming, the church has pioneered the human task. In its halting, awkward way, the Church, at its best, has moved onto secular turf to fill needs, to bind up wounds. It has been a tutor of the world, a schoolmaster—and to call this tutelage imprisonment, and to demean it, is really quite ludicrous.[17]

[17] Delivered in June, 1965. Part of the address may be found in *The Ministers Quarterly*, Vol. XI, No. 4 (Winter 1965–6), pp. 25 ff.

But, secondly, there is always the haunting issue of "Christ and Culture." The quasi-sociologists frequently draw back from their own suggestions for fear of the charge that they are suggesting a "Christ of Culture." And do we not thereby succumb to a belief in the inability of Christ to transform culture? The new theology must suggest that the dichotomy is a false one (and based, incidentally, on suspect reading of Ritschl, the Christian Socialist movement, and the old Social Gospel). It is not a question of Christ in, or Christ transforming, culture, but a question of the gospel which we do not know precisely, being borne by cultural systems in history and transforming them toward a new, enlivened, just, future possibility—pointing ultimately to an eschatological judgment and vindication of history, a final seeing face to face. The eschaton is the only final point of transcendence for man. Until then, he must operate within the boundaries of, and with the meaningful content of, history, although the opening of the present toward the future provides an opportunity for novelty.

If there is to be an adequate new theology for the new social gospel, then, some of its main outlines are clear. A theology for a new social gospel must not, as some of its predecessors frequently did, cut itself off from resources beyond its immediate environment. The work of philosophical theology at the boundaries of experience remains significant and not mere empty speculation. The attempt to explore and define the nature of historical and conceptual *a priori,* the universal phenomenon of "ought" language in every human culture, and the fundamental boundaries of nature or creation, these all remain highly germane, even if the new social gospel claims that what populates these forms with special meanings and brings them to life is the peculiar set of historical conditions that obtain from Jesus Christ, defined, reenacted, pointed to, and anticipated by the church.

However, in pointing out potential allies, it is possible to suggest that particular fundamental accents must become central today. An adequate theology for the new social gospel must involve a theology of history; it must allow a shifting point of reference in the interaction of historical systems; it must entail a new concentration on ecclesiology and polity; and it must demand an eschatological point of reference. Whether such a theology can be fully constructed in the near future remains a question, but the situation remains as Rauschenbusch defined it. "We have a social gospel. We need a systematic theology large enough to match it and vital enough to back it."

The Death of God and the Future of Theology

Harvey Cox

It is scarcely an exaggeration to say that, with the publication of *The Secular City,* Harvey Cox burst meteorlike upon the theological scene. Indications are, however, that unlike most meteors Cox has staying power. Though an exponent of "secular theology," of Bonhoefferian "religionless religion," he has steered clear of the "God-is-dead" dead-end, while acknowledging the contributions of the death-of-God theologians. Indeed, open-endedness, openness to the future, is for Cox the touchstone of a theology adequate for our time: "The only future that theology has, one might say, is to become the theology of the future." In this essay* Cox tells why he regards two thinkers in particular as formidable aids in the development of such a theology: Pierre Teilhard de Chardin and the lesser known (at least to Americans) Ernst Bloch. An ordained Baptist minister, Dr. Cox is now associate professor of Church and Society at Harvard Divinity School. His other writings include *God's Revolution and Man's Responsibility.*

IN ONE SENSE there is no future for theology in an age of the "Death of God," but in another sense we cannot be certain of this until we know what the phrase means and what the function of theology is. For "Death of God" is sometimes used to mean different things, even by the same writer in a single paragraph. My own investigation has isolated three distinct meanings.

The first is nontheistic or atheistic. As Paul van Buren has said, "Christianity is about man and not about God." For van Buren it is futile to say anything at all about "God," since the word has no viable empirical referent. We must therefore construct some form of theology in which we stop talking about God. Religious devotion and even religious language may remain, but the referents are entirely changed.

Van Buren's methodology is borrowed from the rigorous techniques of British and American philosophical analysis. A very different viewpoint is that of Thomas Altizer, who seems to be informed by certain Buddhist and Hegelian themes that have led him to assert that there once was a transcendent, real God, but that this God became immanent in Jesus and finally died in his crucifixion. In contrast to van Buren, Altizer insists that we must not only use the word "God," but we must make the announcement of his death central to our proclamation today. He is not puzzled by the word; he not only knows what it means but is willing to say more about the history of God than most Christian theologies have said in the past. Furthermore, Altizer insists that "only the Christian can experience the death of God." Experiencing the death of God is, for Altizer, close to what has traditionally been associated with conversion.

The second sense in which the phrase "Death of God" is used occurs in the context of cultural analysis. For Gabriel Vahanian and sometimes William Hamilton, it simply means that the culturally conditioned ways in which people have experienced the holy have become eroded. Religious experience is learned in any culture just as other experience is learned, in the unspoken assumptions and attitudes which children absorb from their parents and from their closest environment. Our forbears learned from their forbears to expect the experience of the holy in socially defined ways, whether in the sunset, in a camp-meeting conversion or in holy communion. This experience was structured by a culture of residual Christendom, still bearing traces of what Paul Tillich calls "theonomy." But the coming of modern technology and massive urbanization shook the structures of traditional society and thereby dissipated the cultural ethos within which the holy had been experienced. Hence the "God" of Christendom is "dead." For most modern writers the phrase is metaphorical, but in a culture strongly influenced by pietism, where the reality of God is identified with the experience of God, the phrase may be taken literally as a somber and threatening event.

The third sense in which "God" is "dead" is one that I discussed in the last chapter of my book *The Secular City*, and it is in some respects similar to both Vahanian's and van Buren's viewpoints. For me, the idea of the "Death of God" represents a crisis in our religious language and symbol structure, which makes the word "God" ambiguous. It is not that the word means nothing to "modern man," as van Buren contends, but that it means so many things to different people that it fuzzes communication rather than facilitating it.

For years the doctrine of God has been in trouble. Paul Tillich, who assailed the very idea that God "is" (in his *Systematic Theology*), would never have settled for an undialectical nontheism, although his attempt to move "beyond theism" (in *The Courage to Be*) probably contributed to the present situation in theology. Karl Barth's christological positivism may also have prepared the way. The "Death of God" movement is an inheritance from them, dramatizing the bankruptcy of the categories we have been trying to use. It is more the symptom of a serious failure in theology than a contribution to the next phase.

Modes of religious experience are, as we have noted, shaped by cultural patterns. When social change jars the patterns, conventional ways of experiencing the holy disappear. When the thickly clotted symbol system of a pre-urban society is replaced by a highly differentiated and individuated urban culture, modalities of religious experience shift. When this happens gradually, over a long span of time, the religious symbols have a chance to become adapted to the new cultural patterns. The experience of the death of the gods, or of God, is a consequence of an abrupt transition which causes the traditional symbols to collapse since they no longer illuminate the shifting social reality.

The "Death of God" syndrome can occur only where the

controlling symbols of the culture have been more or less uncritically fused with the transcendent God. When a civilization collapses and its gods topple, theological speculation can move either toward a God whose being lies beyond culture (Augustine, Barth), toward some form of millenarianism or toward a religious crisis that takes the form of the "Death of God."

In our own period, which is marked by man's historical consciousness reaching out and encompassing everything in sight, the nooks and crannies formerly reserved for the transcendent have all been exposed. Pluralism and radical historicism have become our permanent companions. We know that all doctrines, ideals, institutions, and formulations, whether religious or secular, arise within history and must be understood in terms of their historical milieu. How then do we speak of a God who is somehow present in history, yet whose being is not exhausted by the limits of history? How, in short, do we maintain an affirmation of transcendence within the context of a culture whose mood is relentlessly immanentist? Perhaps a rediscovery of the millenarian tradition, a reappropriation of eschatology, is the way we must go.

The crisis in our doctrine of God is a serious one. This cannot be denied. Nevertheless, our continued and correct insistence on the need to encounter God in *all* of life and not just in a "religious" or cultic precinct fails to express anything that really transcends "history," the source of our experiential reference for what we usually talk about. Some theologians, like Schubert M. Ogden, have responded to the present impasse by going back to the only significant constructive work that has been done in recent decades in American theology—the thought of Charles Hartshorne and Henry Nelson Wieman—and to the philosophy of Alfred North Whitehead. This tactic may eventually produce results, but so far it has not really resolved any of the radical criticisms raised by the "death of God" writers.

My own response to the dead-end signaled by the "death of God" mood is to continue to move away from any spatial symbolization of God and from all forms of metaphysical dualism. I am trying to edge cautiously toward a secular theology, a mode of thinking whose horizon is human history and whose idiom is "political" in the widest Aristotelian sense of that term, i.e. the context in which man becomes fully man.

As I move in this direction, there are certain traps I want to try to avoid. First, though it may be satisfactory for some, I want to steer clear of the mystical-atheistic monism of Thomas Altizer. From the perspective of the science of religion, mysticism, and atheism have always been similar. Both lack the elements of encounter with an "Other," a confrontation that is characteristic of most forms of theism. In Altizer this structural similarity has come to explicit expression. Second, I want to avoid the uncritical empiricism of Paul van Buren. I think his methodological starting point, derived from contemporary British and American linguistic analysis, is too constrictive. It does not take sufficient account of the non-empirical functions of many modes of human speech, the open and changing character of all languages, and the place of any language within a larger universe of symbolic, meta-phorical, and poetic modes of expression. Kenneth Burke, in *The Rhetoric of Religion,* has laid out a type of religious language analysis which does embrace these larger cultural dimensions, thus offering a corrective to the analysts' presuppositions.

Finally, I want to steer clear of the inverse pietism of William Hamilton, whose perceptive analysis of the cultural mood[1] is sometimes confused with the theological task itself. Since he often deduces the mood of the culture from a description of his own moods and beliefs, the basis of his theology is extremely experiential. This may be good, especially in view of the unjustly severe disparaging of "experience" which was so characteristic of the followers of Karl Barth, but theology cannot become experiential in this sense without courting the danger of becoming subjective. Thus, while I can accept his diagnosis of the cultural élan, which is often

---

[1] See his essay "The New Optimism" in Hamilton and Altizer, *Radical Theology and the Death of God* (Indianapolis: Bobbs-Merrill, 1966).

correct, I decline to enlarge it into a properly theological claim.

Let me make it clear that I do not condemn the men I have just named. I do not wish to belittle their contributions. As Gordon Kaufman has suggested, many of us are engaged in different "experiments in thought," pushing ahead to think through the implications of this or that set of premises.[2] This theological diversity is a mark of strength, not of weakness. Let me make it clear, too, that if I regard undialectical religious atheism as too easy a way out, I also find most available "theistic" options equally unattractive. The road ahead often seems narrow, dark, and perilous, yet we can neither retreat nor stand still. The best I can do now is to try to indicate where I hope a breakthrough might be found, to point in the direction I want to go, not to a spot where I have arrived.

For me, the way out of the "death of God" miasma which leads forward rather than backward is lighted, however flickeringly, by two of the seminal minds of our era, Pierre Teilhard de Chardin and Ernst Bloch. Both of these men are intellectual vagabonds; neither belongs to the theological club. But if our present decrepitude teaches us anything, it is that the club needs massive transfusions of new blood if it is to survive at all. I believe it is only by listening to such outsiders as these that any new health will come to the faltering enterprise of theology.

Teilhard's theology is only accidentally scientific, in the narrow sense. It is really a Christian cosmology, the first that has really engaged the imagination of modern man. Teilhard correctly saw that for modern man the question of God would focus on the question of man. It would appear in, with and under the issue of man's place in the enormously expanded world of modern science. Teilhard's complex theories about the role of centrifugal and centripetal forces in evolution, the new kind of heredity seen in man as a culture-bearing animal, and the crucial role man's consciousness of evolution

[2] See Gordon D. Kaufman, "Theological Historicism as an Experiment in Thought," *The Christian Century*, March 2, 1966, p. 268.

will play in that evolution—these cannot be discussed here. The point which they suggest, however, is that any thinking about God from now on must begin with the recognition that man now sees himself as the one who can and must carry through many of the responsibilities which men of earlier millenia have assigned to their gods.

Between Teilhard, the maverick Catholic, and Bloch, the renegade Marxist, there are many differences; but one cannot help noticing the similarities. Both of them discuss transcendence in terms of the pressure exerted by the future on the present. Both see the future as that pressure on the present which is only possible where there is a creature who can orient himself toward the future and relate himself to reality by this orientation, in short a "creature who can hope." They both regard reality as a radically open-ended process. Teilhard detected in the logic of evolution an ever-deepening humanization of man and "hominization" of the universe. Bloch concerned himself with "man-as-promise" and mapped out what he called "the ontology of the not-yet."

Teilhard's world of discourse was the breathtakingly massive universe and the appearance within it of the phenomenon of man, that point where the cosmos begins to think and to steer itself. Bloch's place of philosophizing is human history, exhumed from its burial in timelessness and launched on a journey into the future by the "birth of the hope," an orientation introduced into the world by the biblical faith but now lost sight of by Christians. Both Bloch and Teilhard affirmed the centrality of what the Germans now call the *"Impuls der Erwartung,"* or impulse of expectancy. The one examined the way cosmic space and geological time seem to dwarf man, the other how history seems to buffet him. But neither became discouraged; both saw hope in man's growing capacity to apply science and critical reflection to the shaping of his own destiny.

We need a non-nonsense "leveling" in theological discourse. I think that if we can affirm anything real which also transcends history, it will be the future as it lives in man's imagination, nurtured by his memory and actualized by his responsibility. Some theologians have already begun to explore the implications this would have for traditional ideas of eschatology and incarnation. Although I think Teilhard's legacy will increasingly help us in working out this new direction, it is Bloch who I believe will be more influential.

Though difficult and often unclear, Bloch's massive book, *Das Prinzip der Hoffnung* (The Principle of Hope), first published in 1954, supplies the only serious alternative to Martin Heidegger's even more opaque *Sein und Zeit* (Being and Time) of 1927 as a philosophical partner for theology. Heidegger senses life to be hemmed in and radically finite, but he still fiercely presses the desperate question of the "Sein des Seienden," the meaning of the being of that which is. Heidegger's influence on modern theology has been enormous, but as I argued in *The Secular City,* it seems to me almost wholly deleterious. Bloch presses the same difficult questions that Heidegger raises, but he does so within an ontology that seeks to question and subvert the tight finitude of Heidegger's constricted human world.

Thus while Heidegger plumbs the caliginous depths of anxiety, care and "Sein zum Tode" (being toward death), Bloch deals with that "infatuation with the possible" without which human existence is unthinkable. "The basic theme of philosophy," argues Bloch, "is that which is still not culminated, the still unpossessed homeland," and instead of anxiety and death "philosophy's basic categories should be 'frontier,' 'future,' 'the new,' and the 'Traum nach vorwärts.' "[3] Like Heidegger, Bloch considers himself to be an atheist. But just as many theologians such as Rudolf Bultmann, Herbert Braun, and Heinrich Ott have found ideas of worth and interest in Heidegger, so a new group has already begun to find promising hints in the works of Ernst Bloch. Thus Jürgen Moltmann's *Theologie der Hoffnung*[4] obviously owes much to Bloch, as does Gerhard Sauter's *Zukunft und Verheissung.*[5]

One point of continuing interest for the theologians is that

[3] Bloch, *Das Prinzip der Hoffnung* (Berlin: Suhrkampf Verlag, 1954), p. 83. Bloch's expression "Traum nach vorwärts" is simple enough German, but a literal translation would be "dream toward forward" rather than "dream toward the future," which is our closest idiomatic equivalent.

[4] München: Christian Kaiser Verlag, 1964.

[5] Zurich: Zuingl: Verlag, 1965.

Bloch not only engages in a brilliant analysis of man as "the creature who hopes," he also postulates a correspondence between man as the being who hopes and dreams and the historical world itself. He sees this correspondence (*Entsprechung*) between the "subjective of hope" and the "objectively possible," and he even tries (often unsuccessfully) to describe and elucidate it. The relationship between "subjective" and "objective" hope raises in Bloch's mind the question of an "identity" between man-who-hopes and a structure of reality which supports and nourishes such hope.

Here the Christian naturally thinks of qualities sometimes attributed to God. Bloch is not aware of the similarity; indeed he describes the identity between subjective spontaneity and historical possibility as the "demythologized content of that which Christians have revered as God." He therefore insists that atheism is the only acceptable stance today because the Christian God has been imprisoned in the categories of a static ontology.

From a biblical perspective there are many questions to be asked about Bloch's work. He does not provide us with a clear-cut way out of the "death of God" morass. At many points in his argument Bloch's commitment to radical historicism, along with residual traces of his Marxist materialism, seems to collide with his passionate desire to picture a radically open world in which at least the possibility of something "wholly other" is not excluded in principle. There are several places where, for example, he insists that all possibility is already incipiently present in what is, thus betraying an Aristotelian teleological bias. But his main thesis cannot be easily dismissed.

I agree with Wolf-Dieter Marsch's remark that as long as Christians cling to the static "is" as the normative predicate for God, such thinkers as Bloch must rightly continue to regard themselves as theists. But if theology can leave behind the God who "is" and begin its work with the God who "will be" (or in biblical parlance "He who comes"), an exciting new epoch in theology could begin, one in which Ernst Bloch's work would be extraordinarily important.

If the present wake is for the God who *is* (and now *was*), this may clear the decks for the God who *will be*. I cannot say for sure that the opening of such a path will lead anywhere, but the task of opening it would first require a thorough reworking of our major theological categories. We would see Jesus, for example, not as a visitor to earth from some supra-terrestrial heaven, but as the one in whom precisely this two-story dualism is abolished for good, and who becomes the pioneer and first sign of the coming New Age. We would see the community of faith as those "on the way" to this promised reality, "forgetting what is behind and reaching out for that which is ahead" (Phil. 3:14). "Radical" theology would have more radical social consequences than the so-called radical theology of the death of God has produced so far.

The doctrine of God would become theology's answer to the seemingly irrefutable fact that history can only be kept open by "anchoring" that openness somewhere outside history itself, in this case not "above" but *ahead*. Faith in God would be recognized, for our time, in that hope for the future Kingdom of Peace that frees men to suffer and sacrifice meaningfully in the present. Still, I would be the worst of imposters if I pretended that in the God of Hope we can immediately affirm the one who will appear when the corpse of the dead God of metaphysical theism is finally interred. He may not appear at all, and our efforts to work out a new and viable doctrine of God for our time may be fated to fail from the beginning. But before any of us throws in the towel, I hope we will exercise the freedom given us by the present *Götterdämmerung* of the divinities of Christendom, and use this freedom to think as candidly and as rigorously as possible about where we go from here.[6]

The only future that theology has, one might say, is to become the theology of the future. Its attention must turn to that future which God makes possible but for which man

---

[6] Since writing this article I have read Leslie Dewart's brilliant new book *The Post-Christian God: Theism in a World Come of Age* (New York: Herder, 1966). It is a splendid example of a new possibility in theism once we have divested ourselves of static metaphysical categories. Dewart stresses the "presence" rather than the existence of God.

is inescapably responsible. Traditionally, it is prophecy that has dealt with the future. Hence the fate of theology will be determined by its capacity to regain its prophetic role. It must resist the temptation of becoming an esoteric specialty and resume its role as critic and helper of the faithful community as that community grapples with the vexing issues of our day.

The "death of God" syndrome signals the collapse of the static orders and fixed categories by which men have understood themselves in the past. It opens the future in a new and radical way. Prophecy calls man to move into this future with a confidence informed by the tradition but transformed by the present. Theology helps prophecy guide the community of faith in its proper role as the avant garde of humanity. This community must clarify the life-and-death options open to *homo sapiens*, devote itself unsparingly to the humanization of city and cosmos, and keep alive the hope of a kingdom of racial equality, peace among the nations, and bread for all. One could never weep for a dead god. A god who can die deserves no tears. Rather we would rejoice that, freed of another incubus, we now take up the task of fashioning a future made possible not by anything that "is" but by "He who comes."